SHAKESPEARE MADE EASY

MODERN ENGLISH VERSION
SIDE-BY-SIDE WITH FULL ORIGINAL TEXT

King Lear

EDITED AND RENDERED INTO MODERN ENGLISH BY
Alan Durband

BARRON'S

First U.S. edition published 1986 by
Barron's Educational Series, Inc.

Hutchinson & Co. (Publishers) Ltd
An imprint of the Hutchinson Publishing Group
17–21 Conway Street, London W1P 6JD

Hutchinson Publishing Group (Australia) Pty Ltd
PO Box 496, 16–22 Church Street, Hawthorne,
Melbourne, Victoria 3122

Hutchinson Group (NZ) Ltd.
32–34 View Road, PO Box 40–086, Glenfield, Auckland 10

Hutchinson Group (SA) (Pty) Ltd
PO Box 337, Bergvlei 2012, South Africa

First published 1986
© Alan Durband 1986

All inquiries should be addressed to:
Barron's Educational Series, Inc.
250 Wireless Boulevard
Hauppauge, NY 11788
http://www.barronseduc.com

ISBN-13: 978-0-8120-3637-4
ISBN-10: 0-8120-3637-9

Library of Congress Catalog No. 85-22951

Library of Congress Cataloging-in-Publication Data

Shakespeare, William, 1564–1616.
    King Lear.

    (Shakespeare made easy)
    Summary: Presents the original text of Shakespeare's play
side by side with a modern version, discusses the author and
the theater of his time, and provides quizzes and other study
activities.
    1. Shakespeare, William, 1564–1616. King Lear.
2. Shakespeare, William, 1564–1616—Study and teaching.
[1. Shakespeare, William, 1564–1616. King Lear.   2. Shakespeare,
William, 1564–1616—Study and teaching.   3. Plays]   I. Durband,
Alan.   II. Title.   III. Series: Shakespeare, William, 1564–1616.
Shakespeare made easy.
PR2819.A25D87   1986   822.3'3   85-22951
ISBN 0-8120-3637-9

PRINTED IN THE UNITED STATES OF AMERICA
30 29 28 27 26 25 24 23 22

Paper contains a minimum of 15%
post-consumer waste (PCW)

'Reade him, therefore: and againe, and againe: And if then you do not like him, surely you are in some danger, not to understand him . . . .'

John Hemming
Henry Condell

Preface to the 1623 Folio Edition

Shakespeare Made Easy

Titles in the series

Contents

Introduction

Shakespeare Made Easy is intended for readers approaching the plays for the first time, who find the language of Elizabethan poetic drama an initial obstacle to understanding and enjoyment. In the past, the only answer to the problem has been to grapple with the difficulties with the aid of explanatory footnotes (often missing when they are most needed) and a stern teacher. Generations of students have complained that "Shakespeare was ruined for me at school."

Usually a fuller appreciation of Shakespeare's plays comes in later life, when the mind has matured and language skills are more developed. Often the desire to read Shakespeare for pleasure and enrichment follows from a visit to the theater, where excellence of acting and production can bring to life qualities which sometimes lie dormant on the printed page.

Shakespeare Made Easy can never be a substitute for the original plays. It cannot possibly convey the full meaning of Shakespeare's poetic expression, which is untranslatable. *Shakespeare Made Easy* concentrates on the dramatic aspect, enabling the novice to become familiar with the plot and characters, and to experience one facet of Shakespeare's genius. To know and understand the central issues of each play is a sound starting point for further exploration and development.

Discretion can be used in choosing the best method to employ. One way is to read the original Shakespeare first, ignoring the modern translation or using it only when interest or understanding flags. Another way is to read the translation first, to establish confidence and familiarity with plots and characters.

Either way, cross-reference can be illuminating. The modern text can explain "what is being said" if Shakespeare's language is particularly complex or his expression antiquated. The Shakespeare text will show the reader of the modern paraphrase how much more can be expressed in poetry than in prose.

The use of *Shakespeare Made Easy* means that the newcomer need never be overcome by textual difficulties. From first to last, a measure of understanding is at hand – the key is provided for what has been a locked door to many students in the past. And as understanding grows, so an awareness develops of the potential of language as a vehicle for philosophic and moral expression, beauty, and the abidingly memorable.

Even professional Shakespearean scholars can never hope to arrive at a complete understanding of the plays. Each critic, researcher, actor or producer merely adds a little to the work that has already been done, or makes fresh interpretations of the texts for new generations. For everyone, Shakespearean appreciation is a journey. *Shakespeare Made Easy* is intended to help with the first steps.

William Shakespeare

His life

William Shakespeare was born in Stratford-on-Avon, Warwickshire, on April 23, 1564, the son of a prosperous wool and leather merchant. Very little is known of his early life. From parish records we know that he married Ann Hathaway in 1582, when he was eighteen, and she was twenty-six. They had three children, the eldest of whom died in childhood.

Between his marriage and the next thing we know about him, there is a gap of ten years. Probably he became a member of a traveling company of actors. By 1592 he had settled in London and had earned a reputation as an actor and playwright.

Theaters were then in their infancy. The first (called *The Theatre*) was built by the actor James Burbage in 1576, in Shoreditch, then a suburb of London. Two more followed as the taste for theater grew: *The Curtain* in 1577 and *The Rose* in 1587. The demand for new plays naturally increased. Shakespeare probably earned a living adapting old plays and working in collaboration with others on new ones. Today we would call him a "freelance," since he was not permanently attached to one theater.

In 1594, a new company of actors, The Lord Chamberlain's Men, was formed, and Shakespeare was one of the shareholders. He remained a member throughout his working life. The Company was regrouped in 1603 and renamed The King's Men, with James I as their patron.

Shakespeare and his fellow actors prospered. In 1598 they built their own theater, *The Globe*, which broke away from the traditional rectangular shape of the inn and its yard (the early home of traveling bands of actors). Shakespeare described it in *Henry V* as "this wooden O," because it was circular.

Many other theaters were built by investors eager to profit from the new enthusiasm for drama. *The Hope, The Fortune, The Red Bull*, and *The Swan* were all open-air "public" theaters. There were also many "private" (or indoor) theaters, one of which (*The Blackfriars*) was purchased by Shakespeare and his friends because the child actors who performed there were dangerous competitors. (Shakespeare denounces them in *Hamlet*.)

After writing some thirty-seven plays (the exact number is something which scholars argue about), Shakespeare retired to his native Stratford, wealthy and respected. He died on his birthday, in 1616.

His plays

Shakespeare's plays were not all published in his lifetime. None of them comes to us exactly as he wrote it.

In Elizabethan times, plays were not regarded as either literature or good reading matter. They were written at speed (often by more than one writer), performed perhaps ten or twelve times, and then discarded. Fourteen of Shakespeare's plays were first printed in Quarto (17cm × 21cm) volumes, not all with his name as the author. Some were authorized (the "good" Quartos) and probably were printed from prompt copies provided by the theater. Others were pirated (the "bad" Quartos) by booksellers who may have employed shorthand writers, or bought actors' copies after the run of the play had ended.

In 1623, seven years after Shakespeare's death, John Hemming and Henry Condell (fellow actors and shareholders in The King's Men) published a collected edition of Shakespeare's works – thirty-six plays in all – in a Folio (21cm × 34cm) edition. From their introduction it would seem that they used Shakespeare's original manuscripts ("we have scarce received from him a blot in his papers"), but the Folio volumes that still survive are not all exactly alike, nor are the plays printed as we know them today, with act and scene divisions and stage directions.

A modern edition of a Shakespeare play is the result of a great

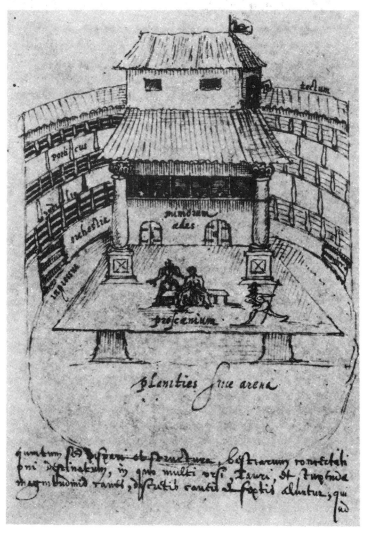

*Interior of the Swan Theatre – from a pen and ink drawing made in
1596 (Mansell Collection)*

deal of scholarly research and editorial skill over several centuries. The aim is always to publish a text (based on the good and bad Quartos and the Folio editions) that most closely resembles what Shakespeare intended. Misprints have added to the problems, so some words and lines are pure guesswork. This explains why some versions of Shakespeare's plays differ from others.

His theater

The first playhouse built as such in Elizabethan London, constructed in 1576, was *The Theatre*. Its co-founders were John Brayne, an investor, and James Burbage, a carpenter turned actor. Like the six or seven "public" (or outdoor) theaters which followed it over the next thirty years, it was situated outside the city, to avoid conflict with the authorities. They disapproved of players and playgoing, partly on moral and political grounds, and partly because of the danger of spreading the plague. (There were two major epidemics during Shakespeare's lifetime, and on each occasion the theaters were closed for lengthy periods.)

The Theatre was a financial success, and Shakespeare's company performed there until 1598, when a dispute over the lease of the land forced Burbage to take down the building. It was re-created in Southwark, as *The Globe*, with Shakespeare and several of his fellow actors as the principal shareholders.

By modern standards, *The Globe* was small. Externally, the octagonal building measured fewer than thirty meters across, but in spite of this it could accommodate an audience of between two and three thousand people. (The largest of the three theaters at the National Theatre complex in London today seats 1160.)

Performances were advertised by means of playbills posted around the city, and they took place during the hours of daylight when the weather was suitable. A flag flew to show that all was well, to save playgoers a wasted journey.

At the entrance, a doorkeeper collected one penny (about 60 cents today) for admission to the "pit" – a name taken from the old inn-yards, where bear-baiting and cock-fighting were popular sports. This was the minimum charge for seeing a play. The "groundlings," as they were called, simply stood around the three sides of the stage, in the open air. Those who were better off could pay extra for a seat under cover. Stairs led from the pit to three tiers of galleries round the walls. The higher one went, the more one paid. The best seats cost one shilling ($7 today). In theaters owned by speculators like Francis Langley and Philip Henslowe, half the gallery takings went to the landlord.

A full house might consist of 800 groundlings and 1500 in the galleries, with a dozen more exclusive seats on the stage itself for the gentry. A new play might run for between six and sixteen performances; the average was about ten. As there were no breaks between scenes, and no intervals, most plays could be performed in two hours. A trumpet sounded three times before the play began.

The acting company assembled in the Tiring House at the rear of the stage. This was where they "attired" (or dressed) themselves: not in costumes representing the period of the play, but in Elizabethan doublet and hose. All performances were therefore in modern dress, though no expense was spared to make the stage costumes lavish. The entire company was male. By law, actresses were not allowed, and female roles were performed by boys.

Access to the stage from the Tiring House was through two doors, one on each side of the stage. Because there was no front curtain, every entrance had to have its corresponding exit, so an actor killed on stage had to be carried off. There was no scenery: the audience used its imagination, guided by the spoken word. Storms and night scenes might well be performed on sunny days in mid-afternoon; the Elizabethan playgoer relied entirely on the play-wright's descriptive skills to establish the dramatic atmosphere.

Once on stage, the actors and their expensive clothes were protected from sudden showers by a canopy, the underside of which was painted blue and spangled with stars to represent the heavens. A trapdoor in the stage made ghostly entrances and the gravedigging scene in *Hamlet* possible. Behind the main stage, in between the two entrance doors, there was a curtained area, concealing a small inner stage, useful for bedroom scenes. Above this was a balcony, which served for castle walls (as in *Henry V*) or a domestic balcony (as in the famous scene in *Romeo and Juliet*).

The acting style in Elizabethan times was probably more declamatory than we favor today, but the close proximity of the audience also made a degree of intimacy possible. In those days soliloquies and asides seemed quite natural. Act and scene divisions did not exist (those in printed versions of the play today have been added by editors), but Shakespeare often indicates a scene-ending by a rhyming couplet.

A company such as The King's Men at *The Globe* would consist of around twenty-five actors, half of whom might be shareholders, and the rest part-timers engaged for a particular play. Among the shareholders in *The Globe* were several specialists – William Kempe, for example, was a renowned comedian and Robert Armin was a singer and dancer. Playwrights wrote parts to suit the actors who were available, and devised ways of overcoming the absence of women. Shakespeare often has his heroines dress as young men, and physical contact between lovers was formal compared with the realism we expect today.

His verse

Shakespeare wrote his plays mostly in blank verse: that is, unrhymed lines consisting of ten syllables, alternately stressed and unstressed. The technical term for this form is the iambic pentameter. When Shakespeare first began to write for the stage, it was fashionable to maintain this regular beat from the first line of the play till the last.

Shakespeare conformed at first, and then experimented. Some of his early plays contain whole scenes in rhyming couplets – in *Romeo and Juliet*, for example, there is extensive use of rhyme, and as if to show his versatility, Shakespeare even inserts a sonnet into the dialogue.

But as he matured, he sought greater freedom of expression than rhyme allowed. Rhyme was still used to indicate a scene-ending, or to stress lines that he wished the audience to remember. Generally, though, Shakespeare moved toward the rhythms of everyday speech. This gave him many dramatic advantages, which he fully and subtly exploits in terms of atmosphere, character, emotion, stress and pace.

It is Shakespeare's poetic imagery, however, that most distinguishes his verse from that of lesser playwrights. It enables him to stretch the imagination, express complex thought-patterns in memorable language, and convey a number of associated ideas in compressed and economical form. A study of Shakespeare's imagery – especially in his later plays – is often the key to a full understanding of his meaning and purposes.

At the other extreme is prose. Shakespeare normally reserves it for servants, clowns, commoners, and pedestrian matters such as lists, messages and letters.

King Lear

Date

The play was entered in the Stationer's Register in November 1607, having been performed before King James in December 1606. It was probably written during the previous year, 1605.

Sources

The main plot of *King Lear* can be traced to several sources: *The Chronicles of England, Scotland and Ireland* by Ralph Holinshed (first published in 1577 and reissued in 1587), which tells the story of "Lear the Sonne of Baldud" and his three daughters "Gonorilla, Regan and Cordeilla"; John Higgins' narrative poem in *Mirror of Magistrates* (1574 edition), which is written from the viewpoint of "Cordila"; an old play called *The True Chronicle History of King Leir* (known to have been performed in 1594, and written at least six years earlier); and Book Two of Edmund Spenser's *The Faerie Queene* (1590).

The Gloucester subplot may have been suggested by an episode in Sir Philip Sidney's *Arcadia* (1950) in which the King of Paphlagonia, blinded by "a hard-hearted sonne of his," seeks a rock from which to "cast himselfe headlong to death," led by his loyal son "poorly arayed and extreamely weather-beaten."

Shakespeare always restructured and developed his source material, and though these texts (and possibly others) were part of his initial working equipment, *King Lear* bears only a token resemblance to the older stories which he worked upon: for example, in Holinshed and the old chronicle play, Lear and the French army are victorious, and in neither does the King go mad.

Text

King Lear was first published in a Quarto version, in 1608. It was reprinted in 1619, when it was spuriously dated 1608: publishers in Elizabethan times often passed off reprints in this fraudulent way. Shakespeare was not involved in either publication. The play next appeared in the Folio edition of 1623. Hemming and Condell, the editors, are thought to have used a manuscript copy or theater prompt-book, together with the first Quarto, in compiling their text.

The Quarto omits about 100 lines that appear in the Folio. The Folio omits about 300 lines that are printed in the Quartos. No definitive text therefore exists; all editors must use discretion in preparing the play for publication. This explains why editions often differ from each other.

King Lear

Original text and modern version

The characters

Lear   King of Britain
King of France
Duke of Burgundy
Duke of Cornwall   Regan's husband
Duke of Albany   Goneril's husband
Earl of Kent
Earl of Gloucester
Edgar   Gloucester's legitimate son
Edmund   Gloucester's bastard son
Curan   a courtier
Old Man   Gloucester's tenant
Doctor
Fool
Oswald   Goneril's steward
A Captain   employed by Edmund
Gentleman   in the service of Cordelia
Herald
Servants   to Cornwall
Goneril ⎫
Regan   ⎬   Lear's daughters
Cordelia ⎭
Knights   attending on Lear; **Officers, Messengers, Soldiers**
and **Attendants**

Act one

Scene 1

King Lear's Palace. Enter **Kent, Gloucester,** *and* **Edmund.**

Kent   I thought the King had more affected the Duke of
Albany than Cornwall.

Gloucester   It did always seem so to us: but now, in the
division of the kingdom, it appears not which of the Dukes
he values most; for equalities are so weighed that curiosity
in neither can make choice of either's moiety.

Kent   Is not this your son, my lord?

Gloucester   His breeding, sir, hath been at my charge. I
have so often blushed to acknowledge him, that now I am
brazed to it.

Kent   I cannot conceive you.

Gloucester   Sir, this young fellow's mother could;
whereupon she grew round-wombed, and had, indeed, sir,
a son for her cradle ere she had a husband for her bed. Do
you smell a fault?

Kent   I cannot wish the fault undone, the issue of it being so
proper.

Gloucester   But I have a son, sir, by order of law, some year
elder than this, who yet is no dearer in my account: though
this knave came something saucily to the world before he
was sent for, yet was his mother fair; there was good sport
at his making, and the whoreson must be acknowledged.
Do you know this noble gentleman, Edmund?

Act one

Scene 1

King Lear's palace. Enter the **Earl of Kent**, *followed by the* **Earl of Gloucester** *and his illegitimate son* **Edmund**. *They are discussing court matters.*

Kent   I thought the King favored the Duke of Albany more than the Duke of Cornwall.

Gloucester   It always seemed so to us. But now that he has divided up his kingdom, it isn't clear which of the Dukes he values more. Their shares are so equal that neither is to be preferred to the other.

Kent   [*indicating* **Edmund**] Isn't this your son, my lord?

Gloucester   I fathered him, sir. I've so often been embarrassed to admit he's mine that now I'm hardened to it.

Kent   I cannot conceive why.

Gloucester   Sir, this young fellow's mother could! So she got pregnant, and had a son for her cradle before she had a husband for her bed. Do you detect a fault?

Kent   I can't wish the fault undone, the result of it being so handsome!

Gloucester   But I have a legitimate son, sir, about a year older than this one, though I don't make any distinction in his favor. [*nodding toward* **Edmund**] Though this fellow was cheeky enough to be born before he was sent for, there's no denying his mother was beautiful. We had a good time begetting him, so the rascal can't be disowned. Do you know this noble gentleman, Edmund?

Edmund   No, my lord.

Gloucester   My Lord of Kent. Remember him hereafter as my honourable friend.

Edmund   My services to your lordship.

Kent   I must love you, and sue to know you better.

Edmund   Sir, I shall study deserving.

Gloucester   He hath been out nine years, and away he shall again. The King is coming.

[*Sennet. Enter* **King Lear, Cornwall, Albany, Goneril, Regan, Cordelia,** *and Attendants*]

Lear   Attend the Lords of France and Burgundy, Gloucester.

Gloucester   I shall, my Liege.

[*Exeunt* **Gloucester** *and* **Edmund**]

Lear   Meantime, we shall express our darker purpose.
  Give me the map there. Know that we have divided
  In three our kingdom; and 'tis our fast intent
  To shake all cares and business from our age,
  Conferring them on younger strengths, while we
  Unburdened crawl toward death. Our son of Cornwall,
  And you, our no less loving son of Albany,
  We have this hour a constant will to publish
  Our daughters' several dowers, that future strife
  May be prevented now. The princes, France and
    Burgundy,
  Great rivals in our youngest daughter's love,
  Long in our court have made their amorous sojourn,
  And here are to be answered. Tell me, my daughters –
  Since now we will divest us both of rule,

Edmund No, my lord.

Gloucester [*introducing him formally*] The Lord of Kent.
Regard him always as my honorable friend.

Edmund [*bowing*] At your service, my lord.

Kent My love to you: I'd like to know you better.

Edmund Sir, I'll try to be worthy of your interest.

Gloucester He's been soldiering abroad these last nine years,
and he'll be off again soon. [*The sound of trumpets is heard*]
The King is coming.

[*A servant enters carrying a coronet, followed by* **King Lear;**
the Dukes of **Albany** *and* **Cornwall;** *their wives* **Goneril** *and*
Regan, *two daughters of the King;* **Cordelia,** *Lear's youngest
daughter; and members of the court.*]

Lear Bring in the Lords of France and Burgundy, Gloucester.

Gloucester I shall, my liege. [*He goes, followed by* **Edmund**]

Lear Meanwhile we'll reveal our plan. Give me that map,
there. [**Servants** *hand him a large map of Britain. He
addresses the court*] Be it known that we have divided our
kingdom into three parts; and it is our firm intention to
shake off all cares and responsibilities in our old age, and to
confer them on younger shoulders while we, freed of our
burdens, crawl toward death. Our son-in-law Cornwall, and
you, our no less loving son-in-law Albany: we have resolved
at this juncture to make public the various doweries of our
daughters, so that future strife can be prevented now. The
King of France and the Duke of Burgundy – keen rivals for
the hand of our youngest daughter – have for a long time
resided at our court as suitors, and they are to have their
answer here. [*To* **Goneril, Regan** *and* **Cordelia**] Tell me, my
daughters – since we shall now divest us of our throne, our

23

Interest of territory, cares of state –
Which of you shall we say doth love us most?
That we our largest bounty may extend
Where nature doth with merit challenge. Goneril,
Our eldest-born, speak first.

Goneril   Sir, I love you more than words can wield the
      matter;
Dearer than eye-sight, space and liberty;
Beyond what can be valued rich or rare;
No less than life, with grace, health, beauty, honour;
As much as child e'er loved, or father found;
A love that makes breath poor and speech unable;
Beyond all manner of so much I love you.

Cordelia   [*aside*] What shall Cordelia speak? Love, and be
      silent.

Lear   Of all these bounds, even from this line to this,
With shadowy forests and with champains riched,
With plenteous rivers and wide-skirted meads,
We make thee lady; to thine and Albany's issues
Be this perpetual. What says our second daughter,
Our dearest Regan, wife of Cornwall? Speak.

Regan   I am made of that self metal as my sister,
And prize me at her worth. In my true heart
I find she names my very deed of love:
Only she comes too short: that I profess
Myself an enemy to all other joys
Which the most precious square of sense possesses,
And find I am alone felicitate
In your dear Highness' love.

Cordelia   [*aside*]   Then poor Cordelia!
And yet not so; since I am sure my love's
More ponderous than my tongue.

territorial possessions and our administrative responsibilities – which of you shall we say is the one who loves us most? Then we can bestow our greatest generosity where natural affection most merits it. Goneril, our eldest child, speak first.

Goneril   Sir, I love you more than words can express: dearer than eyesight, freedom or independence; more than what is utterly priceless or rare; no less than life itself when it has dignity, health, beauty and honor; as much as a child ever loved or a father ever enjoyed affection; a love that makes words weak and speech inadequate. Beyond all such comparisons I love you.

Cordelia   [*aside*] What shall Cordelia say? Just love, and be silent . . .

Lear   [*indicating the boundaries of* **Goneril's** *legacy on the map*] All this region – from this line here to this – rich with shady forests, fertile plains, teeming rivers and broad meadows, we give you to rule. This is for you and your husband Albany's descendants forever. [*He turns to* **Regan**] What has our second daughter to say, our dearest Regan, wife of the Duke of Cornwall? Speak.

Regan   I am made of the same metal as my sister, so value me as you have done her. From the bottom of my heart, I find she describes my own love precisely, except that she understates it. No other pleasure appeals to me: my happiness is solely in the enjoyment of your love.

Cordelia   [*to herself*] Poor Cordelia, then! But not really so, because I'm sure my love is greater than my tongue can express.

Lear   To thee and thine, hereditary ever,
Remain this ample third of our fair kingdom,
No less in space, validity, and pleasure,
Than that conferred on Goneril. Now, our joy,
Although our last, not least; to whose young love
The vines of France and milk of Burgundy
Strive to be interessed; what can you say to draw
A third more opulent than your sisters? Speak.

Cordelia   Nothing, my lord.

Lear   Nothing?

Cordelia   Nothing.

Lear   Nothing will come of nothing: speak again.

Cordelia   Unhappy that I am, I cannot heave
My heart into my mouth: I love your Majesty
According to my bond; no more nor less.

Lear   How, how, Cordelia! Mend your speech a little,
Lest it may mar your fortunes.

Cordelia   Good my lord,
You have begot me, bred me, loved me: I
Return those duties back as are right fit,
Obey you, love you, and most honour you.
Why have my sisters husbands, if they say
They love you all? Happily, when I shall wed,
That lord whose hand must take my plight shall carry
Half my love with him, half my care and duty:
Sure I shall never marry like my sisters,
To love my father all.

Lear   But goes thy heart with this?

Cordelia   Ay, my good lord.

Lear   So young, and so untender?

Lear [*to* **Regan**] To you and yours, in perpetuity, is bestowed this extensive third of our fine kingdom: no smaller, less valuable or pleasurable than that conferred on Goneril. [*Turning to* **Cordelia**] Now our joy; last-born but not least; for whose young love the vineyards of France and the pastures of Burgundy compete: What can you say to attract a third share more valuable than that of your sisters? Speak.

Cordelia   Nothing, my lord.

Lear   Nothing?

Cordelia   Nothing.

Lear   Nothing begets nothing. Speak again.

Cordelia   Wretched as I am, I can't express in words what's in my heart. I love your Majesty according to my duty as a daughter. No more, no less.

Lear   [*his anger rising*] What, what Cordelia? Speak more tactfully, lest you spoil your chances!

Cordelia   My good lord, you have fathered me, brought me up and loved me. I return those duties accordingly: I obey you, love you, and honor you most. Why have my sisters got husbands, if they say they love you absolutely? Be assured that when I wed, the man who has my hand in marriage will have half my love, half my care and duty. Certainly I'll never marry like my sisters, loving my father so totally.

Lear   Is this spoken from the heart?

Cordelia   Yes, my good lord.

Lear   So young, yet so hard-hearted?

Cordelia   So young, my lord, and true.

Lear   Let it be so; thy truth then be thy dower:
    For, by the sacred radiance of the sun,
    The mysteries of Hecate and the night,
    By all the operation of the orbs
    From whom we do exist and cease to be,
    Here I disclaim all my paternal care,
    Propinquity and property of blood,
    And as a stranger to my heart and me
    Hold thee from this for ever. The barbarous Scythian,
    Or he that makes his generation messes
    To gorge his appetite, shall to my bosom
    Be as well neighboured, pitied, and relieved,
    As thou my sometime daughter.

Kent   Good my liege –

Lear   Peace, Kent!
    Come not between the dragon and his wrath.
    I loved her most, and thought to set my rest
    On her kind nursery. Hence, and avoid my sight!
    So be my grave my peace, as here I give
    Her father's heart from her! Call France. Who stirs?
    Call Burgundy. Cornwall and Albany,
    With my two daughters' dowers digest this third;
    Let pride, which she calls plainness, marry her.
    I do invest you jointly with my power,
    Pre-eminence, and all the large effects
    That troop with majesty. Ourself, by monthly course,
    With reservation of an hundred knights
    By you to be sustained, shall our abode
    Make with you by due turn. Only we shall retain
    The name and all th'addition to a king;
    The sway, revenue, execution of the rest,
    Beloved sons, be yours: which to confirm,
    This coronet part between you.

Cordelia   So young, my lord, and truthful.

Lear   Right, then: truth shall be your dowry! By the sun's sacred beams, by the witch-queen's magic rites at night, by all the stars that govern life and death: I here disclaim my fatherly affection, my kinship, my blood relationship! For evermore I shall regard you as a stranger to my heart and me. Barbarians like the Scythians, or those who eat their progeny when they're hungry, shall be as welcomed, pitied and given succor as you, my *former* daughter!

Kent   Your Majesty –

Lear   Silence, Kent! Don't come between the dragon and the object of his wrath! I loved her most, and planned to live with her in my retirement. Go, get out of my sight! Death is my only consolation, since here I give away a father's love! Call the King of France. Quick now! Call Burgundy! Cornwall and Albany, to my two daughters' dowries add this third [*pointing to* **Cordelia's** *territory on the map*]. Let pride – which she calls frankness – get her a husband. I invest you jointly with my power, my absolute authority, and all the ceremony that goes with kingship. We shall live with you alternately on a monthly basis, retaining the right to have a hundred knights maintained at your expense. We'll simply retain the title and all the honors and prerogatives due to a king. Policy, taxation, and all administrative matters, beloved sons, will be yours. In confirmation, this coronet is divided between you. [*The* **Servant** *presents it to the* **Dukes**]

Kent   Royal Lear,
  Whom I have ever honoured as my King,
  Loved as my father, as my master followed,
  As my great patron thought on in my prayers, –

Lear   The bow is bent and drawn; make from the shaft.

Kent   Let it fall rather, though the fork invade
  The region of my heart: be Kent unmannerly,
  When Lear is mad. What would'st thou do, old man?
  Think'st thou that duty shall have dread to speak
  When power to flattery bows? To plainness honour's bound
  When majesty falls to folly. Reserve thy state;
  And, in thy best consideration, check
  This hideous rashness: answer my life my judgment,
  Thy youngest daughter does not love thee least;
  Nor are those empty-hearted whose low sounds
  Reverb no hollowness.

Lear   Kent, on thy life, no more.

Kent   My life I never held but as a pawn
  To wage against thine enemies; nor fear to lose it,
  Thy safety being the motive.

Lear   Out of my sight!

Kent   See better, Lear; and let me still remain
  The true blank of thine eye.

Lear   Now, by Apollo –

Kent   Now, by Apollo, King,
  Thou swear'st thy gods in vain.

Lear   O vassal! Miscreant!

  [*Laying his hand on his sword*]

Alb., Corn.   Dear sir, forbear.

30

Kent   Royal Lear, whom I've always honored as my King,
loved as if he were my father, followed as he is my master,
mentioned in my prayers as my great patron –

Lear   The bow is bent and drawn: keep clear of the arrow!

Kent   Better to let it go, even though it pierces my heart! Kent
must be discourteous when Lear is mad. What are you
doing, old man? Do you think loyal men will fear to speak
when those in power fall for flattery? Honor demands plain
speaking when kings descend to folly. Keep your kingdom,
and think again; let this appalling rashness go no further. I'll
stake my life on it: your youngest daughter does not love
you least, nor are they heartless whose low-key speeches
contain no flattery.

Lear   Kent, on your life, no more!

Kent   I never considered my life as more than a mere pawn, to
be used against your enemies, nor do I fear losing it when
your safety is the issue.

Lear   Out of my sight!

Kent   See better, Lear, and let me – as ever – be clear-sighted
on your behalf!

Lear   Now, by Apollo – !

Kent   Now, by Apollo, King, you invoke your gods in vain!

Lear   Oh, you ruffian! Infidel! [*He puts his hand to his sword*]

Alb., Corn.   Good sir, be patient!

Kent   Do: kill thy physician, and the fee bestow
Upon the foul disease. Revoke thy gift;
Or, whilst I can vent clamour from my throat,
I'll tell thee thou dost evil.

Lear   Hear me, recreant!
On thine allegiance, hear me!
Since thou hast sought to make us break our vow,
Which we durst never yet, and with strained pride
To come betwixt our sentence and our power,
Which nor our nature nor our place can bear,
Our potency made good, take thy reward.
Five days we do allot thee for provision
To shield thee from disasters of the world;
And on the sixth to turn thy hated back
Upon our kingdom: if on the tenth day following
Thy banished trunk be found in our dominions,
The moment is thy death. Away! By Jupiter,
This shall not be revoked.

Kent   Fare thee well, King; sith thus thou wilt appear,
Freedom lives hence, and banishment is here.
[*To* **Cordelia**] The gods to their dear shelter take thee,
    maid,
That justly think'st and has most rightly said!
[*To* **Goneril** *and* **Regan**] And your large speeches may your
    deeds approve,
That good effects may spring from words of love.
Thus Kent, O princes, bids you all adieu;
He'll shape his old course in a country new.

                                                    [*Exit*]

[*Flourish. Re-enter* **Gloucester**, *with* **France, Burgundy,**
and Attendants]

Gloucester   Here's France and Burgundy, my noble lord.

Kent   Kill your doctor and give the fee to the foul
disease! Withdraw your gift, or while I've still got breath to
protest, I'll tell you that you're doing wrong!

Lear   Listen, traitor! On your oath of allegiance, hear me!
Since you have tried to make us break our vow, which we
have never done before, and because, with excessive pride,
you've attempted to come between our sentence and our
authority – which neither our character nor our rank can
tolerate – to confirm our power, take your reward! We give
you five days to prepare yourself for the rigors of the world.
On the sixth, turn your hated back upon our kingdom. If on
the tenth day after that your banished body is to be found
in our realm, that moment is your death. Away! By Jupiter,
this will not be revoked!

Kent   Farewell, King. Since that's how you want it, freedom
lives abroad, and banishment is here. [*To* **Cordelia**] The gods
protect you, maid. Your reasoning's right and you've said
what's true. [*To* **Goneril** *and* **Regan**] As for your grandiose
speeches, may your deeds live up to them! Then some good
might come from loving words. [*To the assembled nobles*]
Thus, Princes, Kent bids you all farewell. He'll continue to
be his old self in a new country.

[*He goes*]

[*A flourish of trumpets heralds the entry of* **Gloucester**, *the*
King of France, *the* **Duke of Burgundy**, *and their Attendants*]

Gloucester   Here are France and Burgundy, my lord.

Lear   My Lord of Burgundy,
    We first address toward you, who with this king
    Hath rivalled for our daughter..What, in the least,
    Will you require in present dower with her,
    Or cease your quest of love?

Burgundy   Most royal Majesty,
    I crave no more than hath your Highness offered,
    Nor will you tender less.

Lear   Right noble Burgundy,
    When she was dear to us, we did hold her so,
    But now her price is fallen. Sir, there she stands:
    If aught within that little-seeming substance,
    Or all of it, with our displeasure pieced,
    And nothing more, may fitly like your grace,
    She's there, and she is yours.

Burgundy   I know no answer.

Lear   Will you, with those infirmities she owes,
    Unfriended, new-adopted to our hate,
    Dowered with our curse and strangered with our oath,
    Take her, or leave her?

Burgundy   Pardon me, royal Sir;
    Election makes not up in such conditions.

Lear   Then leave her, sir; for, by the power that made me,
    I tell you all her wealth. [*To* **France**] For you, great King,
    I would not from your love make such a stray
    To match you where I hate; therefore beseech you
    T'avert your liking a more worthier way
    Than on a wretch whom Nature is ashamed
    Almost to acknowledge hers.

France   This is most strange,
    That she, whom even but now was your best object,
    The argument of your praise, balm of your age,

Lear   My Lord of Burgundy: we address you first. You have competed with this king for our daughter's hand. What is the minimum dowry you will require with her, without which you'd cease to be a suitor?

Burgundy   Most royal Majesty: I beg no more than your Highness has offered. Surely you would not suggest less?

Lear   Right noble Burgundy, when we loved her, we valued her accordingly. Now her price has fallen. Sir, there she stands. If anything in particular about that outspoken object, or all of it – complete with our displeasure, and nothing more – happens to suit your Grace, she's there, and she is yours.

Burgundy   I don't know what to say.

Lear   Will you – with all her imperfections: friendless; our hatred freshly upon her; her dowry our curse; disowned by our vow – take her or leave her?

Burgundy   With respect, royal sir, decisions are not made on terms like those.

Lear   Then leave her, sir, because by the gods that made me, I'm telling you that's all she's worth. [*To* **France**] As for you, great King, I would not distance myself from your love by marrying you to one I hate. Therefore I entreat you to turn your affections in a worthier direction than on a wretch who behaves so unnaturally.

France   It's very strange that she – who just now was your most precious possession, the subject of your praise, the comfort of your old age, the best, the dearest – should

The best, the dearest, should in this trice of time
Commit a thing so monstrous, to dismantle
So many folds of favour. Sure, her offence
Must be of such unnatural degree
That monsters it, or your fore-vouched affection
Fall into taint; which to believe of her,
Must be a faith that reason without miracle
Should never plant in me.

Cordelia   I yet beseech your Majesty –
If for I want that glib and oily art
To speak and purpose not, since what I well intend,
I'll do't before I speak – that you make known
It is no vicious blot, murder or foulness,
No unchaste action, or dishonoured step,
That hath deprived me of your grace and favour,
But even for want of that for which I am richer,
A still-soliciting eye, and such a tongue
That I am glad I have not, though not to have it
Hath lost me in your liking.

Lear   Better thou
Hadst not been born than not t'have pleased me better.

France   Is it but this? A tardiness in nature
Which often leaves the history unspoke
That it intends to do? My Lord of Burgundy,
What say you to the lady? Love's not love
When it is mingled with regards that stand
Aloof from th'entire point. Will you have her?
She is herself a dowry.

Burgundy   Royal King,
Give but that portion which yourself proposed,
And there I take Cordelia by the hand,
Duchess of Burgundy.

Lear   Nothing: I have sworn; I am firm.

suddenly commit something so monstrous as to destroy such deep affection. Either her offense must be atrociously unnatural, or else your former vows of love are suspect. Short of a miraculous revelation, my reason would never allow me to believe that of her.

Cordelia   I appeal to your Majesty – in spite of lacking the glib and oily art of making empty promises, preferring action rather than words – to state publicly that it is no vicious misbehavior, murder or wickedness, no wantonness or dishonorable action, that has deprived me of your grace and favor. Rather it is for lacking what I'm better off without: an eye for seeking favors, and the kind of tongue I'm glad I haven't got, though not having it has ruined me in your affection.

Lear   Better you had never been born than not to have pleased me better.

France   Is this all? A natural reticence that often unintentionally leaves inner thoughts unspoken? My Lord of Burgundy, what do you say to the lady? Love is not true love when it is subject to irrelevant conditions. Will you have her? She's a dowry in herself.

Burgundy   [*to* **Lear**] Royal King, just give the dowry which you yourself proposed, and I'll take Cordelia by the hand – Duchess of Burgundy.

Lear   Nothing. I have made a vow. I am resolute.

Burgundy   I am sorry, then, you have so lost a father
That you must lose a husband.

Cordelia   Peace be with Burgundy!
Since that respect and fortunes are his love,
I shall not be his wife.

France   Fairest Cordelia, that art most rich, being poor;
Most choice, forsaken; and most loved, despised!
Thee and thy virtues here I seize upon:
Be it lawful I take up what's cast away.
Gods, gods! 'Tis strange that from their cold'st neglect
My love should kindle to inflamed respect.
Thy dowerless daughter, King, thrown to my chance,
Is queen of us, of ours, and our fair France.
Not all the dukes of waterish Burgundy
Can buy this unprized precious maid of me.
Bid them farewell, Cordelia, though unkind:
Thou losest here, a better where to find.

Lear   Though hast her, France; let her be thine; for we
Have no such daughter, nor shall ever see
That face of hers again; therefore be gone
Without our grace, our love, our benison.
Come, noble Burgundy.

[*Flourish. Exeunt* **Lear, Burgundy, Cornwall, Albany,
Gloucester,** *and Attendants*]

France   Bid farewell to your sisters.

Cordelia   The jewels of our father, with washed eyes
Cordelia leaves you: I know you what you are;
And like a sister am most loath to call
Your faults as they are named. Love well our father:
To your professed bosoms I commit him:
But yet, alas, stood I within his grace,

Burgundy [*to* **Cordelia**] Then I am sorry: losing a father has lost you a husband.

Cordelia [*wryly*] God bless Burgundy! Since he's in love with respectability and wealth, I shall not be his wife!

France Fairest Cordelia, who is precious, being poor; most exquisite, being forsaken; and most loved, being despised! You and your virtues I here claim. If it is lawful, I will take up what has been cast away. The gods, the gods! It's strange that their cold indifference should ignite my love! Your dowerless daughter, King, by good fortune mine, is queen to me, of all I possess, and of fair France. Not all the dukes of wishy-washy Burgundy could buy this underrated but priceless maid from me. Bid them farewell, Cordelia, unkind though they are. You lose here to gain more elsewhere.

Lear You've got her, France. She's yours. We have no such daughter, nor shall we ever see that face of hers again. Therefore be gone: without our good wishes, our love, or our blessing. Come, noble Burgundy!

[**Lear** *departs, followed by* **Burgundy, Cornwall, Albany, Gloucester** *and the Attendants*]

France [*to* **Cordelia**] Say goodbye to your sisters.

Cordelia My father's precious ones, Cordelia leaves in tears. I know you for what you are, but as your sister I am reluctant to expose you. Love our father well. I entrust him to your so-called care. However, if I were still in favor, I'd find him

I would prefer him to a better place.
So farewell to you both.

Regan   Prescribe not us our duty.

Goneril   Let your study
Be to content your lord, who hath received you
At fortune's alms; you have obedience scanted,
And well are worth the want that you have wanted.

Cordelia   Time shall unfold what plighted cunning hides;
Who cover faults, at last shame them derides.
Well may you prosper!

France   Come, my fair Cordelia.

[Exeunt **France** *and* **Cordelia***]*

Goneril   Sister, it is not little I have to say of what most
nearly appertains to us both. I think our father will hence
to-night.

Regan   That's most certain, and with you; next month with
us.

Goneril   You see how full of changes his age is; the
observation we have made of it hath not been little: he
always loved our sister most; and with what poor judgment
he hath now cast her off appears too grossly.

Regan   'Tis the infirmity of his age; yet he hath ever but
slenderly known himself.

Goneril   The best and soundest of his time hath been but
rash; then must we look from his age to receive not alone
the imperfections of long-engraffed condition, but
therewithal the unruly waywardness that infirm and
choleric years bring with them.

somewhere better to stay. So farewell to you both.

Regan   Don't tell us what to do!

Goneril   Concentrate on pleasing your husband, who took you
as a handout from fortune. You have been less than
obedient, and you well deserve what's happened to you.

Cordelia   Time will reveal what deceit conceals.
Tricksters get exposed in the end. Good luck to you.

France   Come, my fair Cordelia.

[**France** *and* **Cordelia** *leave*]

Goneril   Sister, I have a lot to say of mutual interest. I think
our father will leave tonight.

Regan   That's for certain – and with you. Next month he'll
stay with us.

Goneril   You see how fickle he can be in his old age. We've
seen plenty of examples. He always loved our sister most.
His poor judgment is very obvious from the way he now
casts her off.

Regan   His age is the trouble. But then he has always lacked
self-control.

Goneril   Even in his prime he was hot-headed. So now we
must expect not only his deep-rooted faults, but also the
willfulness that comes with feeble and crochety old age.

Regan   Such unconstant starts are we like to have from him
   as this of Kent's banishment.

Goneril   There is further compliment of leave-taking between
   France and him. Pray you, let us hit together: if our father
   carry authority with such disposition as he bears, this last
   surrender of his will but offend us.

Regan   We shall further think of it.

Goneril   We must do something, and i' th 'heat.

[*Exeunt*]

Scene 2

The Earl of Gloucester's castle. Enter **Edmund,** *with a letter.*

Edmund   Thou, Nature, art my goddess; to thy law
   My services are bound. Wherefore should I
   Stand in the plague of custom, and permit
   The curiosity of nations to deprive me,
   For that I am some twelve or fourteen moonshines
   Lag of a brother? Why bastard? Wherefore base?
   When my dimensions are as well compact,
   My mind as generous, and my shape as true,
   As honest madam's issue? Why brand they us
   With base? with baseness? bastardy? base, base?
   Who in the lusty stealth of nature take
   More composition and fierce quality
   Than doth, within a dull, stale, tired bed,
   Go to the creating a whole tribe of fops,
   Got 'tween asleep and wake? Well then,

Regan   We're likely to get more sudden whims like Kent's banishment.

Goneril   And there's the way he rudely took leave of France. Well then, let's work together. If our father continues to exercise power in his condition, his abdication will be a problem to us.

Regan   We'll give it some more thought.

Goneril   We must strike while the iron is hot.

[*They go*]

Scene 2

The Earl of Gloucester's castle. **Edmund** *enters, carrying a letter.*

Edmund   Nature, you are my goddess! I obey your laws. Why should I be plagued by convention and let the narrow-mindedness of society keep me from my rights, just because I'm some twelve or fourteen months younger than my brother? Why am I "bastard"? Why inferior? I'm as well-proportioned, my mind is as vigorous, my build as similar, as the married lady's offspring. Why do they brand us as inferior? With inferiority? Illegitimacy? Inferior, inferior? What, we – who get sounder constitutions and more guts from hot-blooded fornication than goes into the making of a whole tribe of idiots conceived between bedtime and morning in a dull and tedious marriage bed?

Legitimate Edgar, I must have your land;
Our father's love is to the bastard Edmund
As to the legitimate. Fine word, 'legitimate'!
Well, my legitimate, if this letter speed,
And my invention thrive, Edmund the base
Shall top the legitimate. I grow, I prosper:
Now, gods, stand up for bastards!

[*Enter* **Gloucester**]

Gloucester   Kent banished thus! And France in choler
parted!
And the King gone to-night! Prescribed his power!
Confined to exhibition! All this done
Upon the gad! Edmund, how now! What news?

Edmund   So please your lordship, none.   [*Putting up the letter*]

Gloucester   Why so earnestly seek you to put up that letter?

Edmund   I know no news, my lord.

Gloucester   What paper were you reading?

Edmund   Nothing, my lord.

Gloucester   No? What needed then that terrible dispatch of
it into your pocket? The quality of nothing hath not such
need to hide itself. Let's see: come; if it be nothing, I shall
not need spectacles.

Edmund   I beseech you, sir, pardon me; it is a letter from my
brother that I have not all o'erread, and for so much as I
have perused, I find it not fit for your o'erlooking.

Gloucester   Give me the letter, sir.

Edmund   I shall offend, either to detain or give it. The
contents, as in part I understand them, are to blame.

Well, then, legitimate Edgar, I must have your inheritance!
Our father loves the bastard Edmund as much as the
legitimate Edgar. Fine word, "legitimate"! Well, my
legitimate, if this letter [*he flourishes it*] works properly, and
my plan prospers, Edmund the bastard will beat the
legitimate. I progress; I prosper. Now, gods – stand up for
bastards!

[*His father, the* **Earl of Gloucester,** *enters, thinking aloud*]

Gloucester   Kent banished like that! And France has left in
anger! And the King departed tonight, his power limited,
restricted to a token force! All this done on the spur of the
moment! [*He notices his son*] Greetings, Edmund. What
news?

Edmund   [*hiding his letter very obviously*] May it please your
lordship, none.

Gloucester   Why are you trying so hard to hide that letter?

Edmund   I've no news, my lord.

Gloucester   What was the document you were reading?

Edmund   Nothing, my lord.

Gloucester   No? Then why the indecent haste to put it into
your pocket? What's "nothing" has no such need to hide
itself. Let's see; come on; if it's nothing, I won't need
spectacles.

Edmund   I beg you, sir, excuse me: it's a letter from my
brother that I haven't finished reading, and from what I've
scanned, I believe it's not for your eyes.

Gloucester   Give me the letter, sir!

Edmund   I'll give offense whether I keep it or give it. The
contents, as far as I can follow them, are objectionable.

Gloucester   Let's see, let's see.

Edmund   I hope, for my brother's justification, he wrote this but as an essay or taste óf my virtue.

Gloucester   [*reads*] *This policy and reverence of age makes the world bitter to the best of our times; keeps our fortunes from us till our oldness cannot relish them. I begin to find an idle and fond bondage in the oppression of aged tyranny, who sways, not as it hath power, but as it is suffered. Come to me, that of this I may speak more. If our father would sleep till I waked him, you should enjoy half his revenue for ever, and live the beloved of your brother,* Edgar.

Hum! Conspiracy! 'Sleep till I waked him, you should enjoy half his revenue.' My son Edgar! Had he a hand to write this? A heart and brain to breed it in? When came you to this? Who brought it?

Edmund   It was not brought me, my lord; there's the cunning of it; I found it thrown in at the casement of my closet.

Gloucester   You know the character to be your brother's?

Edmund   If the matter were good, my lord, I durst swear it were his; but, in respect of that, I would fain think it were not.

Gloucester   It is his.

Edmund   It is his hand, my lord; but I hope his heart is not in the contents.

Gloucester   Has he never before sounded you in this business?

Edmund   Never, my lord. But I have heard him oft maintain it to be fit that, sons at perfect age, and fathers declined, the father should be as ward to the son, and the son manage his revenue.

Gloucester   Let's see, let's see!

Edmund   I hope – to make excuses for my brother – that he wrote this as a test or trial of my honesty.

Gloucester   [*reading aloud*] *This practice of revering old people makes the best years of our lives a misery. It keeps our legacies from us till we're too old to enjoy them. I'm beginning to feel that oppression by an aged tyrant is stupid and foolish slavery. It operates not through strength, but through the victim's willingness to suffer. Come and see me, so I can explain further. If our father would only sleep till I awakened him, you'd enjoy half his income forever – and be beloved of your brother,* Edgar.

Hmm! Conspiracy! ''Sleep till I awakened him, you'd enjoy half his income . . .'' My son Edgar! Could he have written this? Had he a heart and a brain to think it up? When did this come to you? Who brought it?

Edmund   It wasn't brought to me, my lord. There's the cunning of it. I found it thrown through the window of my bedroom.

Gloucester   You recognize the handwriting as your brother's?

Edmund   If the contents were acceptable, my lord, I'd swear it was his. But in connection with that [*he indicates the letter*] I'd prefer to think it wasn't.

Gloucester   It *is* his!

Edmund   It's his writing, my lord, but I hope his heart isn't in the contents.

Gloucester   Has he ever sounded you out on this business before?

Edmund   Never, my lord. But I've often heard him maintain it to be only right that, once sons reach maturity and fathers are past their prime, the father should be in the custody of the son, and the son should manage his affairs.

Gloucester O villain, villain! His very opinion in the letter!
   Abhorred villain! Unnatural detested, brutish villain!
   Worse than brutish! Go, sirrah, seek him; I'll apprehend
   him. Abominable villain! Where is he?

Edmund I do not well know, my lord. If it shall please you
   to suspend your indignation against my brother till you can
   derive from him better testimony of his intent, you should
   run a certain course; where, if you violently proceed against
   him, mistaking his purpose, it would make a great gap in
   your own honour, and shake in pieces the heart of his
   obedience. I dare pawn down my life for him, that he hath
   writ this to feel my affection to your honour, and to no
   other pretence of danger.

Gloucester Think you so?

Edmund If your honour judge it meet, I will place you
   where you shall hear us confer of this, and by an auricular
   assurance have your satisfaction; and that without any
   further delay than this very evening.

Gloucester He cannot be such a monster.

Edmund Nor is not, sure.

Gloucester To his father, that so tenderly and entirely loves
   him. Heaven and earth! Edmund, seek him out; wind me
   into him, I pray you: frame the business after your own
   wisdom. I would unstate myself to be in a due resolution.

Edmund I will seek him, sir, presently; convey the business
   as I shall find means, and acquaint you withal.

Gloucester These late eclipses in the sun and moon portend
   no good to us: though the wisdom of nature can reason it
   thus and thus, yet nature finds itself scourged by the
   sequent effects. Love cools, friendship falls off, brothers
   divide: in cities, mutinies; in countries, discord; in palaces,

Gloucester   Oh, the villain, the villain! That's exactly what he says in the letter! The hated villain! The unnatural, detestable, brutish villain! Worse than brutish! Go, sir, find him. I'll arrest him. The detestable villain! Where is he?

Edmund   I don't really know, my lord. If you could contain your anger against my brother till you can extract from him a clearer indication of his intentions, you'd be better advised. On the other hand, if you react violently against him, mistaking his purpose, your own honor will be greatly damaged, and his loyalty shaken to the core. I'd stake my life on him: he's written this to test my love for your honor, and not with dangerous intent.

Gloucester   Do you think so?

Edmund   If your honor thinks it's a good idea, I'll place you where you can hear us discuss this, and by hearing for yourself you can settle your doubts this very evening at the latest.

Gloucester   He can't be such a monster –

Edmund   Nor is he, surely.

Gloucester   – to his own father, who loves him so tenderly and entirely! Heaven and earth! Edmund, find him. Get his confidence, do. Use your discretion. I'd give my all to be assured of his innocence.

Edmund   I'll look for him, sir, immediately: work things as best I can, and report back.

Gloucester   These recent eclipses of the sun and moon are bad omens for us. Though human reason can explain such things away, nonetheless mankind has to suffer the natural consequences. Love cools off. Friendship declines. Brothers are divided. In cities there are riots; in countries, civil war; in

treason; and the bond cracked 'twixt son and father. This
villain of mine comes under the prediction; there's son
against father: the King falls from bias of nature; there's
father against child. We have seen the best of our time:
machinations, hollowness, treachery, and all ruinous
disorders follow us disquietly to our graves. Find out this
villain, Edmund; it shall lose thee nothing: do it carefully.
And the noble and true-hearted Kent banished! His offence,
honesty! 'Tis strange.

[*Exit*]

Edmund   This is the excellent foppery of the world, that,
when we are sick in fortune, often the surfeit of our own
behaviour, we make guilty of our disasters the sun, the
moon, and stars; as if we were villains by necessity, fools by
heavenly compulsion; knaves, thieves, and treachers by
spherical predominance; drunkards, liars, and adulterers by
an enforced obedience of planetary influence; and all that we
are evil in, by a divine thrusting on. An admirable evasion
of whoremaster man, to lay his goatish disposition to the
charge of a star! My father compounded with my mother
under the Dragon's tail, and my nativity was under Ursa
Major; so that it follows I am rough and lecherous. Tut! I
should have been that I am had the maidenliest star in the
firmament twinkled on my bastardizing. Edgar –

[*Enter* **Edgar**]

Pat he come, like the catastrophe of the old comedy: my
cue is villainous melancholy, with a sigh like Tom o'
Bedlam. O, these eclipses do portend these divisions.

Edgar   How now, brother Edmund! What serious
contemplation are you in?

palaces, treason; and the bond between son and father is broken. This villain of mine fits the pattern: there's son against father. The King goes against his natural instincts: there's father against child. We've had the best years: intrigue, insincerity, treachery and chaos follow us distressingly to our graves. Sound out this villain, Edmund; you'll lose nothing by it. Do it discreetly. And the noble and loyal Kent is banished: his offense, honesty! It's strange.

[*He goes*]

Edmund   How typically stupid: when things go wrong, often through our own fault, we blame our troubles on the sun, moon and stars! As though we are villains through no choice of our own; fools by order of heaven; knaves, thieves and traitors through the dominance of a planet at our births; drunkards, liars and adulterers by compulsion from the stars; and that all our evil acts come from divine provocation! An admirable alibi for lecherous man, to blame his lustful disposition on a star! My father tumbled my mother under a waning moon and I was born under the Great Bear: so it follows that I'm rough and lecherous? Pah! I'd be what I am had the most chaste star in the firmament twinkled over my illegitimacy! Edgar –

[**Edgar** *enters*]

– and here he comes, as predictably as the ending of an old-fashioned play. My role requires deep melancholy – with a sigh like that of a lunatic beggar. [*He assumes a suitably solemn face and manner of speech*] Oh, these eclipses are premonitions of disorder . . . [*He hums to himself as if deep in philosophic thought*]

Edgar   Greetings, brother Edmund! What's the big problem on your mind?

51

Edmund   I am thinking, brother, of a prediction I read this other day, what should follow these eclipses.

Edgar   Do you busy yourself about that?

Edmund   I promise you, the effects he writes of succeed unhappily; as of unnaturalness between the child and the parent; death, dearth, dissolutions of ancient amities; divisions in state; menaces and maledictions against king and nobles; needless diffidences, banishment of friends, dissipation of cohorts, nuptial breaches, and I know not what.

Edgar   How long have you been a sectary astronomical?

Edmund   When saw you my father last?

Edgar   The night gone by.

Edmund   Spake you with him?

Edgar   Ay, two hours together.

Edmund   Parted you in good terms? Found you no displeasure in him by word nor countenance?

Edgar   None at all.

Edmund   Bethink yourself wherein you may have offended him; and at my entreaty forbear his presence until some little time hath qualified the heat of his displeasure, which at this instant so rageth in him that with the mischief of your person it would scarcely allay.

Edgar   Some villain hath done me wrong.

Edmund   That's my fear. I pray you have a continent forbearance till the speed of his rage goes slower; and as I say, retire with me to my lodging, from whence I will fitly bring you to hear my lord speak. Pray ye, go; there's my key. If you do stir abroad, go armed.

Edgar   Armed, brother!

Edmund   I'm thinking, brother, of a prediction I read the other day about what will follow from these eclipses.

Edgar   Do you worry about things like that?

Edmund   I assure you that the consequences written about turn out to be disagreeable: such as unnaturalness between child and parent; death, famine and the ending of longstanding friendships; disunity in countries; threats and curses against King and nobles; unfounded suspicions; the banishment of friends; desertion of troops; matrimonial strife; and I don't know what.

Edgar   How long have you been a student of astrology?

Edmund   When did you last see my father?

Edgar   Last night.

Edmund   Did you speak to him?

Edgar   Yes. Fully two hours.

Edmund   Did you part on friendly terms? Did he seem displeased by the way he spoke or looked?

Edgar   Not at all.

Edmund   Try to think how you may have offended him. Do me the favor of avoiding him till his temper has cooled. At the moment he's so furious that injury to your person would hardly cool his anger.

Edgar   Some villain has wronged me!

Edmund   That's what I fear. I advise you to keep at a discreet distance till he calms down: and as I say, come back with me to my place, where at an opportune time I'll let you overhear what my lord says. Please – go! There's my key. If you do go out, go armed.

Edgar   Armed, brother?

Edmund   Brother, I advise you to the best. I am no honest
    man if there be any good meaning towards you; I have told
    you what I have seen and heard: but faintly, nothing like
    the image and horror of it; pray you, away.

Edgar   Shall I hear from you anon?

Edmund   I do serve you in this business.

                                  [*Exit* **Edgar**]

    A credulous father, and a brother noble,
    Whose nature is so far from doing harms
    That he suspects none; on whose foolish honesty
    My practices ride easy! I see the business.
    Let me, if not by birth, have lands by wit:
    All with me's meet that I can fashion fit.

                                    [*Exit*]

Scene 3

The Duke of Albany's palace. Enter **Goneril,** *and* **Oswald,** *her
Steward.*

Goneril   Did my father strike my gentleman for chiding of
    his Fool?

Oswald   Ay, madam.

Goneril   By day and night, he wrongs me; every hour
    He flashes into one gross crime or other,
    That sets us all at odds: I'll not endure it:
    His knights grow riotous, and himself upbraids us

Edmund Brother, I advise you for the best. I'd be a liar if I said there's any good will toward you. I've told you what I've seen and heard, but toned it down – nothing like the horrible reality. Please, go!

Edgar Shall I hear from you soon?

Edmund Leave everything to me. [**Edgar** *goes.* **Edmund** *laughs out loud*] A credulous father and a noble brother! He's so incapable of mischief himself that he suspects none. His foolish honesty is no match for my wiles. It's very simple: if I can't get property through inheritance, I'll get it by using my wits. Anything goes that suits my purposes.

Scene 3

The Duke of Albany's palace. Enter **Goneril** *and her steward* **Oswald.**

Goneril Did my father strike my officer for rebuking his Fool?

Oswald Yes, madam.

Goneril He does me wrong by day and night. Not an hour passes but he commits one flagrant offense or another that has us all at loggerheads. I won't put up with it. His knights are getting riotous, and he himself scolds us about

On every trifle. When he returns from hunting
I will not speak with him; say I am sick:
If you come slack of former services,
You shall do well; the fault of it I'll answer.

Oswald He's coming, madam; I hear him.

[*Horns within*]

Goneril Put on what weary negligence you please,
You and your fellows; I'd have it come to question:
If he distaste it, let him to my sister,
Whose mind and mine, I know, in that are one,
Not to be over-ruled. Idle old man,
That still would manage those authorities
That he hath given away! Now, by my life,
Old fools are babes again, and must be used
With checks as flatteries, when they are seen abused.
Remember what I have said.

Oswald   Well, madam.

Goneril And let his knights have colder looks among you;
What grows of it, no matter; advise your fellows so:
I would breed from hence occasions, and I shall,
That I may speak: I'll write straight to my sister
To hold my very course. Prepare for dinner.

[*Exeunt*]

every little thing. When he returns from hunting, I won't speak to him. Say I'm sick. If you're less dutiful than formerly, that will be quite all right. I'll take the responsibility.

[*Hunting horns can be heard*]

Oswald   He's coming, madam. I can hear him.

Goneril   Be as offhand as you like, you and your colleagues. I want to make an issue of it. If he doesn't like it, let him go to my sister. She and I are of one mind, not to give in to him. Silly old man, who wants to be in charge of what he's given away! Upon my soul, old fools are babies again, and must be restrained when they are deluded. Remember what I've said.

Oswald   I will indeed, madam.

Goneril   Be cooler to his knights. Ignore the consequences. Spread the word among your colleagues. I'll make capital out of such incidents; I will, so I can speak out. I'll write to my sister at once to do the same. Prepare for dinner.

[*They go*]

Scene 4

A hall in the same. Enter **Kent,** *disguised.*

Kent   If but as well I other accents borrow,
That can my speech defuse, my good intent
May carry through itself to that full issue
For which I razed my likeness. Now, banished Kent,
If thou canst serve where thou dost stand condemned,
So may it come, thy master, whom thou lovest,
Shall find thee full of labours.

[*Horns within. Enter* **Lear,** *Knights, and Attendants*]

Lear   Let me not stay a jot for dinner: go, get it ready.

[*Exit an Attendant*]

How now! What art thou?

Kent   A man, sir.

Lear   What dost thou profess? What would'st thou with us?

Kent   I do profess to be no less than I seem; to serve him
truly that will put me in trust; to love him that is honest; to
converse with him that is wise, and says little; to fear
judgment; to fight when I cannot choose; and to eat no fish.

Lear   What art thou?

Kent   A very honest-hearted fellow, and as poor as the King.

Lear   If thou be'st as poor for a subject as he is for a King,
thou art poor enough. What would'st thou?

Kent   Service.

Lear   Who would'st thou serve?

Scene 4

Another room in the palace. Enter **Kent**, *in disguise*

Kent   If I can also alter my voice, I may be able to carry out the worthy purpose which prompted my disguise. Well now, banished Kent, if you can serve where you stand condemned, it may well be that your master, whom you love, will discover you are a dedicated servant.

[*Hunting horns herald the entrance of the* **King** *and his Knights*]

Lear   [*to his* **Servant**] Don't keep me waiting for dinner! Go and get it ready. [*The* **Servant** *goes*] Well now, who are you?

Kent   A man, sir.

Lear   What's your profession? What's your business with us?

Kent   I profess to be no less than I appear to be; to serve any man loyally who'll trust me; to love the man who is honest; to consort with the man who is wise but says little; to fear being judged; to fight when I have no alternative; and to eat no fish.

Lear   What are you?

Kent   A very genuine fellow, and as poor as the King.

Lear   If you are as poor a subject as he is a King, that's pretty poor! What are you seeking?

Kent   Employment.

Lear   With whom?

Kent   You.

Lear   Dost thou know me, fellow?

Kent   No, sir; but you have that in your countenance which I would fain call master.

Lear   What's that?

Kent   Authority.

Lear   What services canst thou do?

Kent   I can keep honest counsel, ride, run, mar a curious tale in telling it, and deliver a plain message bluntly; that which ordinary men are fit for, I am qualified in, and the best of me is diligence.

Lear   How old art thou?

Kent   Not so young, sir, to love a woman for singing, nor so old to dote on her for anything; I have years on my back forty-eight.

Lear   Follow me; thou shalt serve me; if I like thee no worse after dinner I will not part from thee yet. Dinner, ho! Dinner! Where's my knave? My Fool? Go you and call my Fool hither.

[Exit an Attendant]

[Enter **Oswald**]

You, you, sirrah, where's my daughter?

Oswald   So please you –

[Exit]

Lear   What says the fellow there? Call the clotpoll back.

[Exit a **Knight**]

Kent   You.

Lear   Do you know me, man?

Kent   No, sir, but there's something in your bearing that I respect.

Lear   What's that?

Kent   Authority.

Lear   What services can you perform?

Kent   I can keep a secret; ride; run; spoil a good story in the telling of it; and deliver a simple message bluntly. What ordinary men are fit for, I'm good at. My best quality is determination.

Lear   How old are you?

Kent   Not so young, sir, that I'd love a woman for singing, nor so old as to dote on her for anything. I'm forty-eight.

Lear   Follow me. You can be my servant. If I like you no less after dinner, I'll take you on permanently. Dinner! hey there! Dinner! Where's my knave? My Fool? [*To an Attendant*] Go and fetch my Fool.

[*The Attendant leaves.* **Oswald** *enters*]

You. You, fellow. Where's my daughter?

Oswald   [*brushing past him*] Excuse me – [*he goes*]

Lear   What did the fellow say? Call the blockhead back! [*A* **Knight** *goes in pursuit*] Where's my Fool, eh? I think the

Where's my Fool, ho? I think the world's asleep.

[*Re-enter* **Knight**]

How now! Where's that mongrel?

Knight   He says, my lord, your daughter is not well.

Lear   Why came not the slave back to me when I called him?

Knight   Sir, he answered me in the roundest manner, he would not.

Lear   He would not!

Knight   My lord, I know not what the matter is; but, to my judgment, your Highness is not entertained with that ceremonious affection as you were wont; there's a great abatement of kindness appears as well in the general dependants as in the Duke himself also and your daughter.

Lear   Ha! say'st thou so?

Knight   I beseech you, pardon me, my lord, if I be mistaken; for my duty cannot be silent when I think your Highness wronged.

Lear   Thou but rememberest me of mine own conception: I have perceived a most faint neglect of late; which I have rather blamed as mine own jealous curiosity than as a very pretence and purpose of unkindness: I will look further into't. But where's my Fool? I have not seen him this two days.

Knight   Since my young lady's going into France, sir, the Fool hath much pined away.

Lear   No more of that; I have noted it well. Go you, and tell

world's asleep. [*The* **Knight** *returns alone*] Well, where's
that mongrel?

Knight   He says, my lord, that your daughter isn't well.

Lear   Why didn't the slave come back to me when I called
him?

Knight   Sir, he answered in the rudest manner that he would
not.

Lear   He would not?

Knight   My lord, I don't know why, but in my opinion your
Highness is not being treated with the same respectful
ceremony as you are used to. There's a distinct unfriend-
liness among the staff, as well as in the Duke himself and
your daughter.

Lear   Hm? Do you think so?

Knight   Please forgive me, my lord, if I'm mistaken. My
duty won't allow me to be silent when I think your Highness
is being wronged.

Lear   You are only reminding me of what I've noticed myself. I
have observed a hint of neglect lately. I'd put it down to my
own jealous sensitivity rather than a deliberate intention to
be uncivil. I'll look further into it. But where's my Fool? I
haven't seen him these last two days.

Knight   Since my young lady went to France, sir, the Fool has
pined away considerably.

Lear   Enough of that. I've taken good note of it. [*To an*

my daughter I would speak with her.

[*Exit an Attendant*]

Go you, call hither my Fool.

[*Exit an Attendant*]

[*Enter* **Oswald**]

Oh, you sir, you, come you hither, sir. Who am I, sir?

Oswald   My lady's father.

Lear   'My lady's father!' My lord's knave: you whoreson dog! You slave! You cur!

Oswald   I am none of these, my lord; I beseech your pardon.

Lear   Do you bandy looks with me, you rascal?   [*Striking him*]

Oswald   I'll not be struck, my lord.

Kent   Nor tripped neither, you base football player.   [*Tripping up his heels*]

Lear   I thank thee, fellow; thou servest me, and I'll love thee.

Kent   Come, sir, arise, away! I'll teach you differences: away, away! If you will measure your lubber's length again, tarry; but away! Have you wisdom? [*Exit* **Oswald**] So.

Lear   Now, my friendly knave, I thank thee: there's earnest of thy service.   [*Gives* **Kent** *money*].

[*Enter* **Fool**]

Fool   Let me hire him too: here's my coxcomb.   [*Offers* **Kent** *his cap*]

Lear   How now, my pretty knave! How dost thou?

Attendant] Go and tell my daughter I want to speak to her. [*The Attendant leaves*] You [*to another*], go and bring my Fool here. [*The Attendant goes*]

[**Oswald** *enters*]

Oh, you, sir. You. Come here, sir. Who am I, sir?

Oswald   My lady's father.

Lear   "My lady's father"! My lord's lackey, you lousy dog! You wretch! You cur!

Oswald   I am none of these, my lord; I beg your pardon.

Lear   Do you exchange looks with me, you rascal? [*He strikes* **Oswald** *angrily*]

Oswald   I won't be struck, my lord.

Kent   Or tripped, either, you contemptible lout? [**Oswald** *falls to the ground*]

Lear   Thank you, fellow. You're my servant, and I'll take care of you.

Kent   [*to Oswald*] Come on, sir, get up and go! I'll teach you your place! Be off with you: go! If you want to be stretched out full length again, stay. But away with you! Use your common sense. [**Oswald** *runs off*] That's right.

Lear   Now, my friendly fellow, thank you: there's something on account. [*He gives* **Kent** *some money*]

[*The* **Fool** *enters*]

Fool   Let me hire him too: here's my coxcomb. [*He offers* **Kent** *his jester's cap, which resembles a cock's comb in shape and color*]

Lear   Hello, there, my pretty fellow! How have you been?

Fool   Sirrah, you were best take my coxcomb.

Kent   Why, Fool?

Fool   Why, for taking one's part that's out of favour. Nay, and thou canst not smile as the wind sits, thou'lt catch cold shortly: there, take my coxcomb. Why, this fellow has banished two on 's daughters, and did the third a blessing against his will: if thou follow him thou must needs wear my coxcomb. How now, nuncle! Would I had two cox-combs and two daughters!

Lear   Why, my boy?

Fool   If I gave them all my living, I'd keep my coxcombs myself. There's mine; beg another of thy daughters.

Lear   Take heed, sirrah; the whip.

Fool   Truth's a dog must to kennel; he must be whipped out when Lady the brach may stand by the fire and stink.

Lear   A pestilent gall to me!

Fool   Sirrah, I'll teach thee a speech.

Lear   Do.

Fool   Mark it, nuncle:

Have more than thou showest,
Speak less than thou knowest,
Lend less than thou owest,
Ride more than thou goest,
Learn more than thou trowest,
Set less than thou throwest;
Leave thy drink and thy whore

Fool   Sir, you had better have my coxcomb.

Kent   Why, Fool?

Fool   Why? For siding with someone who's out of favor. No, if you can't side with the winners, you'll be in trouble shortly. So there: take my coxcomb. Why, this fellow [*indicating* **Lear**] has alienated two of his daughters and done the third one a blessing without intending to. If you join his service, you'll have to wear my coxcomb. [*To* **Lear**] Greetings, uncle. I wish I had two coxcombs and two daughters.

Lear   Why, my boy?

Fool   If I gave them all my possessions, I'd keep my coxcombs for myself. [*He offers his cap to* **Lear**] There's mine. Beg the second off your daughters.

Lear   Watch it, now: you'll be whipped!

Fool   Truth is a dog that's sent to his kennel. He gets whipped, whereas flattery, the hound bitch, is allowed to stand in front of the fire, and stink.

Lear   [*brooding*] It's quite insufferable!

Fool   Sir, I'll tell you something.

Lear   Do.

Fool   Listen carefully, uncle:

>Own more than you show,
>Don't tell all you know,
>Lend less than you've got,
>Ride more than you trot,
>Don't believe all you're told,
>Don't risk all your gold;
>Give up drink and your whores,

And keep in-a-door,
And thou shalt have more
Than two tens to a score.

Kent   This is nothing, Fool.

Fool   Then 'tis like the breath of an unfee'd lawyer; you give
me nothing for't. Can you make no use of nothing, nuncle?

Lear   Why no, boy; nothing can be made out of nothing.

Fool   [*to* **Kent**] Prithee, tell him, so much the rent of his
land comes to: he will not believe a Fool.

Lear   A bitter Fool!

Fool   Dost thou know the difference, my boy, between a
bitter Fool and a sweet one?

Lear   No, lad; teach me.

Fool   That lord that counselled thee
       To give away thy land,
Come place him here by me;
       Do thou for him stand:
The sweet and bitter fool
       Will presently appear;
The one in motley here,
       The other found out there.

Lear   Dost thou call me fool, boy?

Fool   All thy other titles thou hast given away; that thou wast
born with.

Kent   This is not altogether fool, my lord.

Fool   No, faith, lords and great men will not let me; if I had
a monopoly out, they would have part on't: and ladies too,

Don't stray out of doors,
And you will have more
Than two tens to the score.

Kent   This is a lot of nothing, Fool.

Fool   Then it's like the advice of a lawyer working without
a fee: you get it for nothing. Can't you make use of nothing,
uncle?

Lear   Why no, boy. Nothing can be made out of nothing.

Fool   [*to* **Kent**] Do me a favor. Tell him that's what his
income amounts to. He won't believe a Fool.

Lear   A bitter Fool!

Fool   [*to* **Lear**] Do you know the difference, my boy, between a
bitter Fool and a sweet one?

Lear   No, lad, tell me.

Fool   Whoever counselled you
    To give away your land,
Come place him here by me,
    While you for him there stand:
The sweet and bitter fool
    Will instantly appear;
The one in motley here –
    The other standing there!

[*He points to* **Lear** *as the bitter one*]

Lear   Are you calling me a fool, boy?

Fool   All your other titles you have given away. That one you
were born with.

Kent   He's not all fool, my lord.

Fool   No, indeed. Lords and great men won't let me be. If I
had the monopoly, they'd want their share of the profits.

they will not let me have all the fool to myself: they'll be snatching. Nuncle, give me an egg, and I'll give thee two crowns.

Lear   What two crowns shall they be?

Fool   Why, after I have cut the egg i' th' middle and eat up the meat, the two crowns of the egg. When thou clovest thy crown i' th' middle, and gavest away both parts, thou borest thine ass on thy back o'er the dirt: thou hadst little wit in thy bald crown when thou gavest thy golden one away. If I speak like myself in this, let him be whipped that first find it so.

[*Singing*]

>   *Fools had ne'er less grace in a year;*
>   *For wise men are grown foppish,*
>   *And know not how their wits to wear,*
>   *Their manners are so apish.*

Lear   When were you wont to be so full of songs, sirrah?

Fool   I have used it, nuncle, ever since thou madest thy daughters thy mothers; for when thou gavest them the rod and puttest down thine own breeches,

[*Singing*]

>   *Then they for sudden joy did weep,*
>   *And I for sorrow sung,*
>   *That such a king should play bo-peep,*
>   *And go the fools among.*

Prithee, nuncle, keep a schoolmaster than can teach thy Fool to lie: I would fain learn to lie.

Lear   An you lie, sirrah, we'll have you whipped.

Fool   I marvel what kin thou and thy daughters are: they'll have me whipped for speaking true, thou't have me whipped for lying; and sometimes I am whipped for holding my peace. I had rather be any kind o' thing than a Fool;

And ladies, too: they wouldn't let me monopolize fooling; they'd be snatching. Uncle, give me an egg, and I'll give you two crowns.

Lear   What two crowns would they be?

Fool   Why, after I'd cut the egg down the middle, and eaten the yolk, the two halves of the eggshell! When you chopped your crown in two and gave both parts away, you were like the man in the fable who carried his ass on his back over the mire. You had little common sense in that bald crown of yours when you gave your golden one away. If I'm speaking like a fool, whip the man who's responsible. [*He sings*]

> Fools have never fared so ill
>   'Cos wise men have turned dopey,
> Fools don't know how to sell their skill,
>   When it's not hard to copy.

Lear   Since when have you been so full of songs, eh?

Fool   I've been in the mood, uncle, ever since you made your daughters your mothers. When you gave them a cane and dropped your trousers [*he sings*]

> They suddenly both wept for joy,
>   And I in sorrow sang,
> That such a King should play the dunce,
>   And join the foolish gang.

Please, uncle, employ a schoolmaster to teach your Fool how to lie. I'd like to learn how to lie.

Lear   If you lie, laddie, we'll have you whipped.

Fool   I can't make out the relationship between you and your daughters. They'll have me whipped for speaking the truth; you'll have me whipped for lying. Sometimes I'm whipped for saying nothing at all. I'd rather be anything at all than a

and yet I would not be thee, nuncle; thou hast pared thy wit
o' both sides, and left nothing i' th' middle: here comes one
o' the parings.

[*Enter* **Goneril**]

Lear   How now, daughter! What makes that frontlet on? You
are too much of late i' th' frown.

Fool   Thou was a pretty fellow when thou hadst no need to
care for her frowning; now thou art an O without a figure. I
am better than thou art now; I am a Fool, thou art nothing.
[*To* **Goneril**] Yes, forsooth, I will hold my tongue; so your
face bids me, though you say nothing.

Mum, mum:
He that keeps nor crust nor crumb,
Weary of all, shall want some.

[*Pointing to* **Lear**] That's a shealed peascod.

Goneril   Not only, sir, this your all-licenced Fool,
But other of your insolent retinue
Do hourly carp and quarrel, breaking forth
In rank and not-to-be-endured riots. Sir,
I had thought, by making this well known unto you,
To have found a safe redress; but now grow fearful,
But what yourself too late have spoke and done,
That you protect this course, and put it on
By your allowance; which if you should, the fault
Would not 'scape censure, nor the redress sleep,
Which, in the tender of a wholesome weal,
Might in their working do you that offence,
Which else were shame, that then necessity
Will call discreet proceeding.

Fool   For you know, nuncle,

The hedge-sparrow fed the cuckoo so long,

Fool. But I wouldn't be you, uncle. You have sliced your brains in two and left nothing in the middle. Here comes one of the halves.

[**Goneril** *enters*]

Lear   Well, now, daughter. Why the face? You frown too much lately.

Fool   You were a lucky fellow when you didn't need to care about her frowning. Now you are a nonentity. I'm better than you are now. I'm a Fool. You are nothing. [*To* **Goneril**] Yes indeed. I'll hold my tongue. That's what your face is saying, though you haven't spoken.

> Hush, hush:
> The man who gives away his all,
> May find his kindness turns to gall.

[*Pointing to* **Lear**] He's an empty pea-pod.

Goneril   Not merely, sir, your free-speaking Fool, but others among your insolent followers are bickering and quarreling hour by hour, erupting into gross and intolerable rioting. Sir, I thought that by bringing this to your notice I'd get things put right. Now I'm beginning to fear, from what you yourself all too recently have said and done, that you are covering up this behavior, and encouraging it by your tolerance. If this is the case, the offense would not go uncriticized. Nor would disciplinary measures for the good of society be slow in coming: much as they'll offend you, and might in other circumstances seem humiliating, if it were not that necessity justified them.

Fool   'Cos you know, uncle:

> The hedge-sparrow fed the cuckoo for so long

That it had its head bit off by its young.

So out went the candle, and we were left darkling.

Lear   Are you our daughter?

Goneril   I would you would make use of your good wisdom,
Whereof I know you are fraught; and put away
These dispositions which of late transport you
From what you rightly are.

Fool   May not an ass know when the cart draws the horse?
Whoop, Jug! I love thee.

Lear   Does any here know me? This is not Lear:
Does Lear walk thus? Speak thus? Where are his eyes?
Either his notion weakens, his discernings
Are lethargied – Ha! waking? 'tis not so.
Who is it that can tell me who I am?

Fool   Lear's shadow.

Lear   I would learn that; for by the marks of sovereignty,
knowledge and reason, I should be false persuaded I had
daughters.

Fool   Which they will make an obedient father.

Lear   Your name, fair gentlewoman?

Goneril   This admiration, sir, is much o' th' savour
Of other your new pranks. I do beseech you
To understand my purposes aright:
As you are old and reverend, you should be wise.
Here you do keep a hundred knights and squires;
Men so disordered, so deboshed, and bold,
That this our court, infected with their manners,
Shows like a riotous inn: epicurism and lust
Makes it more like a tavern or a brothel
Than a graced palace. The shame itself doth speak

That it had its head bitten off by its young.

So out went the light and we were in darkness!

Lear   [*to* **Goneril**] Are you really our daughter?

Goneril   I wish you would use your common sense, which I know you possess, and that you'd cast off these temperamental moods which recently have changed your personality.

Fool   Can't a fool tell when the cart draws the horse? Gee-up, Joan! I love you!

Lear   Does anyone here recognize me? This can't be Lear. Does Lear walk like this? Speak like this? Where are his eyes? Either his brain is getting weak or his senses are sluggish. What, awake? It can't be so. Is there anyone here who can tell me who I am?

Fool   [*aside*] Lear's shadow . . .

Lear   [*not heeding the comment*] I'd really like to know, because from the evidence of sanity, knowledge and reason I'd be misled into believing I had daughters.

Fool   Who will make you into an obedient father.

Lear   [*to* **Goneril** *with heavy sarcasm*] Your name, fair lady?

Goneril   This play-acting, sir, is much in line with these other new pranks of yours. I want you to understand me clearly. As you are old and respected, you should be wise. Here you keep a hundred knights and squires, men so disorderly, so debauched and insolent, that our court – influenced by their conduct – resembles a rowdy inn. Luxurious living and pleasure-seeking make it more like a tavern or a brothel than a respectable palace. It's so shameful as to demand instant

For instant remedy; be then desired
By her, that else will take the thing she begs,
A little to disquantity your train;
And the remainders that shall still depend,
To be such men as may besort your age,
Which know themselves and you.

Lear   Darkness and devils!
Saddle my horses; call my train together.
Degenerate bastard! I'll not trouble thee:
Yet have I left a daughter.

Goneril   You strike my people, and your disordered rabble
Make servants of their betters.

[*Enter* **Albany**]

Lear   Woe, that too late repents! [*To* **Albany**] O sir, are you
   come?
Is it your will? Speak, sir. Prepare my horses.
Ingratitude, thou marble-hearted fiend,
More hideous, when thou show'st thee in a child,
Than the sea-monster!

Albany   Pray, sir, be patient.

Lear   [*to* **Goneril**] Detested kite, thou liest!
My train are men of choice and rarest parts,
That all particulars of duty know,
And in the most exact regard support
The worships of their name. O most small fault,
How ugly didst thou in Cordelia show!
Which, like an engine, wrenched my frame of nature
From the fixed place, drew from my heart all love,
And added to the gall. O Lear, Lear, Lear!
Beat at this gate, that let thy folly in [*striking his head*]
And thy dear judgment out! Go, go, my people.

[*Exeunt* **Kent** *and Knights*]

redress. Therefore, be requested by one who'll otherwise
take what she's politely asking for: reduce the size of your
retinue somewhat, and keep as your remaining attendants
men appropriate to your age, who can control themselves
and you.

Lear   Hell and damnation! Saddle my horses! Call my troop
together! [*To* **Goneril**] You misbegotten bastard! I won't
trouble you. I still have one daughter left!

Goneril   You strike my servants, and your rowdy rabble order
their betters around.

[**Albany** *enters*]

Lear   Woe to him who repents too late! [*To* **Albany**] Oh, sir, so
you're here. Is this your doing? Answer me, sir! [*To his
Servants*] Get my horses ready. Oh, ingratitude! You're a
fiend with a heart of stone, more hideous than any monster
of the sea when you reveal yourself in a child.

Albany   Really, sir, compose yourself!

Lear   [*to* **Goneril**] Vulture! You tell lies. My troops are men of
rare distinction, who know their duties, and are meticulous
in living up to their honorable reputations. Oh, how a
relatively small defect seemed repugnant in Cordelia! It
wrenched me apart as if I were on the rack, drew all my love
from my heart, and generated bitterness. Oh, Lear, Lear,
Lear! [*He slaps his forehead in despair*] Knock at this door
that let your folly in, and your discretion out! [*Gesturing to
his followers*] Go, go, my people. [**Kent** *and the Knights
leave*]

Albany   My lord, I am guiltless, as I am ignorant
Of what hath moved you.

Lear   It may be so, my lord.
Hear, Nature, hear! Dear goddess, hear!
Suspend thy purpose, if thou didst intend
To make this creature fruitful!
Into her womb convey sterility!
Dry up in her the organs of increase,
And from her derogate body never spring
A babe to honour her! If she must teem,
Create her child of spleen, that it may live
And be a thwart disnatured torment to her!
Let it stamp wrinkles in her brow of youth,
With cadent tears fret channels in her cheeks,
Turn all her mother's pains and benefits
To laughter and contempt that she may feel
How sharper than a serpent's tooth it is
To have a thankless child! Away, away!

                                                        [*Exit*]

Albany   Now, gods that we adore, whereof comes this?

Goneril   Never afflict yourself to know more of it:
But let his disposition have that scope
As dotage gives it.

[*re-enter* **Lear**]

Lear   What! fifty of my followers at a clap!
Within a fortnight!

Albany   What's the matter, sir?

Lear   I'll tell thee. [*To* **Goneril**] Life and death! I am
ashamed

Albany   My lord, I am as guiltless as I am ignorant of what has upset you.

Lear   Possibly so, my lord. [*He turns again to* **Goneril**] Hear, Nature, hear! Dear goddess, hear! If you intended her to be fertile, change your mind! Make her sterile! Dry up her womb, and may her despicable body never honor her with a baby! If she must breed, make her child all malice, so it will live to be a peevish, cold-hearted torment to her! May it put wrinkles in her young brow; may tears cut channels in her cheeks; all her maternal care turn into mockery and contempt, so that she realizes how sharper than a serpent's tooth it is to have a thankless child! Let's away, away . . . [*He rushes off, overcome with emotion*]

Albany   Now by all the gods, what started that?

Goneril   Don't bother yourself to find out. Let his old age have its fling.

[**Lear** *returns*]

Lear   What, fifty of my followers at a stroke? Within a fortnight?

Albany   What do you mean, sir?

Lear   I'll tell you. [*To* **Goneril**] Life and death! I am ashamed

That thou hast power to shake my manhood thus,
That these hot tears, which break from me perforce,
Should make thee worth them. Blasts and fogs upon thee!
Th'untented woundings of a father's curse
Pierce every sense about thee! Old fond eyes,
Beweep this cause again, I'll pluck ye out,
And cast you, with the waters that you loose,
To temper clay. Yea, is't come to this?
Ha! Let it be so: I have another daughter,
Who, I am sure, is kind and comfortable:
When she shall hear this of thee, with her nails
She'll flay thy wolvish visage. Thou shalt find
That I'll resume the shape which thou dost think
I have cast off for ever.

[*Exit*]

Goneril   Do you mark that?

Albany   I cannot be so partial, Goneril,
To the great love I bear you, –

Goneril   Pray you, content. What, Oswald, ho!
[*To the* **Fool**] You, sir, more knave than fool, after your
master.

Fool   Nuncle Lear, Nuncle Lear! Tarry, take the Fool with
thee.

A fox, when one has caught her,
And such a daughter,
Should sure to the slaughter,
If my cap would buy a halter;
So the Fool follows after.

[*Exit*]

that you can shake my manly dignity like this, as though you
are worthy of these hot tears that burst from me. Storms
and fogs upon you! May the deep wounds of a father's
curse pierce all your senses! Foolish old eyes, if you persist
in weeping, I'll pluck you out, and trample you and your
tears into the ground. Has it really come to this? Right. So
be it. I have another daughter who I'm sure is kind and
comforting. When she hears about you, she'll scratch your
wolvish face with her nails. You'll discover that I'll resume
the role that you think I've cast off forever.

[*He staggers off, overwhelmed*]

Goneril   Did you note that?

Albany   For all the great love I have for you, Goneril, I can't be
so biased as −

Goneril   [*stopping him*] That's enough. [*Calling*] Oswald there!
[*To the* **Fool**] You, sir − more rascal than fool − be off after
your master.

Fool   Uncle Lear, Uncle Lear! Hold on, take the Fool with you!

A fox, when one has caught her,
And such a daughter,
Should surely go for slaughter,
If my cap would buy a halter.
So the Fool chases after . . .

[*He runs off in pursuit of* **Lear**]

Goneril   This man hath had good counsel. A hundred
    knights!
    'Tis politic and safe to let him keep
    At point a hundred knights; yes, that on every dream,
    Each buzz, each fancy, each complaint, dislike,
    He may enguard his dotage with their powers,
    And hold our lives mercy. Oswald, I say!

Albany   Well, you may fear too far.

Goneril   Safer than trust too far.
    Let me still take away the harms I fear,
    Not fear still to be taken: I know his heart.
    What he hath uttered I have writ my sister;
    If she sustain him and his hundred knights,
    When I have showed th'unfitness –

    [*Enter* **Oswald**]

                              How now, Oswald!
    What, have you writ that letter to my sister?

Oswald   Ay, madam.

Goneril   Take you some company, and away to horse:
    Inform her full of my particular fear;
    And thereto add such reasons of your own
    As may compact it more. Get you gone,
    And hasten your return.

                              [*Exit* **Oswald**]

                    No, no, my lord.
    This milky gentleness and course of yours
    Though I condemn not, yet, under pardon,
    You are much more attasked for want of wisdom
    Than praised for harmful mildness.

Albany   How far your eyes may pierce I cannot tell:
    Striving to better, oft we mar what's well.

Goneril   This man [*she means her father*] has been well
advised. A hundred knights! [*Sarcastically*] It's sensible and
safe to let him keep a hundred fully armed knights! Yes – so
that after every wild dream, each rumor, each fantasy,
each complaint or dislike, he can back up his senile ways
with their power, and put our lives in jeopardy. Oswald,
I say!

Albany   Well, you may be worrying too much.

Goneril   That's safer than trusting too much. I'd rather
eliminate the dangers that worry me than live continually in
fear. I know his character. I've written to my sister reporting
what he has said. If she accommodates him and his hundred
knights after I've explained the undesirability –

[**Oswald** *returns*]

Well, Oswald: have you written that letter to my sister?

Oswald   Yes, madam.

Goneril   Take some companions with you and ride off. Inform
her fully of my personal fear. Add such reasons of your own
as may make it more convincing. Be off with you and return
quickly.

[**Oswald** *goes*]

This very tolerant attitude of yours, my lord, though I don't
condemn it, yet – if I may say so – you are much more
criticized for your naivety than praised for your dangerous
leniency.

Albany   How far you are right I don't know. Sometimes things
are best left alone.

Goneril   Nay, then –

Albany   Well, well; th'event.

[*Exeunt*]

Scene 5

Court before the same. Enter **Lear, Kent,** *and* **Fool.**

Lear   Go you before to Gloucester with these letters.
Acquaint my daughter no further with anything you know
than comes from her demand out of the letter. If your
diligence be not speedy I shall be there afore you.

Kent   I will not sleep, my lord, till I have delivered your
letter.

[*Exit*]

Fool   If a man's brains were in 's heels, were't not in danger
of kibes?

Lear   Ay, boy.

Fool   Then, I prithee, be merry; thy wit shall not go
slipshod.

Lear   Ha, ha, ha!

Fool   Shalt see thy other daughter will use thee kindly; for
though she's as like this as a crab's like an apple, yet I can
tell what I can tell.

Lear   What canst tell, boy?

Goneril   So –

Albany   Well, well. Let's see how things develop.

[*They go*]

Scene 5

A room in the Duke of Albany's palace. Enter **Lear**, **Kent**, *and the* **Fool**.

Lear   [*to* **Kent**] Go ahead to Gloucester with this letter. Tell my daughter only what's needed to answer questions arising from the letter. If you're not quick, I'll be there before you.

Kent   I will not sleep, my lord, till I've delivered your letter. [*He goes*]

Fool   If a man's brains were in his heels, wouldn't they be in danger of chilblains?

Lear   Yes, boy.

Fool   Then cheer up. You'll never need to wear soft slippers with your intelligence.

Lear   Ha, ha, ha!

Fool   You'll see your other daughter will treat you just as kindly. Because though she's as like this one [*jerking his thumb in the direction of* **Goneril**] as a crab-apple is to an apple, yet I can tell what I can tell.

Lear   What *can* you tell, boy?

Fool   She will taste as like this as a crab does to a crab. Thou canst tell why one's nose stands i' th' middle on 's face?

Lear   No.

Fool   Why, to keep one's eyes on either side 's nose, that what a man cannot smell out, he may spy into.

Lear   I did her wrong –

Fool   Canst tell how an oyster makes his shell?

Lear   No.

Fool   Nor I neither; but I can tell why a snail has a house.

Lear   Why?

Fool   Why, to put 's head in; not to give it away to his daughters, and leave his horns without a case.

Lear   I will forget my nature. So kind a father! Be my horses ready?

Fool   Thy asses are gone about 'em. The reason why the seven stars are no more than seven is a pretty reason.

Lear   Because they are not eight?

Fool   Yes, indeed: thou would'st make a good Fool.

Lear   To take't again perforce! Monster ingratitude!

Fool   If thou wert my Fool, nuncle, I'd have thee beaten for being old before thy time.

Lear   How's that?

Fool   Thou should'st not have been old till thou hadst been wise.

Lear   O! let me not be mad, not mad, sweet heaven; Keep me in temper; I would not be mad!

Fool The taste will be the same. You know why one's nose is in the middle of one's face?

Lear No.

Fool Why, to keep one's eyes on either side of one's nose. Then what a man can't smell out, he can look into.

Lear I wronged her . . . [*thinking of* **Cordelia**]

Fool Do you know how an oyster makes its shell?

Lear No.

Fool I don't either. But I can say why a snail has a house.

Lear Why?

Fool To put his head in, of course, not to give it away to his daughters, and leave himself exposed.

Lear I'll forget what's in my nature. Me, so kind a father! Are my horses ready?

Fool Your asses are preparing them. The reason why the Pleiades are only seven stars is a good one . . .

Lear Because they aren't eight?

Fool Yes, indeed. You'd make a good Fool!

Lear To take it all back again! [*He's thinking of regaining the throne*] Monstrous ingratitude!

Fool If you were my Fool, uncle, I'd have you beaten for being old too soon.

Lear How do you mean?

Fool You shouldn't have got old till you'd acquired some sense.

Lear Oh, don't let me go mad; not mad, sweet heaven! Keep me sane. I don't want to be mad!

[*Enter* **Gentleman**]

How now! Are the horses ready?

Gentleman   Ready, my lord.

Lear   Come, boy.

Fool   She that's a maid now, and laughs at my departure,
Shall not be a maid long, unless things be cut shorter.

[*Exeunt*]

[*A* **Gentleman** *enters*]

Well, are the horses ready?

Gentleman   Ready, my lord.

Lear   [*to the* **Fool**] Come on, boy . . .

Fool   [*to the audience*]

The virgin of today, who laughs at my departure,
Won't be one much longer, unless something's cut
    shorter.

[*They go*]

Act two

Scene 1

The castle of the Earl of Gloucester. Enter **Edmund** *and* **Curan,** *meeting.*

Edmund   Save thee, Curan.

Curan   And you, sir. I have been with your father, and given
him notice that the Duke of Cornwall and Regan his
Duchess will be here with him this night.

Edmund   How comes that?

Curan   Nay, I know not. You have heard of the news abroad?
I mean the whispered ones, for they are yet but ear-kissing
arguments.

Edmund   Not I: pray you, what are they?

Curan   Have you heard of no likely wars toward, 'twixt the
Dukes of Cornwall and Albany?

Edmund   Not a word.

Curan   You may do then, in time. Fare you well, sir.

[*Exit*]

Edmund   The Duke be here to-night! The better! Best!
This weaves itself perforce into my business.
My father hath set guard to take my brother;
And I have one thing, of a queasy question,
Which I must act. Briefness and fortune, work!
Brother, a word; descend: brother, I say!

[*Enter* **Edgar**]

Act two

Scene 1

Inside the castle of the **Earl of Gloucester**. **Edmund** *enters and meets* **Curan**, *a courtier*.

Edmund   God be with you, Curan.

Curan   And you, sir. I've been with your father, and informed him that the Duke of Cornwall, and his Duchess Regan, will be here with him tonight.

Edmund   How has that come about?

Curan   I don't know. You've heard the latest? I mean the rumors, since at the moment they're only idle gossip.

Edmund   No, I haven't. What are they?

Curan   Haven't you heard of the impending wars between the Dukes of Cornwall and Albany?

Edmund   Not a word.

Curan   You probably will soon. Fare you well, sir.

[He goes]

Edmund   The Duke coming here tonight! So much the better! Marvelous! This fits in with my scheme. My father has hidden himself to overhear my brother and I've got some delicate business to do. Speed and good fortune, come to my aid! *[He calls up the adjacent stairs]* Brother, a word with you! Come down! Brother, I say!

*[***Edgar*** descends]*

My father watches: O sir, fly this place;
Intelligence is given where you are hid;
You have now the good advantage of the night.
Have you not spoken 'gainst the Duke of Cornwall?
He's coming hither, now, i' th' night, i' th' haste,
And Regan with him; have you nothing said
Upon his party 'gainst the Duke of Albany?
Advise yourself.

Edgar   I am sure on 't, not a word.

Edmund   I hear my father coming; pardon me;
In cunning I must draw my sword upon you;
Draw; seem to defend yourself; now quit you well.
Yield; come before my father. Light, ho! here!
Fly, brother. Torches! Torches! So, farewell.

[*Exit* **Edgar**]

Some blood drawn on me would beget opinion
Of my more fierce endeavour: I have seen drunkards
Do more than this in sport. Father! Father!
Stop, stop! No help?

[*Enter* **Gloucester,** *and Servants with torches*]

Gloucester   Now, Edmund, where's the villain?

Edmund   Here stood he in the dark, his sharp sword out,
Mumbling of wicked charms, conjuring the moon
To stand 's auspicious mistress.

Gloucester   But where is he?

Edmund   Look, sir, I bleed.

Gloucester   Where is the villain, Edmund?

Edmund   Fled this way, sir, when by no means he could –

[*To the audience*] My father is watching. [*Whispering to* **Edgar**, *and assuming an agitated manner*] Sir, run away! Your hiding place has been discovered. You have the advantage of night cover. Have you not been speaking out against the Duke of Cornwall? He's coming here now, overnight, in great haste, and Regan is with him. Have you said anything supportive of his case against the Duke of Albany? Think hard.

Edgar   I'm sure of it. Not a word.

Edmund   I can hear my father coming. Excuse me: I must pretend to draw my sword upon you. [*He does so*] Draw yours. Make as if to defend yourself. [**Edgar**, *bewildered, does as he is told*] Do your best. [*Speaking out loud for* **Gloucester** *to hear*] Surrender! Come to my father! Light there! [*Whispering*] Run, brother. [*Aloud*] Torches, torches! [*Pushing* **Edgar** *out*] So, farewell. [**Edgar** *runs off*] Some blood on me would be convincing evidence of my tough struggle. [*He cuts his arm*] I've seen drunkards do more than this in fun. [*Calling pathetically*] Father, father! [*After* **Edgar**] Stop, stop! Will no one help?

[**Gloucester** *enters with Servants and torches*]

Gloucester   Now, Edmund, where's the villain?

Edmund   He was standing here in the dark, his sharp sword drawn, mumbling wicked spells, and making incantations to the moon to seek her favor.

Gloucester   But where is he?

Edmund   [*playing for time*] Look, sir, I'm bleeding.

Gloucester   Where *is* the villain, Edmund?

Edmund   [*pointing*] He fled this way, sir, when he was quite unable –

Gloucester   [*To Servants*] Pursue him, ho! Go after. 'By no
    means' what?

Edmund   Persuade me to the murder of your lordship;
    But that I told him the revenging gods
    'Gainst parricides did all the thunder bend;
    Spoke with how manifold and strong a bond
    The child was bound to th' father; sir, in fine,
    Seeing how loathly opposite I stood
    To his unnatural purpose, in fell motion,
    With his prepared sword he charges home
    My unprovided body, lanced mine arm:
    But when he saw my best alarumed spirits
    Bold in the quarrel's right, roused to th'encounter,
    Or whether gasted by the noise I made,
    Full suddenly he fled.

Gloucester   Let him fly far:
    Not in this land shall he remain uncaught;
    And found – dispatch. The noble Duke my master,
    My worthy arch and patron, comes to-night:
    By his authority I will proclaim it,
    That he which finds him shall deserve our thanks,
    Bringing the murderous coward to the stake;
    He that conceals him, death.

Edmund   When I dissuaded him from his intent,
    And found him pight to do it, with curst speech
    I threatened to discover him: he replied,
    'Thou unpossessing bastard! Dost thou think,
    If I would stand against thee, would the reposal
    Of any trust, virtue, or worth in thee
    Make thy words faithed? No: what I should deny –
    As this I would; ay, though thou didst produce
    My very character – I'ld turn it all
    To thy suggestion, plot, and damned practice:
    And thou must make a dullard of the world,

Gloucester Follow him, quick! Go after him! [*Servants rush off in pursuit*] "Quite unable" to do what?

Edmund Persuade me to murder your lordship. And I told him the vengeful gods deal ruthlessly with parricides. I spoke about how the bond between father and son was complex and strong. Sir, in short, seeing how bitterly opposed I was to his unnatural plan, with a deadly thrust he lunged at my defenseless body with his naked sword and wounded my arm. But when he saw my energetic response to the challenge, inspired by the justice of the cause – or perhaps aghast at the noise I made – he suddenly ran off.

Gloucester No matter how far he goes, there's nowhere in this land where he can stay free. Once found, kill him. The noble Duke, my master and chief patron, comes here tonight. With his authority I'll announce that whoever finds him will be rewarded for bringing the murderous coward to his execution. For anyone who hides him, death!

Edmund When I tried to dissuade him from his plan, and found he was determined to proceed, with angry words I threatened to expose him. He replied, "You poverty-stricken bastard! Do you think anyone would believe a word you said if I spoke to the contrary? No. I'd deny it all – indeed I would, even if you produced my own handwriting – and say it was your scheme, plot and treacherous proposal. People would have to be very stupid not to see that the profits from

If they not thought the profits of my death
Were very pregnant and potential spirits
To make thee seek it.'

Gloucester   O strange and fastened villain!
Would he deny his letter, said he? I never got him.

[*Tucket within*]

Hark! the Duke's trumpets. I know not why he comes.
All ports I'll bar; the villain shall not 'scape;
The Duke must grant me that: besides his picture
I will send far and near, that all the kingdom
May have due note of him: and of my land,
Loyal and natural boy, I'll work the means
To make thee capable.

[*Enter* **Cornwall, Regan,** *and Attendants*]

Cornwall   How now, my noble friend! Since I came hither
Which I can call but now, I have heard strange news.

Regan   If it be true, all vengeance comes too short
Which can pursue th'offender. How dost, my lord?

Gloucester   O, madam, my old heart is cracked, it's cracked.

Regan   What! did my father's godson seek your life?
He whom my father named, your Edgar?

Gloucester   O, lady, lady, shame would have it hid.

Regan   Was he not companion with the riotous knights
That tended upon my father?

Gloucester   I know not, madam; 'tis too bad, too bad.

Edmund   Yes, madam, he was of that consort.

Regan   No marvel then, though he were ill affected;
'Tis they have put him on the old man's death,

my death give you an obvious and powerful motive for seeking it.''

Gloucester   Oh, that unnatural and confirmed villain! He'd deny his letter, did he say? He's no child of mine.

[*The* **Duke of Cornwall's** *trumpet-call is heard*]

Listen! The Duke's trumpets. I don't know why he's come. I'll block all seaports. The villain won't escape. The Duke must grant me that. Also, I'll send a picture of him far and wide so that all the kingdom will take note of him. And I'll devise a way of your inheriting my lands, you loyal and true son.

[**Cornwall, Regan** *and their Attendants enter*]

Cornwall   Greetings, my noble friend! Since I arrived just now, I've heard strange news.

Regan   If it's true, no vengeance is adequate in pursuit of the offender. How are you, my lord?

Gloucester   Oh, madam, my old heart is broken. It's broken!

Regan   What, did my father's godson seek your life? The one my father named: your Edgar?

Gloucester   Oh, lady, lady. Shame would have it hidden.

Regan   Wasn't he a companion of the riotous knights who served my father?

Gloucester   I don't know, madam. It's too awful. Too awful.

Edmund   [*taking his cue from Regan*] Yes, madam, he was one of that lot.

Regan   No wonder, then, that he was so disloyal. *They've* incited him to plan the old man's death, so that he can

To have th'expense and waste of his revenues.
I have this present evening from my sister
Been well informed of them, and with such cautions
That if they come to sojourn at my house,
I'll not be there.

Cornwall   Nor I, assure thee, Regan.
Edmund, I hear that you have shown your father
A child-like office.

Edmund   It was my duty, sir.

Gloucester   He did bewray his practise, and received
This hurt you see, striving to apprehend him.

Cornwall   Is he pursued?

Gloucester   Ay, my good lord.

Cornwall   If he be taken he shall never more
Be feared of doing harm; make your own purpose,
How in my strength you please. For you, Edmund,
Whose virtue and obedience doth this instant
So much commend itself, you shall be ours:
Natures of such deep trust we shall much need;
You we first seize on.

Edmund   I shall serve you, sir,
Truly, however else.

Gloucester   For him I thank your Grace.

Cornwall   You know not why we came to visit you –

Regan   Thus out of season, threading dark-eyed night:
Occasions, noble Gloucester, of some prize,
Wherein we must have use of your advice.
Our father he hath writ, so hath our sister,
Of differences, which I best thought it fit
To answer from our home; the several messengers

squander his wealth. Just this very evening I've been told about them by my sister, with such warnings that if they come to stay at my house, I won't be there.

Cornwall   Nor I, Regan, that's for sure. Edmund, I hear you have behaved like a good son to your father.

Edmund   It was my duty, sir.

Gloucester   He revealed Edgar's plot, and received the wound you see while trying to arrest him.

Cornwall   Is he being pursued?

Gloucester   Yes, my good lord.

Cornwall   If he's captured, never fear his doing harm again. Make your own plans, using my resources as you please. As for you, Edmund, whose virtuous loyalty is so commendable at this present time, you shall be one of us. Trustworthy natures such as yours we have great need of. We seize upon your services.

Edmund   [bowing] I shall serve you truly, sir, whatever else.

Gloucester   On his behalf I thank your Grace.

Cornwall   You don't know why we came to visit you –

Regan   – so unexpectedly, traveling through the darkness of the night. Business of some importance, Gloucester, requiring your advice. Our father has written to us – and so has our sister – about certain quarrels. I thought it best to answer him away from home. The messengers are waiting

From hence attend dispatch. Our good old friend,
Lay comforts to your bosom, and bestow
Your needful counsel to our business,
Which craves the instant use.

Gloucester   I serve you, madam.
Your Graces are right welcome.

[Flourish. Exeunt]

Scene 2

Before Gloucester's castle. Enter **Kent** *and* **Oswald,** *severally.*

Oswald   Good dawning to thee, friend: art of this house?

Kent   Ay.

Oswald   Where may we set our horses?

Kent   I' th' mire.

Oswald   Prithee, if thou lovest me, tell me.

Kent   I love thee not.

Oswald   Why, then I care not for thee.

Kent   If I had thee in Lipsbury pinfold, I would make thee
care for me.

Oswald   Why dost thou use me thus? I know thee not.

Kent   Fellow, I know thee.

Oswald   What dost thou know me for?

Kent   A knave, a rascal, an eater of broken meats; a base,

to be dispatched. Our good old friend, be of good cheer, and give us your much-needed advice about these matters, which require instant action.

Gloucester   Your servant, madam. Your Graces are most welcome.

[*Trumpets sound as they leave*]

Scene 2

Outside Gloucester's castle. **Kent** *and* **Oswald** *meet. Dawn has not yet broken.*

Oswald   Good morning to you, friend. Are you a servant here?

Kent   Yes.

Oswald   Where may we put our horses?

Kent   In the mud.

Oswald   Please, if you love me, tell me.

Kent   I don't love you.

Oswald   Well, then, I don't much care for you.

Kent   Any more of your lip, and I'll make you care.

Oswald   Why the abuse? I don't know you.

Kent   I know you, man.

Oswald   What do you know of me?

Kent   You're a rogue, a rascal, a scrap-food guzzler. A low, proud, shallow, beggarly, three-suited, hundred-pound, filthy worsted-stocking knave; a lily-livered, action-taking whoreson, glass-gazing, super-serviceable, finical rogue; one-trunk-inheriting slave; one that wouldst be a bawd in way of good service, and art nothing but the composition of a knave, beggar, coward, pandar, and the son and heir of a mongrel bitch: one whom I will beat into clamorous whining if thou deniest the least syllable of thy addition.

Oswald   Why, what a monstrous fellow art thou, thus to rail on one that is neither known of thee nor knows thee!

Kent   What a brazen-faced varlet art thou, to deny thou knowest me! Is it two days since I tripped up thy heels and beat thee before the King? Draw, you rogue; for though it be night, yet the moon shines: I'll make a sop o' th' moonshine of you. You whoreson cullionly barber-monger, draw.

Oswald   Away! I have nothing to do with thee.

Kent   Draw, you rascal; you come with letters against the King, and take vanity the puppet's part against the royalty of her father. Draw, you rogue, or I'll so carbonado your shanks: draw, you rascal; come your ways.

Oswald   Help, ho! Murder! Help!

Kent   Strike, you slave; stand, rogue, stand; you neat slave, strike.

[*Beating him*]

Oswald   Help, ho! Murder! Murder!

[*Enter* **Edmund,** *with his rapier drawn*]

Edmund   How now! What's the matter? Part!

Kent   With you, goodman boy, if you please: come, I'll flesh ye; come on, young master.

proud, shallow, beggarly, scruffy, upstart of a dirty, shabby, cowardly, officious, mincing rogue. A down-and-out slave. A man who'd be a pimp to get a good job, and who's nothing but a mixture of knave, beggar, coward, procurer, and the son and heir of a mongrel bitch. A fellow I'll beat till he shrieks if he denies one syllable of what I've said!

Oswald   Why, what a terrible fellow you are, to curse someone who is neither known to you, nor knows you!

Kent   What a hard-faced rascal you are, to deny you know me! Is it two days since I tripped you up in front of the King? Draw your sword, you rogue, 'cos though it may be night, the moon's shining. I'll pierce you so the moonlight shines through you! [*He draws*] You lousy, rascally phony! Draw!

Oswald   Go away! I'll have nothing to do with you!

Kent   Draw, you rascal! You're here with letters critical of the King, and you side with Lady Stuck-Up against her royal father. Draw, you rogue, or I'll give you a real roasting! Draw, you rascal! Come on!

Oswald   Help! Murder! Help!

Kent   Fight, you coward! Stand your ground, you rogue! You foppish coward, fight! [*He beats* **Oswald** *with the flat of his sword*]

Oswald   Help! Murder! Murder!

[**Edmund** *enters with his rapier drawn*]

Edmund   Hey, what's all this about? Break!

Kent   I'll deal with you, young shaver, if you like! Come on, I'll teach you a few things! Come on, laddie! [*He challenges* **Edmund** *too*]

[*Enter* **Cornwall, Regan, Gloucester,** *and Servants*]

Gloucester   Weapons! Arms! What's the matter here?

Cornwall   Keep peace, upon your lives. He dies that strikes again. What is the matter?

Regan   The messengers from our sister and the King.

Cornwall   What is your difference? Speak.

Oswald   I am scarce in breath, my lord.

Kent   No marvel, you have so bestirred your valour. You cowardly rascal, nature disclaims in thee: a tailor made thee.

Cornwall   Thou art a strange fellow; a tailor make a man?

Kent   A tailor, sir: a stone-cutter or a painter could not have made him so ill, though they had been but two years o' th' trade.

Cornwall   Speak yet, how grew your quarrel?

Oswald   This ancient ruffian, sir, whose life I have spared at suit of his grey beard –

Kent   Thou whoreson zed! Thou unnecessary letter! My lord, if you will give me leave, I will tread this unbolted villain into mortar, and daub the wall of a jakes with him. Spare my grey beard, you wagtail?

Cornwall   Peace, sirrah! You beastly knave, know you no reverence?

Kent   Yes, sir; but anger hath a privilege.

Cornwall   Why art thou angry?

Kent   That such a slave as this should wear a sword,
Who wears no honesty. Such smiling rogues as these,
Like rats, oft bite the the holy cords a-twain

[**Cornwall** *enters, with* **Regan, Gloucester** *and Servants*]

Gloucester   Weapons! Fighting! What's all this?

Cornwall   No more, upon your lives: the next to strike dies! What's the matter?

Regan   They are the messengers from our sister and the King.

Cornwall   What's the quarrel? Speak.

Oswald   I'm out of breath, my lord.

Kent   No wonder; your courage was so aroused. You cowardly rascal, you're not natural. Some tailor stitched you together.

Cornwall   You're an odd fellow. A tailor make a man?

Kent   Yes, a tailor, sir. A stone-cutter or a painter couldn't have done such a botched job, even if he'd only been working for a couple of years.

Cornwall   So tell me, how did your quarrel start?

Oswald   This ancient ruffian, sir, whose life I have spared on account of his grey beard –

Kent   You useless wretch! You good-for-nothing! My lord, with your permission I'll grind this coarse villain into mortar, and plaster the wall of a privy with him. Spare my grey beard, you dodo bird?

Cornwall   Quiet, man! You uncouth hooligan: have you no respect?

Kent   Yes, sir. But anger takes precedent.

Cornwall   Why are you so angry?

Kent   Because such a wretch as this should display a sword but not show any honesty. Smiling rogues such as these often gnaw like rats through bonds of love that are too tight

Which are too intrinse t'unloose; smooth every passion
That in the natures of their lords rebel;
Bring oil to fire, snow to their colder moods;
Renege, affirm, and turn their halcyon beaks
With every gale and vary of their masters,
Knowing nought, like dogs, but following.
A plague upon your epileptic visage!
Smile you my speeches, as I were a fool?
Goose, if I had you upon Sarum plain,
I'd drive ye cackling home to Camelot.

Cornwall   What, art thou mad, old fellow?

Gloucester   How fell you out? Say that.

Kent   No contraries hold more antipathy
Than I and such a knave.

Cornwall   Why dost thou call him knave? What is his fault?

Kent   His countenance likes me not.

Cornwall   No more, perchance, does mine, nor his, nor hers.

Kent   Sir, 'tis my occupation to be plain:
I have seen better faces in my time
Than stands on any shoulder that I see
Before me at this instant.

Cornwall   This is some fellow,
Who, having been praised for bluntness, doth affect
A saucy roughness, and constrains the garb
Quite from his nature: he cannot flatter, he,
An honest mind and plain, he must speak truth:
And they will take it, so; if not, he's plain.
These kind of knaves I know, which in this plainness
Harbour more craft and more corrupter ends
Than twenty silly ducking observants,
That stretch their duties nicely.

to be undone by other means. They satisfy the lusts of their
debauched masters. They add fuel to anger; they bring chill
to moods of dejection; they deny, affirm, and turn with
the wind according to their masters' moods – knowing
nothing but how to follow, like dogs. Damn your twitching
face! Are you laughing at me, as if I were a fool? You goose,
if you were on Salisbury Plain I'd make you cackle your way
back home to Winchester.

Cornwall   What, are you mad, old fellow?

Gloucester   How did you come to quarrel? Explain that.

Kent   No two men hate each other more than I and that rogue.

Cornwall   Why do you call him a rogue? What has he done
wrong?

Kent   I don't like his face.

Cornwall   Or mine, or his, or hers, probably.

Kent   Sir, I'm a plain man. I *have* seen better faces in my time
than any I see before me now.

Cornwall   This is a fellow who, having been praised for
bluntness, has assumed a cheeky impertinence; but he
misuses it. [*Sarcastically*] Oh no, he can't flatter. Not he!
He has a plain, honest mind. He has to speak the truth. If
people will take it, fine. If not, it's just his way. I know
these rogues. Behind this bluntness they conceal more
craftiness, and have corrupter purposes, than twenty
groveling bootlickers who never put a foot wrong.

Kent   Sir, in good sooth, in sincere verity,
　　　Under th'allowance of your great aspect,
　　　Whose influence, like the wreath of radiant fire
　　　On flickering Phoebus' front –

Cornwall　　　　　　　　　What mean'st by this?

Kent   To go out of my dialect, which you discommend so
　　　much. I know, sir, I am no flatterer: he that beguiled you in
　　　a plain accent was a plain knave; which for my part I will not
　　　be, though I should win your displeasure to entreat me to't.

Cornwall   What was the offence you gave him?

Oswald   I never gave him any:
　　　It pleased the King his master very late
　　　To strike at me, upon his misconstruction;
　　　When he, compact, and flattering his displeasure,
　　　Tripped me behind; being down, insulted, railed,
　　　And put upon him such a deal of man,
　　　That worthied him, got praises of the King
　　　For him attempting who was self-subdued;
　　　And, in the fleshment of this dread exploit,
　　　Drew on me here again.

Kent　　　　　　　　None of these rogues and cowards
　　　But Ajax is their fool.

Cornwall　　　　　　Fetch forth the stocks!
　　　You stubborn ancient knave, you reverend braggart,
　　　We'll teach you.

Kent　　　　　　Sir, I am too old to learn.
　　　Call not your stocks for me; I serve the King,
　　　On whose employment I was sent to you;
　　　You shall do small respect, show too bold malice
　　　Against the grace and person of my master,
　　　Stocking his messenger.

Kent   [*mockingly overpolite*] Sir, in all good faith, in sincere
truthfulness, with the gracious approval of your mightiness,
whose power – like the great ball of fire round the sun –

Cornwall   [*interrupting*] What's your game?

Kent   [*reverting to normality*] To change my manner of
speech, which you disapprove of so much: I know, sir, that
I'm no flatterer. The man who tricked you with plain-
speaking was a plain rogue. That I'll never be, even if you
begged me and I risked your displeasure by turning you
down.

Cornwall   [*to* **Oswald**] What offense did you give him?

Oswald   I didn't give him any. Recently, through a
misunderstanding, his master the King chose to strike me.
Then, backing his Majesty up and pandering to his anger, he
tripped me from behind. While I was down, he insulted me,
abused me, and made himself out to be such a hero that he
got credit from it, and was praised by the King for tackling a
man who was offering no aggression. And, inspired by this
amazing achievement, he drew on me here again.

Kent   All rogues and cowards think the noble Ajax is a coward
compared with them.

Cornwall   Bring the stocks here! You fierce old rogue, you
elderly braggart! We'll teach you!

Kent   Sir, I'm too old to learn. Don't call your stocks for me. I
serve the King, on whose business I was sent to you. In
stocking his messenger, you would be showing scant
respect, insulting the King personally, and his office.

Cornwall   Fetch forth the stocks!
  As I have life and honour, there shall he sit till noon.

Regan   Till noon! Till night, my lord; and all night too.

Kent   Why, madam, if I were your father's dog,
  You should not use me so.

Regan   Sir, being his knave, I will.

Cornwall   This is a fellow of the self-same colour
  Our sister speaks of. Come, bring away the stocks.

[*Stocks brought out*]

Gloucester   Let me beseech your Grace not to do so.
  His fault is much, and the good King his master
  Will check him for't: your purposed low correction
  Is such as basest and contemned'st wretches
  For pilferings and most common trespasses
  Are punished with: the King must take it ill,
  That he, so slightly valued in his messenger,
  Should have him thus restrained.

Cornwall   I'll answer that.

Regan   My sister may receive it much more worse
  To have her gentleman abused, assaulted,
  For following her affairs. Put in his legs.'

[**Kent** *is put in the stocks*]

Cornwall   Come, my lord, away.

[*Exeunt all but* **Gloucester** *and* **Kent**]

Gloucester   I am sorry for thee, friend; 'tis the Duke's
    pleasure,

Cornwall   Bring the stocks! Upon my life and honor, he'll sit there till noon.

Regan   Till noon? Till night, my lord, and all night too.

Kent   Why, madam, if I were your father's dog you wouldn't treat me like that.

Regan   Sir, you being his stooge, I will.

Cornwall   This is a fellow of the very sort our sister wrote about. Come, bring along the stocks.

[*They are carried in*]

Gloucester   Let me plead with your Grace not to do this. He's greatly at fault, and the good King, his master, will rebuke him for it. The undignified punishment you propose is the sort that the most disreputable and discredited wretches are punished with, for petty pilfering and minor misdemeanors. The King won't take kindly to having his messenger shackled like this.

Cornwall   I'll answer for that.

Regan   My sister might be far more offended, having her servant abused and assaulted for carrying out her business. Put his legs in.

[**Kent** *is put in the stocks*]

Cornwall   Let's go, my lord.

[*All but* **Gloucester** *and* **Kent** *leave*]

Gloucester   I'm sorry for you, friend. It's the Duke's whim. As

Whose disposition, all the world well knows,
Will not be rubbed nor stopped: I'll entreat for thee.

Kent   Pray, do not, sir. I have watched and travelled hard;
Some time I shall sleep out, the rest I'll whistle.
A good man's fortune may grow out at heels:
Give you good morrow!

Gloucester   The Duke's to blame in this; 'twill be ill taken.

[*Exit*]

Kent   Good King, that must approve the common saw,
Thou out of heaven's benediction comest
To the warm sun!
Approach, thou beacon to this under globe,
That by thy comfortable beams I may
Peruse this letter. Nothing almost sees miracles,
But misery: I know 'tis from Cordelia,
Who hath most fortunately been informed
Of my obscured course; and shall find time
From this enormous state, seeking to give
Losses their remedies. All weary and o'erwatched,
Take vantage, heavy eyes, not to behold
This shameful lodging.
Fortune, good night; smile once more; turn thy wheel!

[*He sleeps*]

all the world well knows, his temperament will brook no
restraint or obstacle. I'll plead for you.

Kent   Please don't, sir. I've gone without sleep and traveled a
rough road. I'll sleep away some of the time; the rest I'll
whistle. Even a good man's fortunes can get down at the
heels. Good day to you!

Gloucester   The Duke's at fault in this. It will be taken badly.

[*He goes*]

Kent   Good King, who should have heeded the old proverb:
you've gone from the frying pan into the fire! Come, moon,
so that I can read this letter by your comforting beams!
Miracles are mostly related to misery; I know this is from
Cordelia, who fortunately has been informed of my disguise.
She will find an opportune time to put things right in this
monstrous state. Take this opportunity, heavy eyes – all
weary and fatigued – not to look upon these shameful
stocks. Good night, Fortune! Smile once more: then turn
your wheel!

[*He sleeps*]

Scene 3

A wood. Enter **Edgar.**

Edgar   I heard myself proclaimed;
    And by the happy hollow of a tree
    Escaped the hunt. No port is free; no place
    That guard, and most unusual vigilance,
    Does not attend my taking. Whiles I may 'scape,
    I will preserve myself; and am bethought
    To take the basest and most poorest shape
    That ever penury, in contempt of man,
    Brought near to beast; my face I'll grime with filth,
    Blanket my loins, elf all my hairs in knots,
    And with presented nakedness outface
    The winds and persecutions of the sky.
    The country gives me proof and precedent
    Of Bedlam beggars, who, with roaring voices,
    Strike in their numbed and mortified bare arms
    Pins, wooden pricks, nails, sprigs of rosemary;
    And with this horrible object, from low farms,
    Poor pelting villages, sheep-cotes, and mills,
    Sometime with lunatic bans, sometime with prayers,
    Enforce their charity. Poor Turlygod! Poor Tom!
    That's something yet: Edgar I nothing am.

[Exit]

Scene 3

A wood. **Edgar** *enters.*

Edgar   I heard myself proclaimed an outlaw. By hiding in the
   convenient hollow of a tree, I escaped the hunt. No seaport
   is free. There's nowhere that isn't tightly guarded in order to
   capture me. While I can still escape, I'll protect myself. I
   intend to assume the role of the lowest and poorest man
   that poverty at its most degrading ever dragged down to the
   level of a beast. I'll begrime my face with filth, wear a
   loin-cloth, matt all my hair in knots, and brave the winds and
   sufferings of the elements in the full exposure of my
   nakedness. There are many examples around the
   countryside of lunatic beggars who, with roaring voices,
   stick pins, wooden skewers, nails and sprigs of rosemary in
   their cold and numbed bare arms. Using this horrible
   spectacle, they extort charity from humble farms, poor
   poverty-stricken villages, sheepfarms and mills, sometimes
   with lunatic curses, sometimes with prayers. [*He speaks like
   a Bedlam beggar*] Poor Turlygod! Poor Tom! [*In his normal
   voice*] There's that much left for me; as Edgar I'm nothing.

[*He goes*]

Scene 4

Before Gloucester's castle. **Kent** *in the stocks. Enter* **Lear, Fool,**
and a **Gentleman.**

Lear   'Tis strange that they should so depart from home,
And not send back my messenger.

Gentleman   As I learned,
The night before there was no purpose in them
Of this remove.

Kent   Hail to thee, noble master!

Lear   Ha!
Mak'st thou this shame thy pastime?

Kent   No, my lord.

Fool   Ha, ha! He wears cruel garters. Horses are tied by the
heads, dogs and bears by the neck, monkeys by the loins,
and men by the legs: when a man's over-lusty at legs then
he wears wooden nether-stocks.

Lear   What's he that hath so much thy place mistook
To set thee here?

Kent   It is both he and she,
Your son and daughter.

Lear   No.

Kent   Yes.

Lear   No, I say.

Kent   I say, yea.

Lear   No, no; they would not.

Kent   Yes, yes, they have.

Scene 4

Outside **Gloucester's** *castle.* **Kent** *is in the stocks.* **Lear,** *the* **Fool** *and a* **Gentleman** *enter.*

Lear   It's strange that they should leave home like that, and not send back my messenger.

Gentleman   I heard that the night before they had no intention of going.

Kent   Greetings, noble master!

Lear   What, is this sort of disgrace a hobby with you?

Kent   No, my lord.

Fool   Ha, ha, he's wearing cruel [*a pun on "crewel," that is, "worsted"*] garters! Horses are tied by the heads, dogs and bears by the neck, monkeys by the waist, and men by the legs. When a man gets too frisky, then he has to wear wooden stockings.

Lear   Who has so mistaken your status that he has placed you here?

Kent   It's both "he" and "she": your son-in-law and daughter.

Lear   No.

Kent   Yes.

Lear   No, I say!

Kent   I say yes.

Lear   No, no. They would not!

Kent   Yes, yes. They have.

Lear   By Jupiter, I swear, no.

Kent   By Juno, I swear, ay.

Lear   They durst not do't.
They could not, would not do't; 'tis worse than murder,
To do upon respect such violent outrage.
Resolve me, with all modest haste, which way
Thou might'st deserve, or they impose, this usage,
Coming from us.

Kent   My lord, when at their home
I did commend your Highness' letters to them,
Ere I was risen from the place that showed
My duty kneeling, came there a reeking post,
Stewed in his haste, half breathless, panting forth
From Goneril his mistress salutations;
Delivered letters, spite of intermission,
Which presently they read: on whose contents
They summoned up their meiny, straight took horse;
Commanded me to follow, and attend
The leisure of their answer; gave me cold looks:
And meeting here the other messenger,
Whose welcome, I perceived, had poisoned mine –
Being the very fellow which of late
Display'd so saucily against your Highness –
Having more man than wit about me, drew:
He raised the house with loud and coward cries.
Your son and daughter found this trespass worth
The shame which here it suffers.

Fool   Winter's not gone yet, if the wild-geese fly that way.

Fathers that wear rags
   Do make their children blind,
But fathers that bear bags
   Shall see their children kind.
Fortune, that arrant whore,
Ne'er turns the key to the poor,

Lear   By Jupiter, I swear no!

Kent   By Juno, I swear yes.

Lear   They wouldn't dare do it. They could not – would
not – do it! It's worse than murder to do such a violent
outrage against the King's officer. Tell me, with reasonable
haste, how you could have deserved – or they imposed –
this treatment, coming as you did from me.

Kent   My lord, when I delivered your Highness's letters to
them at their home, I'd no sooner risen from my bow than a
sweating courier, anxious in his haste, half breathless, came
panting greetings from his mistress Goneril. He delivered
letters, ignoring the fact that he was interrupting me, which
they read at once. On noting the contents, they summoned
their servants and immediately took to their horses. They
ordered me to follow and await an answer at their leisure.
They gave me cold looks. So when I met the other
messenger here – whose welcome, I realized, had poisoned
mine – and observed that he was the very same fellow who
had recently behaved so insolently before your Highness,
having more courage than sense, I drew my sword. He
awakened the servants with his loud and cowardly cries.
Your son-in-law and daughter found this offense worthy of
the shame I'm now suffering.

Fool   Winter isn't over while there are wild geese about like
that!

> Fathers who've no money
>   Have children who ignore 'em.
> But fathers who are rich
>   Have children who adore 'em.
> Luck, that shameless whore,
> Never helps the poor.

But for all this thou shalt have as many dolours for thy
daughters as thou canst tell in a year.

Lear   O, how this mother swells up toward my heart!
Hysterica passio, down, thou climbing sorrow;
Thy element's below. Where is this daughter?

Kent   With the Earl, sir; here within.

Lear   Follow me not; stay here.

[*Exit*]

Gentleman   Made you no more offence but what you
speak of?

Kent   None.
How chance the King comes with so small a number?

Fool   And thou hadst been set i' th' stocks for that question,
thou'dst well deserved it.

Kent   Why, Fool?

Fool   We'll set thee to school to an ant, to teach thee there's
no labouring i' th' winter. All that follow their noses are
led by their eyes but blind men; and there's not a nose
among twenty but can smell him that's stinking. Let go thy
hold when a great wheel runs down a hill, lest it break thy
neck with following; but the great one that goes upward, let
him draw thee after. When a wise man gives thee better
counsel, give me mine again: I would have none but knaves
follow it, since a fool gives it.

> That sir which serves and seeks for gain,
>   And follows but for form,
> Will pack when it begins to rain,
>   And leave thee in the storm.
> But I will tarry; the Fool will stay,
>   And let the wise man fly:

So, you'll have more income [*a pun*: *dolours* (*sorrows*) *versus dollars* (*money*)]from your daughters than you can cope with in one year.

Lear   Oh, how this smothering feeling spreads up towards my heart! [*He opens his collar*] The choking disease! Stay down, you spreading sorrow, keep your lowly place! Where is this daughter?

Kent   With the Earl, sir, indoors.

Lear   Don't follow me. Stay here.

[*He rushes off*]

Gentleman   Did you really give no more offense than that?

Kent   None. How come the King has so few with him?

Fool   If you'd been put in the stocks for that question, you would have well deserved it.

Kent   Why, Fool?

Fool   You must learn from the ant: there's nothing to be gained from toiling on behalf of a lost cause. All who follow their noses are guided by their eyes, except blind men, and most of *them* can smell a man who stinks. When a huge wheel runs down a hill, don't hold onto it lest you break your neck trying to keep up with it. When it's going upwards, though, let it pull you with it. When a wise man gives you better advice, return mine. It's really only for knaves, since it's given by a Fool.

> The man who works in hope of gain,
>   And has no sense of loyalty,
> Will quit when fortune's on the wane,
>   And leave you in calamity.
> But I won't leave. The Fool will stay,
>   And let the wise man go;

>The knave turns Fool that runs away;
>   The Fool no knave, perdy.

Kent   Where learned you this, Fool?

Fool   Not i' th' stocks, fool.

[*Re-enter* **Lear,** *with* **Gloucester**]

Lear   Deny to speak with me? They are sick? They are
   weary?
   They have travelled all the night? Mere fetches,
   The images of revolt and flying off.
   Fetch me a better answer.

Gloucester   My dear lord,
   You know the fiery quality of the Duke;
   How unremovable and fixed he is
   In his own course.

Lear   Vengeance! Plague! Death! Confusion!
   Fiery! What quality? Why, Gloucester, Gloucester,
   I'd speak with the Duke of Cornwall and his wife.

Gloucester   Well, my good lord, I have informed them so.

Lear   Informed them! Dost thou understand me, man?

Gloucester   Ay, my good lord.

Lear   The King would speak with Cornwall; the dear father
   Would with his daughter speak, commands her service:
   Are they informed of this? My breath and blood!
   Fiery? the fiery Duke? Tell the hot Duke that –
   No, but not yet; may be he is not well:
   Infirmity doth still neglect all office
   Whereto our health is bound; we are not ourselves
   When nature, being oppressed, commands the mind
   To suffer with the body. I'll forbear;

The knave turns Fool who runs away;
This Fool's no knave, you know.

Kent   Where did you learn this, Fool?

Fool   Not in the stocks, fool.

[**Lear** *returns with* **Gloucester**]

Lear   Refused to speak to me! They are sick? They are tired?
They've traveled all night? Mere excuses: yes, the
symbols of revolt and desertion. Bring me a better answer.

Gloucester   My dear lord, you know the fiery temperament of
the Duke; how obstinate and determined he is in having his
own way.

Lear   Vengeance! Plague! Death! Confusion! ''Fiery''! What
''temperament''? Why, Gloucester, Gloucester, I want to
speak to the Duke of Cornwall and his wife.

Gloucester   Well, my good lord, I have informed them so.

Lear   ''Informed'' them! Do you understand me, man?

Gloucester   Yes, my good lord.

Lear   The King wishes to speak to Cornwall. . . . The dear
father wants to speak to his daughter, commands her
obedience! Are they informed of this? My breath and blood!
''Fiery''? The ''fiery Duke''? Tell the hot-tempered Duke
that – [*he stops short*] No, but not yet. Perhaps he isn't
well. Illness does cause neglect of the duties we perform
when we are fit. We are not ourselves when illness causes
the mind to suffer as well as the body. I'll restrain myself

And am fallen out with my more headier will,
To take the indisposed and sickly fit
For the sound man. [*Looking on* **Kent**] Death on my
   state! Wherefore
Should he sit here? This act persuades me
That this remotion of the Duke and her
Is practice only. Give me my servant forth.
Go and tell the Duke and 's wife I'd speak with them,
Now, presently: bid them come forth and hear me,
Or at their chamber-door I'll beat the drum
Till it cry sleep to death.

Gloucester   I would have all well betwixt you.

                                              [*Exit*]

Lear   O, me! My heart, my rising heart! But, down!

Fool   Cry to it, nuncle, as the cockney did to the eels when
she put 'em i' th' paste alive; she knapped 'em o' th'
coxcombs with a stick, and cried, 'Down, wantons, down!'
'Twas her brother that, in pure kindness to his horse,
buttered his hay.

[*Re-enter* **Gloucester,** *with* **Cornwall, Regan,** *and Servants*]

Lear   Good morrow to you both.

Cornwall   Hail to your Grace!

[**Kent** *is set at liberty*]

Regan   I am glad to see your Highness.

Lear   Regan, I think you are; I know what reason
I have to think so: if thou shouldst not be glad,
I would divorce me from thy mother's tomb,
Sepulchring an adultress. [*To* **Kent**] O, are you free?

and check my impetuous inclination to think what's done in sickness represents the healthy man. [*He looks at* **Kent** *in the stocks and flares up again*] Death to my royal power! Why should he be sitting here? This deed convinces me that this aloofness of the Duke and her is pure deceit. I want my servant out of the stocks! Go and tell the Duke and his wife that I want to speak to them. Now. At once! Tell them to come out and hear me, or I'll beat a drum at their bedroom door till they think they'll never sleep again!

Gloucester   I'd like all to be well between you.

[*He goes*]

Lear   [*holding his chest*] Oh, me! My heart is rising. But, down!

Fool   Give it its orders, uncle, as the cockney woman did the eels, when she put them in the fish paste alive! She rapped them over the head with a stick, and cried, "Down, you playful creatures, down!" It was her brother who, out of pure kindness to his horse, put butter on his hay.

[**Gloucester** *returns, with* **Cornwall**, **Regan** *and Servants*]

Lear   Good morning to you both.

Cornwall   Hail to your Grace!

[**Kent** *is set free*]

Regan   I am glad to see your Highness.

Lear   Regan, I believe you are. I well know the reason for thinking so. If you were not glad, I would denounce the grave of your mother, because it would be the tomb of an adulteress. [*To* **Kent**] Oh, are you free? We'll discuss that

Some other time for that. [*Exit* **Kent**] Beloved Regan.
Thy sister's naught: O Regan! she hath tied
Sharp-toothed unkindness, like a vulture, here. [*Points to
his heart*]
I can scarce speak to thee; thou'lt not believe
With how depraved a quality – O Regan!

Regan   I pray you, sir, take patience. I have hope
You less know how to value her desert
Than she to scant her duty.

Lear   Say? How is that?

Regan   I cannot think my sister in the least
Would fail her obligation. If, sir, perchance
She have restrained the riots of your followers,
'Tis on such ground, and to such wholesome end,
As clears her from all blame.

Lear   My curses on her!

Regan   O sir, you are old;
Nature in you stands on the very verge
Of her confine: you should be ruled and led
By some discretion that discerns your state
Better than you yourself. Therefore I pray you
That to our sister you do make return;
Say you have wronged her.

Lear   Ask her forgiveness?
Do you but mark how this becomes the house:
[*Kneeling*] 'Dear daughter, I confess that I am old;
Age is unnecessary: on my knees I beg
That you'll vouchsafe me raiment, bed, and food.'

Regan   Good sir, no more; these are unsightly tricks.
Return you to my sister.

Lear   Never, Regan.
She hath abated me of half my train;

some other time. [**Kent** *leaves*] Beloved Regan, your sister is wicked. Oh, Regan, her sharp-toothed unkindness has stabbed at my heart like a vulture that's been tied there. I can hardly speak to you. You won't believe the depraved manner with which – [*he chokes*] Oh, Regan!

Regan   Really, sir, have patience. I hope that you are undervaluing her, not she falling short of her duty.

Lear   What did you say? How do you mean?

Regan   I can't believe my sister would fail in her obligation to you in the least. If, sir, she has indeed checked the rioting of your followers, it would be on such grounds, and to such a desirable end, as to clear her from all blame.

Lear   My curses on her!

Regan   Oh, sir, you are old. You are at the end of your life. You should be governed and led by some wiser person who knows you better than you do yourself. Therefore I beg you return to our sister. Tell her you have wronged her.

Lear   Ask her forgiveness? How becoming this would be to royalty! ''Dear daughter, I admit that I am old. Old people are a nuisance. On my knees I beg you to grant me clothes, bed and food.'' [*He kneels to drive his point home*]

Regan   Good sir, no more of this. These are unseemly tricks. Return to my sister.

Lear   [*rising*] Never, Regan. She has deprived me of half my

Looked black upon me; struck me with her tongue,
Most serpent-like, upon the very heart.
All the stored vengeances of heaven fall
On her ingrateful top! Strike her young bones,
You taking airs, with lameness!

Cornwall   Fie, sir, fie!

Lear   You nimble lightnings, dart you blinding flames
Into her scornful eyes! Infect her beauty,
You fen-sucked fogs, drawn by the powerful sun
To fall and blast her pride!

Regan   O the blest gods! So will you wish on me,
When the rash mood is on.

Lear   No, Regan, thou shalt never have my curse:
Thy tender-hefted nature shall not give
Thee o'er to harshness: her eyes are fierce, but thine
Do comfort and not burn. 'Tis not in thee
To grudge my pleasures, to cut off my train,
To bandy hasty words, to scant my sizes,
And in conclusion to oppose the bolt
Against my coming in: thou better know'st
The offices of nature, bond of childhood,
Effects of courtesy, dues of gratitude;
Thy half o' th' kingdom hast thou not forgot,
Wherein I thee endowed.

Regan   Good sir, to th' purpose.

Lear   Who put my man i' th' stocks? [*Tucket within*]

Cornwall   What trumpet's that?

Regan   I know't, my sister's: this approves her letter,
That she would soon be here.

  [*Enter* **Oswald**]

                    Is your lady come?

retinue, given me black looks, and lashed me with her tongue most viciously upon the heart itself. May the entire stock of heaven's vengeances drop on her ungrateful head! Strike her unborn children with lameness, you infectious winds!

Cornwall   Come, sir, come!

Lear   Swift-moving lightning, aim your blinding flames into her eyes! Infect her beauty, you fogs sucked up from the fens by the heat of the powerful sun, to strike and make her ugly!

Regan   Oh, the blessed gods! That's what you'll wish on me when you're in one of your rash moods!

Lear   No, Regan, I will never curse you. Your tender-hearted nature couldn't turn to harshness. Her eyes are fierce, but yours are comforting, and do not smolder. It's not in your nature to begrudge me my pleasures, to reduce my retinue, to exchange hasty words, to cut down my allowances, and finally to lock me out. You know your natural duties; the obligations of child to parent; the ways of good manners; the responsibilities of gratitude. You haven't forgotten the half of the kingdom that I gave to you.

Regan   Good sir, get to the point.

Lear   Who put my man in the stocks? [*A trumpet sounds*]

Cornwall   Whose trumpet is that?

Regan   I recognize it: my sister's. This confirms her letter, that she'd be here soon.

[**Oswald** *enters*]

Has your lady arrived?

Lear   This is a slave, whose easy-borrowed pride
Dwells in the fickle grace of her he follows.
Out, varlet, from my sight!

Cornwall   What means your Grace?

Lear   Who stocked my servant? Regan, I have good hope
Thou didst not know on't. Who comes here?

  [*Enter* **Goneril**]

                                              O heavens,
If you do love old men, if your sweet sway
Allow obedience, if you yourselves are old,
Make it your cause; send down and take my part!
[*To* **Goneril**] Art not ashamed to look upon this beard?
O Regan, will you take her by the hand?

Goneril   Why not by th' hand, sir? How have I offended?
All's not offence that indiscretion finds
And dotage terms so.

Lear   O sides, you are too tough!
Will you yet hold? How came my man i' th' stocks?

Cornwall   I set him there, sir; but his own disorders
Deserved much less advancement.

Lear   You! Did you?

Regan   I pray you, father, being weak, seem so.
If, till the expiration of your month,
You will return and sojourn with my sister,
Dismissing half your train, come then to me:
I am now from home, and out of that provision
Which shall be needful for your entertainment.

Lear   Return to her? And fifty men dismissed?
No, rather I abjure all roofs, and choose
To wage against the enmity o' th' air;

Lear   [*glowering at* **Oswald**] This is the wretch whose
impudence depends on the fickle patronage of his mistress.
Get out of my sight, rascal!

Cornwall   What does your Grace mean?

Lear   Who put my servant in the stocks? Regan, I trust you
didn't know about it. [**Goneril** *approaches*] Who comes
here? Oh, gods: if you love old men; if your gracious
power approves of obedience; if you yourselves are old;
make this an issue. Intercede, and take up my cause! [*To*
Goneril] Are you not ashamed to look upon this beard? [*The
sisters embrace*] Oh, Regan, will you hold her hand?

Goneril   Why not my hand, sir? What have I done wrong? All is
not "offense" simply because it's so-called by the
irresponsible and those in their dotage.

Lear   [*holding his heart*] Is there no release? [*To* **Cornwall**]
How did my man come to be in the stocks?

Cornwall   *I* put him there, sir. His misconduct merited worse.

Lear   You! Did you?

Regan   Really, father, being weak, act accordingly. If you will
return with my sister and stay with her till the end of your
month – dismissing half your retinue – you can then come
to me. I am away from home now, and unable to provide
properly for your maintenance.

Lear   Return to her? With fifty men dismissed? No! Instead, I
reject all shelter, and choose to fight the elements, befriend

To be a comrade with the wolf and owl,
Necessity's sharp pinch! Return with her!
Why, the hot-blooded France, that dowerless took
Our youngest born, I could as well be brought
To knee his throne, and, squire-like, pension beg
To keep base life afoot. Return with her!
Persuade me rather to be slave and sumpter
To this detested groom. [*Pointing at* **Oswald**]

Goneril   At your choice, sir.

Lear   I prithee, daughter, do not make me mad:
I will not trouble thee, my child; farewell.
We'll no more meet, no more see one another;
But yet thou art my flesh, my blood, my daughter;
Or rather a disease that's in my flesh,
Which I must needs call mine: thou art a boil,
A plague-sore, or embossed carbuncle,
In my corrupted blood. But I'll not chide thee;
Let shame come when it will, I do not call it;
I do not bid the thunder-bearer shoot,
Nor tell tales of thee to high-judging Jove.
Mend when thou canst; be better at thy leisure;
I can be patient; I can stay with Regan,
I and my hundred knights.

Regan   Not altogether so;
I looked not for you yet, nor am provided
For your fit welcome. Give ear, sir, to my sister;
For those that mingle reason with your passion
Must be content to think you old, and so –
But she knows what she does.

Lear   Is this well spoken?

Regan   I dare avouch it, sir: what, fifty followers?
Is it not well? What should you need of more?

the wolf and owl, suffer hardship! Return with her? Why, I could as well be made to kneel before the throne of passionate France, who took our youngest-born without a dowry, and beg a pension from him, like some petty squire, to make ends meet. Return with her? I'd rather you persuaded me to be slave and drudge to this detested servant! [*He points at* **Oswald**]

Goneril   Please yourself, sir.

Lear   I beg you, daughter, do not make me mad. I won't trouble you, my child. Farewell. We'll meet no more. We'll see each other no more. [*His anger returns*] But still you *are* my flesh and blood, my daughter; or rather, a disease that's in my flesh, which is mine whether I like it or not. You're a boil, a plague-sore, a swollen tumor in my infected blood! [*Calm again*] But I won't curse you. Let shame choose its own time – I won't summon it. I do not call on Jupiter for vengeance, or tell tales about you to Jove, whose judgment is supreme. Reform when you can. Be better at your leisure. I can be patient. I can stay with Regan, I and my hundred knights.

Regan   Not quite. I wasn't expecting you yet, nor am I prepared for a fitting welcome. Listen to my sister. Anyone considering your words dispassionately would conclude you are old, and therefore – but she knows what she is doing.

Lear   Is this well said?

Regan   It certainly is, sir. What, fifty followers? Isn't that plenty? Why should you need more? Yes, or so many, since

Yea, or so many, sith that both charge and danger
Speak 'gainst so great a number? How, in one house,
Should many people, under two commands,
Hold amity? 'Tis hard; almost impossible.

Goneril   Why might not you, my lord, receive attendance
From those that she calls servants, or from mine?

Regan   Why not, my lord? If then they chanced to slack you,
We could control them. If you will come to me,
For now I spy a danger, I entreat you
To bring but five-and-twenty; to no more
Will I give place or notice.

Lear   I gave you all –

Regan   And in good time you gave it.

Lear   Made you my guardians, my depositaries,
But kept a reservation to be followed
With such a number. What, must I come to you
With five-and-twenty? Regan, said you so?

Regan   And speak't again, my lord; no more with me.

Lear   Those wicked creatures yet do look well-favoured
When others are more wicked; not being the worst
Stands in some rank of praise. [*To* **Goneril**] I'll go with
   thee:
Thy fifty yet doth double five-and-twenty,
And thou art twice her love.

Goneril   Hear me, my lord:
What need you five-and-twenty, ten, or five,
To follow in a house where twice so many
Have a command to tend you?

Regan   What need one?

Lear   O, reason not the need; our basest beggars

the expense and the danger both argue against so great a number? How, in one house, could so many people under two commands live in harmony? It's difficult – almost impossible.

Goneril   Why couldn't you, my lord, be attended by *her* servants, or by mine?

Regan   Why not, my lord? If they happened to become neglectful, we could correct them. If you want to come to me, because now I perceive a danger, I would ask you to bring only twenty-five. I'll accommodate and recognize no more.

Lear   I gave you everything . . .

Regan   And you took your time about it!

Lear   . . . made you my stewardesses and trustees, but with a proviso that I should have a retinue of such a number. What? Must I come to you with twenty-five? Regan, is that what you said?

Regan   And say it again, my lord. No more with me.

Lear   Some wicked creatures seem attractive when compared with others more wicked still. Not being the worst is some measure of praise. [*To* **Goneril**] I'll go with you. Your fifty is twice twenty-five, and your love is double hers.

Goneril   Listen to me, my lord. Why do you need twenty-five – ten – or five – to attend you, in a house where twice as many are at your service?

Regan   What need have you of one?

Lear   Oh, don't argue about ''need''! Our lowliest beggars

Are in the poorest thing superfluous:
Allow not nature more than nature needs,
Man's life's as cheap as beast's. Thou art a lady;
If only to go warm were gorgeous,
Why, nature needs not what thou gorgeous wear'st,
Which scarcely keeps thee warm. But, for true need –
You heavens, give me that patience, patience I need! –
You see me here, you gods, a poor old man,
As full of grief as age; wretched in both!
If it be you that stirs these daughters' hearts
Against their father, fool me not so much
To bear it tamely; touch me with noble anger,
And let not women's weapons, water-drops,
Stain my man's cheeks! No, you unnatural hags,
I will have such revenges on you both
That all the world shall – I will do such things,
What they are, yet I know not, but they shall be
The terrors of the earth. You think I'll weep;
No, I'll not weep:
I have full cause of weeping, but this heart
Shall break into a hundred thousand flaws
Or ere I'll weep. O Fool! I shall go mad.

[*Exeunt* **Lear, Gloucester, Gentleman,** *and* **Fool.** *Storm and*
tempest]

Cornwall   Let us withdraw; 'twill be a storm.

Regan   This house is little: the old man and 's people
Cannot be well bestowed.

Goneril   'Tis his own blame; hath put himself from rest,
And must needs taste his folly.

Regan   For his particular, I'll receive him gladly,
But not one follower.

have something they could do without. If you argue for the
bare necessities, then man's life would be no better than a
beast's. You are a lady: if being warm were the purpose of
being well-dressed, well then, there'd be no physical reason
for the fashionable clothes you are wearing, which hardly
keep you warm. Whereas true need – [*he breaks off*]
Heavens, give me patience, the patience I require! You see
me here, you gods, a poor old man, as full of grief as I am of
age; wretched in both respects! If you are responsible for
turning these daughters' hearts against their father, don't
make me such a fool as to bear it tamely! Inspire me with
noble anger, and don't let women's weapons – tears –
stain my man's cheeks! No, you unnatural hags, I'll do such
things in revenge – I can't say what at present, but they will
be earth-shattering! You think I'll cry? No, I won't cry. I've
got every reason to cry [*thunder claps are heard in the
distance*], but this heart of mine will break into a hundred
thousand pieces before I'll cry. Oh, Fool! I shall go mad! [*He
staggers out, followed by* Gloucester, *the* Gentleman *and
the* Fool]

Cornwall   Let us go in. There's going to be a storm.

Regan   This is a small house. The old man and his retinue
can't be adequately lodged.

Goneril   It's his own fault. He's upset himself, and he must
suffer for his folly.

Regan   For himself, I'll take him gladly. But not one follower.

Goneril   So am I purposed.
Where is my Lord of Gloucester?

Cornwall   Followed the old man forth. He is returned.

[*Re-enter* **Gloucester**]

Gloucester   The King is in high rage.

Cornwall   Whither is he going?

Gloucester   He calls to horse; but will I know not whither.

Cornwall   'Tis best to give him way; he leads himself.

Goneril   My lord, entreat him by no means to stay.

Gloucester   Alack! The night comes on, and the bleak winds
Do sorely ruffle; for many miles about
There's scarce a bush.

Regan   O sir, to wilful men,
The injuries that they themselves procure
Must be their schoolmasters. Shut up your doors;
He is attended with a desperate train,
And what they may incense him to, being apt
To have his ear abused, wisdom bids fear.

Cornwall   Shut up your doors, my lord; 'tis a wild night.
My Regan counsels well: come out o' th' storm.

[*Exeunt*]

Goneril   That's my attitude exactly. Where is my Lord of Gloucester?

Cornwall   He followed the old man out. He's back.

[**Gloucester** *enters*]

Gloucester   The King is in a terrible rage.

Cornwall   Where is he going?

Gloucester   He's summoned the horses. Where he's going, I don't know.

Cornwall   Best give him his own way. He's his own master.

Goneril   My lord, by no means plead with him to stay.

Gloucester   Alas! It's almost night, and the bleak winds are blustering fiercely. There's hardly a bush for miles around.

Regan   Oh, sir, willful men can only learn by suffering from their own actions. Shut your doors. His attendants are a desperate lot, and it's only sensible to fear what they might provoke him into doing. He's apt to be misled.

Cornwall   Shut your doors, my lord. It's a wild night. My Regan's advice is sound. Come out of the storm.

[*They leave*]

Act three

Scene 1

A heath. A storm, with thunder and lightning. Enter **Kent** *and a* **Gentleman,** *meeting.*

Kent   Who's there, besides foul weather?

Gentleman   One minded like the weather, most unquietly.

Kent   I know you. Where's the King?

Gentleman   Contending with the fretful elements;
  Bids the wind blow the earth into the sea,
  Or swell the curled waters 'bove the main,
  That things might change or cease; tears his white hair,
  Which the impetuous blasts, with eyeless rage,
  Catch in their fury, and make nothing of;
  Strives in his little world of man to out-scorn
  The to-and-fro-conflicting wind and rain.
  This night, wherein the cub-drawn bear would couch,
  The lion and the belly-pinched wolf
  Keep their fur dry, unbonneted he runs,
  And bids what will take all.

Kent   But who is with him?

Gentleman   None but the Fool, who labours to out-jest
  His heart-struck injuries.

Kent   Sir, I do know you;
  And dare, upon the warrant of my note,
  Commend a dear thing to you. There is division,
  Although as yet the face of it is covered
  With mutual cunning, 'twixt Albany and Cornwall;

Act three

Scene 1

A heath during a violent storm. **Kent** *and a* **Gentleman** *meet.*

Kent   Who's there, besides foul weather?

Gentleman   Someone as disturbed as the weather is.

Kent   I know you. Where's the King?

Gentleman   He's battling with the angry elements. He tells the wind to blow the earth into the sea, or raise the waves above the mainland, to bring chaos or destruction. He tears his white hair, which violent blasts, blind with rage, seize in their fury and treat with scant respect. He strives with his puny human frame to out-storm the wind and rain as it swirls to and fro in conflict. Tonight, when even the hungry mother-bear takes cover, and the lion and the starving wolf keep their fur dry, he runs bareheaded, and cries out in reckless desperation.

Kent   But who is with him?

Gentleman   Only the Fool, who tries to joke away his master's heartfelt injuries.

Kent   Sir, I know you, and on that account I'll risk entrusting something important to you. Although it's concealed by their craftiness, there is a rift between *Albany* and *Cornwall*.

Who have – as who have not, that their great stars
Throned and set high? – servants, who seem no less,
Which are to France the spies and speculations
Intelligent of our state; what hath been seen,
Either in snuffs and packings of the Dukes,
Or the hard rein which both of them have borne
Against the old kind King; or something deeper,
Whereof perchance these are but furnishings;
But, true it is, from France there comes a power
Into this scattered kingdom; who already,
Wise in our negligence, have secret feet
In some of our best ports, and are at point
To show their open banner. Now to you:
If on my credit you dare build so far
To make your speed to Dover, you shall find
Some that will thank you, making just report
Of how unnatural and bemadding sorrow
The King hath cause to plain.
I am a gentleman of blood and breeding,
And from some knowledge and assurance offer
This office to you.

Gentleman   I will talk further with you.

Kent   No, do not.
For confirmation that I am much more
Than my out-wall, open this purse and take
What it contains. If you shall see Cordelia –
As fear not but you shall – show her this ring,
And she will tell you who that fellow is
That yet you do not know. Fie on this storm!
I will go seek the King.

Gentleman   Give me your hand. Have you no more to say?

Kent   Few words, but, to effect, more than all yet;
That, when we have found the King – in which your pain

They have servants – which great ones have not? – who seem genuine, but who are spies supplying information about our kingdom to the King of France: either concerning the quarrels and intrigues of the Dukes; or the tough way both have handled the kind old King; or something more profound, of which these are perhaps the outward manifestations. But the fact is that an army has arrived, from France, in this divided kingdom. Taking advantage of our negligence, they have already established a secret foothold in some of our best ports, and are on the point of revealing themselves. Now, as for you, if you'll trust me to the extent of hastening to Dover, you'll find men there who'll thank you for delivering a true account of the unnatural and maddening sorrow which the King is suffering from. I am a gentleman of noble blood and good breeding, and I offer this commission to you on reliable information.

Gentleman   I'd like to discuss this further.

Kent   No, don't. For confirmation that I am more than my outward appearance suggests, open this purse and take what it contains. [*The* **Gentleman** *finds a ring inside*] If you should see Cordelia – and no doubt you will – show her this ring, and she will tell you who the fellow is who's now unknown to you. Damn this storm! I'll look for the King.

Gentleman   Give me your hand. Have you nothing to add?

Kent   Few words, but of prime importance. When we find the King – you go that way, and I'll go this – whoever sees him

That way, I'll this – he that first lights on him
Holla the other.

[*Exeunt severally*]

Scene 2

Another part of the heath. Storm still. Enter **Lear** *and* **Fool.**

Lear   Blow, winds, and crack your cheeks! rage! blow!
You cataracts and hurricanoes, spout
Till you have drenched our steeples, drowned the cocks!
You sulphurous and thought-executing fires,
Vaunt-couriers of oak-cleaving thunderbolts,
Singe my white head! And thou, all-shaking thunder,
Strike flat the thick rotundity o' th' world!
Crack nature's moulds, all germens spill at once
That makes ingrateful man!

Fool   O nuncle, court holy-water in a dry house is better
than this rain-water out o'door. Good nuncle, in, and ask
thy daughters' blessing; here's a night pities neither wise
men nor fools.

Lear   Rumble thy bellyful! Spit, fire! Spout, rain!
Nor rain, wind, thunder, fire, are my daughters;
I tax you not, you elements, with unkindness;
I never gave you kingdom, called you children,
You owe me no subscription: then let fall
Your horrible pleasure; here I stand, your slave,
A poor, infirm, weak, and despised old man.
But yet I call you servile ministers,

first, shout to the other.

[*They leave separately*]

Scene 2

Another part of the heath. The storm still rages. **Lear** *and the*
Fool *enter.*

Lear   Blow, winds, and burst your cheeks! Rage! Blow! You
floodgates and waterspouts: gush till you've drenched our
church steeples and drowned the weathercocks! You
searing and mind-dazzling flashes – forerunners of
oak-splitting thunderbolts – singe my white head! And you,
all-shaking thunder: flatten the globe! Crack the molds
which Nature uses for replenishment! Destroy in an instant
the seeds from which ungrateful man is born!

Fool   Oh, uncle, flattery in a house that's dry is better than
a drenching out in the open. Good uncle, go in and ask a
blessing from your daughters. This is a night fit for neither
wise men nor fools.

Lear   Rumble your bellyful! Spit, fire! Spout, rain! Rain, wind,
thunder, fire – they're not my daughters! I don't accuse you,
you natural elements, of unkindness! I never gave you a
kingdom, or called you children. You owe me no deference.
So enjoy yourselves: Here I stand, your victim – a poor,
infirm, weak and despised old man! You're no better than
servile lackeys if you'll conspire with two pernicious

145

That will with two pernicious daughters join
Your high-engendered battles 'gainst a head
So old and white as this. O, 'tis foul!

Fool   He that has a house to put 's head in has a good head-
piece.

The cod-piece that will house
    Before the head has any,
The head and he shall louse;
    So beggars marry many.
The man that makes his toe
    What he his heart should make,
Shall of a corn cry woe,
    And turn his sleep to wake.

For there was never yet fair woman but she made mouths
in a glass.

[*Enter* **Kent**]

Lear   No, I will be the pattern of all patience;
I will say nothing.

Kent   Who's there?

Fool   Marry, here's grace and a cod-piece, that's a wise man
and a fool.

Kent   Alas, sir, are you here? Things that love night
Love not such nights as these; the wrathful skies
Gallow the very wanderers of the dark,
And make them keep their caves. Since I was man,
Such sheets of fire, such bursts of horrid thunder,
Such groans of roaring wind and rain, I never
Remember to have heard; man's nature cannot carry
Th'affliction nor the fear.

Lear   Let the great gods,

daughters to use your heavenly battalions against a head so old and white as mine! Oh, it's despicable!

Fool The man who has a house to put his head in has got a hat with brains under it.

> The horny man who fornicates
>   Before he saves a penny,
> His life to lice he dedicates
>   So beggars marry many.

> The foolish man who cherishes
>   His toe more than his heart,
> Will think from corns he perishes
>   And wake up with a start.

There never yet was a beautiful woman who didn't preen herself in front of a mirror.

[**Kent** *enters*]

Lear [*to himself*] No, I will be a model of patience. I'll say nothing.

Kent Who's there?

Fool Indeed, here's graciousness and vulgarity – that is, a wise man and a Fool.

Kent Alas, sir, are you here? Even nocturnal things dislike such nights as these. The angry skies terrify even the wild animals and make them keep to their caves. Since I was grown, I don't remember ever having seen such sheets of fire, or heard such peals of thunder, such groans of roaring wind and rain. Man is not made to endure such suffering and fear.

Lear Let the almighty gods, who are making this dreadful

That keep this dreadful pudder o'er our heads,
Find out their enemies now. Tremble, thou wretch,
That has within thee undivulged crimes,
Unwhipped of justice; hide thee, thou bloody hand,
Thou perjured, and thou simular man of virtue
That art incestuous; caitiff, to pieces shake,
That under covert and convenient seeming
Hast practised on man's life; close pent-up guilts
Rive your concealing continents, and cry
These dreadful summoners grace. I am a man
More sinned against than sinning.

Kent   Alack, bare-headed!
Gracious my lord, hard by here is a hovel;
Some friendship will it lend you 'gainst the tempest;
Repose you there while I to this hard house –
More harder than the stones whereof 'tis raised,
Which even but now, demanding after you,
Denied me to come in – return and force
Their scanted courtesy.

Lear   My wits begin to turn.
Come on, my boy. How dost, my boy? Art cold?
I am cold myself. Where is this straw, my fellow?
The art of our necessities is strange,
And can make vile things precious. Come, your hovel.
Poor Fool and knave, I have one part in my heart
That's sorry yet for thee.

Fool   [*Singing*]   *He that has and a little tiny wit,*
             With hey, ho, the wind and the rain,
          Must make content with his fortunes fit,
             Though the rain it raineth every day.

Lear   True, my good boy. Come, bring us to this hovel.

[*Exeunt* **Lear** *and* **Kent**]

hubbub over our heads, identify their enemies now! Tremble, you wretch, with your undiscovered crimes as yet unpunished! Hide yourself, you murderer; you perjurer; you incestuous humbug! Rogue, shiver yourself to pieces: under cover of convenient hypocrisy you've tricked your way through life! Well-hidden crimes, burst out from your concealment, and plead for mercy from those dreadful ministers of vengeance! [*Removing his hat to show he has nothing to fear himself*] I am a man who's been more sinned against than ever he has sinned.

Kent   Alas, bare-headed! My gracious lord, there is a shed close by here. It will afford you some friendly protection against the tempest. Rest there, while I return to this cruel house – whose occupants, harder-hearted than the stone of which it is made, recently refused me admittance when I inquired after you – to wrest from them the courtesy they have failed to show.

Lear   My mind is going. [*To the* **Fool**] Come on, my boy. [*He puts his arm around him*] How are you, my boy? Are you cold? I'm cold myself. [*To* **Kent**] Where is this straw, my fellow? Need transforms things strangely. It can make what's paltry, precious. Come then, to your shed. Poor Fool and knave, there's one part of my heart that's sorry still for you.

Fool   [*he sings*] *He whose brain is somewhat dim,*
     With hey, ho, the wind and the rain,
   Must take what Fortune gives to him
     Though the rain keeps raining every day.

Lear   True, boy. [*To* **Kent**] Come, take us to this shed. [**Lear** *and* **Kent** *go*]

Fool   This is a brave night to cool a courtezan.
   I'll speak a prophecy ere I go:

> When priests are more in word than matter;
> When brewers mar their malt with water;
> When nobles are their tailors' tutors;
> No heretics burned, but wenches' suitors;
> When every case in law is right;
> No squire in debt, nor no poor knight;
> When slanders do not live in tongues;
> Nor cut-purses come not to throngs;
> When usurers tell their gold i' th' field;
> And bawds and whores do churches build;
> Then shall the realm of Albion
> Come to great confusion:
> Then comes the time, who lives to see't,
> That going shall be used with feet.

  This prophecy Merlin shall make; for I live before his time.

[Exit]

Scene 3

Gloucester's castle. Enter **Gloucester** *and* **Edmund,** *with lights.*

Gloucester   Alack, alack! Edmund, I like not this unnatural dealing. When I desired their leave that I might pity him, they took from me the use of mine own house; charged me, on pain of perpetual displeasure, neither to speak of him, entreat for him, or any way sustain him.

Fool   This is a fine night for cooling down a lustful wench. I'll
   speak a prophecy before I go:

> When priests are theorists, not doers;
> When beer is watered by the brewers;
> When nobles teach their tailors stitches;
> And lusty lads all suffer itches;
> When every case is right in law;
> No gentry-folk say they are poor;
> When tongues aren't used for slanderous tales;
> And thieves aren't caught and sent to jails;
> When moneylenders show their hoards;
> And churches are endowed by bawds;
> Then shall all the British nation
> Come to its humiliation.
> That's when, if you are still around,
> Feet will be used to walk on ground.

Merlin the magician will make this prophecy one day. I was
born before his time.

[*He goes*]

Scene 3

A room in Gloucester's castle after dark. **Gloucester** *and*
Edmund *enter, carrying torches.*

Gloucester   Alas, alas! Edmund, I don't like this unnatural
   behavior. When I asked their permission to take pity on
   him, they commandeered my house, and ordered me – on
   pain of their permanent displeasure – neither to speak of
   him, plead for him, or in any way sustain him.

Edmund   Most savage and unnatural!

Gloucester   Go to; say you nothing. There is division
between the Dukes, and a worse matter than that. I have
received a letter this night; 'tis dangerous to be spoken; I
have locked the letter in my closet. These injuries the King
now bears will be revenged home; there is part of a power
already footed; we must incline to the King. I will seek him
and privily relieve him; go you and maintain talk with the
Duke, that my charity be not of him perceived. If he ask
for me, I am ill and gone to bed. If I die for it, as no less is
threatened me, the King, my old master, must be relieved.
There is strange things toward, Edmund; pray you, be
careful.

[*Exit*]

Edmund   This courtesy, forbid thee, shall the Duke
Instantly know, and of that letter too:
This seems a fair deserving, and must draw me
That which my father loses; no less than all:
The younger rises when the old doth fall.

[*Exit*]

Scene 4

The heath. Before the hovel. Enter **Lear, Kent,** *and* **Fool.**

Kent   Here is the place, my lord: good my lord, enter:
The tyranny of the open night's too rough
For nature to endure.

Edmund   How savage and unnatural!

Gloucester   Sh! Say nothing. The Dukes have quarreled, and
   something worse: I've had a letter about it tonight. It's too
   dangerous to talk about; I've locked it in my bedroom. These
   wrongs the King is suffering will be revenged to the full.
   Part of an army has already landed; we must take the King's
   side. I'll look for him and aid him secretly. Go and keep the
   Duke talking, so that he won't observe my charity. If he asks
   for me, say I'm ill and gone to bed. Even if I die for it – as
   they've threatened me – the King, my old master, must be
   given help. Strange things are about to happen, Edmund. Do
   be careful.

[*He goes in search of* **Lear**]

Edmund   I'll tell the Duke at once about this kindness, which
   you have been forbidden to do. And the letter, too. This
   should be worth something to me, and must gain me what
   my father will lose: nothing less than everything! The young
   rise when the old fall.

[*He goes*]

Scene 4

The heath, in front of the shed. **Lear** *enters, with* **Kent** *and
the* **Fool.**

Kent   Here's the place, my lord. Good my lord, go in. The
   suffering of a night out in the open is too much for flesh and
   blood to endure.

Lear   Let me alone.

Kent Good my lord, enter here.

Lear   Wilt break my heart?

Kent I had rather break mine own. Good my lord, enter.

Lear Thou think'st 'tis much that this contentious storm
Invades us to the skin: so 'tis to thee;
But where the greater malady is fixed,
The lesser is scarce felt. Thou'ldst shun a bear;
But if thy flight lay toward the roaring sea,
Thou'ldst meet the bear i' th' mouth. When the mind's free
The body's delicate; this tempest in my mind
Doth from my senses take all feeling else
Save what beats there – filial ingratitude!
Is it not as this mouth should tear this hand
For lifting food to't? But I will punish home:
No, I will weep no more. In such a night
To shut me out! Pour on; I will endure.
In such a night as this! O Regan, Goneril!
Your old kind father, whose frank heart gave all –
O, that way madness lies; let me shun that;
No more of that.

Kent   Good my lord, enter here.

Lear Prithee, go in thyself; seek thine own ease:
This tempest will not give me leave to ponder
On things would hurt me more. But I'll go in.
[*To the* **Fool**] In, boy; go first. You houseless poverty –
Nay, get thee in. I'll pray, and then I'll sleep.

[**Fool** *goes in*]

Poor naked wretches, whereso'er you are,
That bide the pelting of this pitiless storm,
How shall your houseless heads and unfed sides,

[*The storm rages on unabated*]

Lear   Leave me alone.

Kent   Good my lord, go in.

Lear   Will you break my heart?

Kent   I'd rather break my own. Good my lord, enter.

Lear   You think it's remarkable that this raging storm soaks us to the skin. So it is, to you. But where there's a greater suffering, the lesser is hardly felt. You'd avoid a bear; but if your escape lay toward the roaring sea, you'd tackle the bear face to face. When there's nothing on your mind, you are conscious of your ailments; this tempest going on in my mind obliterates all feeling other than what's tormenting me – the ingratitude of my daughters! Isn't it equivalent to my mouth biting my hand for lifting food to it? I'll punish ruthlessly! No, I'll weep no more. To shut me out on a night like this! [*To the rain*] Pour on – I can take it! [*To Kent*] On such a night as this! Oh, Regan, Goneril! Your kind old father, whose open-heartedness gave you all! Oh, that way leads to madness! Let me avoid that! I mustn't think of that!

Kent   Good my lord, go in here.

Lear   Please go in yourself: seek some comfort. This tempest prevents me from thinking about things that would hurt me more. But I'll go in. [*To the* **Fool**] In, boy. Go first. [*He returns to his thoughts*] You who are poor and homeless – [*noting the* **Fool** *is hesitant*] No – go in. I'll pray and then I'll sleep. [*The* **Fool** *obeys*] Poor naked wretches, wherever you are, that endure the pelting of this pitiless storm: how shall your bare heads and bony bodies, your

Your looped and windowed raggedness, defend you
From seasons such as these? O, I have ta'en
Too little care of this! Take physic, Pomp;
Expose thyself to feel what wretches feel,
That thou mayst shake the superflux to them,
And show the Heavens more just.

Edgar [*within*] Fathom and half, fathom and half!
Poor Tom! [*The* **Fool** *runs out from the hovel*]

Fool   Come not in here, nuncle; here's a spirit.
Help me, help me!

Kent   Give me thy hand. Who's there?

Fool   A spirit, a spirit: he says his name's poor Tom.

Kent   What art thou that dost grumble there i' th' straw?
Come forth.

[*Enter* **Edgar,** *disguised as a madman*]

Edgar   Away! The foul fiend follows me! Through the sharp
hawthorn blows the cold winds. Hum! Go to thy bed and
warm thee.

Lear   Didst thou give all to thy daughters?
And art thou come to this?

Edgar   Who gives any thing to poor Tom? Whom the foul
fiend hath led through fire and through flame, through ford
and whirlpool, o'er bog and quagmire; that hath laid knives
under his pillow, and halters in his pew; set ratsbane by his
porridge; made him proud of heart, to ride on a bay
trotting-horse over four-inched bridges, to course his own
shadow for a traitor. Bless thy five wits! Tom's a-cold. O,
do de, do de, do de. Bless thee from whirlwinds, star-

tattered-and-torn raggedness, protect you from storms such as these? Oh, I've cared too little about this! Take a dose of this medicine, great ones! Expose yourself to feel what wretches feel, so that you can share their extra wealth, and show that the gods are just!

Edgar   [*from inside, as if he's taking soundings from a sinking ship*] Fathom and a half! Fathom and a half! Poor Tom!

[*The **Fool** rushes out, terrified*]

Fool   Don't come in here, uncle. There's a ghost. Help me, help me!

Kent   Give me your hand. [*Calling inside*] Who's there?

Fool   A spirit, a spirit! He says his name's Poor Tom.

Kent   Who are you, grumbling there in the straw? Come out.

[**Edgar** *appears, disguised as a madman*]

Edgar   [*talking dementedly*] Go away! The foul fiend follows me! The cold winds blow through the prickly hawthorn bushes. Hmm. [*To **Lear***] Go to your bed and get warm.

Lear   Did you give everything to your daughters? And have you come down to this?

Edgar   Who gives anything to Poor Tom? The foul fiend has led him through fire and through flame, through ford and whirlpool, over bog and quagmire. He's put knives under his pillow, and hung nooses from his balconies. He's put poison by his soup; made him overproud, riding a brown trotting-horse over narrow bridges, chasing his own shadow as if it were a traitor. Bless your five wits! Tom's cold. [*He shivers and stamps his feet, making noises to warm himself*] Oh, do-de, do-de, do-de! Bless you against whirlwinds,

157

blasting, and taking! Do poor Tom some charity, whom the foul fiend vexes. There could I have him now, and there, and there again, and there.

Lear   What! have his daughters brought him to this pass? Could'st thou save nothing? Would'st thou give 'em all?

Fool   Nay, he reserved a blanket, else we had been all shamed.

Lear   Now all the plagues that in the pendulous air
Hang fated o'er men's faults light on thy daughters!

Kent   He hath no daughters, sir.

Lear   Death, traitor! Nothing could have subdued nature
To such a lowness but his unkind daughters.
Is it the fashion that discarded fathers
Should have thus little mercy on their flesh?
Judicious punishment! 'twas this flesh begot
Those pelican daughters.

Edgar   Pillicock sat on Pillicock hill:
Alow, alow, loo, loo!

Fool   This cold night will turn us all to fools and madmen.

Edgar   Take heed o' th' foul fiend. Obey thy parents: keep thy word justly; swear not; commit not with man's sworn spouse; set not thy sweet heart on proud array. Tom's a-cold.

Lear   What hast thou been?

Edgar   A servingman, proud in heart and mind; that curled my hair, wore gloves in my cap, served the lust of my

shooting stars and evil influences! Do Poor Tom a favor, who's tormented by the foul fiend. [*He swipes at an imaginary attacker*] I could catch him now – and there – and there again – and there!

[*The storm rages on*]

Lear   What, have his daughters brought him to this? Could you save nothing? Did you give them everything?

Fool   No, he kept a blanket, or he would all have been shamed.

Lear   May all the plagues that hover menacingly in the air over men's faults now descend upon your daughters!

Kent   He has no daughters, sir.

Lear   Death to you, traitor! Nothing could have brought him down to this but his unkind daughters! Is it the fashion now for discarded fathers to endure such sufferings of the flesh? How just the punishment! It was this very flesh that conceived those father-killing daughters!

Edgar   [*reciting an old rhyme*] "Pillycock sat on Pillycock Hill." [*The second line is "If he's not gone, he sits there still," but* **Edgar** *replaces it with howling noises*] Alow, alow! Loo! Loo!

Fool   This cold night will turn us all into fools or madmen.

Edgar   Beware of the foul fiend. Obey your parents. Tell no lies. Don't swear. Commit no adultery. Do not yearn for splendid clothes. [*He shudders*] Tom feels cold.

Lear   What were you?

Edgar   A lover, proud in heart and mind. I curled my hair, wore love-tokens in my hat, fulfilled the heart's desire of my loved

mistress' heart, and did the act of darkness with her; swore
as many oaths as I spake words, and broke them in the
sweet face of Heaven; one that slept in the contriving of
lust, and waked to do it. Wine loved I deeply, dice dearly,
and in woman out-paramoured the Turk: false of heart, light
of ear, bloody of hand; hog in sloth, fox in stealth, wolf in
greediness, dog in madness, lion in prey. Let not the
creaking of shoes nor the rustling of silks betray thy poor
heart to woman: keep thy foot out of brothels, thy hand out
of plackets, thy pen from lenders' books, and defy the foul
fiend. Still through the hawthorn blows the cold wind; says
suum, mun, hey no nonny. Dolphin my boy, boy; sessa! let
him trot by.

Lear   Thou wert better in a grave than to answer with thy
uncovered body this extremity of the skies. Is man no more
than this? Consider him well. Thou owest the worm no
silk, the beast no hide, the sheep no wool, the cat no
perfume. Ha! here's three on 's are sophisticated; thou art
the thing itself; unaccommodated man is no more but such a
poor, bare, forked animal as thou art. Off, off, you lendings!
Come; unbutton here.   [*Tearing off his clothes*]

Fool   Prithee, nuncle, be contented; 'tis a naughty night to
swim in. Now a little fire in a wide field were like an old
lecher's heart; a small spark, all the rest on 's body cold.
Look! here comes a walking fire.

[*Enter* **Gloucester** *with a torch*]

one and slept with her. I made vows with every word I spoke, and broke them openly. My dreams were fantasies of lust; I awoke to practice them. Wine I loved deeply; gambling, dearly; as for women, I had more mistresses than the Sultan of Turkey. I was deceitful; interested in scandal; quick to draw blood; as lazy as a hog, stealthy as a fox, greedy as a wolf, mad as a dog, ruthless as a lion. Don't be turned on by the creaking of shoes or the sound of rustling silks. Keep your feet out of brothels, your hand away from petticoats, your signature from moneylenders' ledgers, and defy the foul fiend. The cold wind blows through the hawthorn bushes: it says [*imitating the sound*] "suum, mum, hey-no-nonny." [*He seems to recognize a presence*] The devil, my boy, boy! [*He puts his finger to his lips*] Sh! Let him pass by.

[*The storm rages on*]

Lear   You'd be better off in your grave than trying to endure this extreme weather in your nakedness. Is man no more than this? [*To the* **Fool**] Note him well. [*To* **Edgar**] You're not indebted to the silkworm for its silk; or the ox for its hide; the sheep for its wool; or the civet cat for its perfume. [*Pointing to himself,* **Edgar** *and the* **Fool**] We three are tainted, but you are the genuine article! Basic man is only a poor, bare, two-legged animal such as you are. [*He begins to take off his clothes*] Off, off, you borrowings! Come, unbutton here!

Fool   Please, uncle, don't do that! It's a wicked night to go swimming in. [*He sees* **Gloucester** *approaching carrying a torch*] Now a little fire in a big field is like the heart of an old lecher: a small spark of life with all the rest of his body cold. Look, here comes a walking fire!

[**Gloucester** *enters with a torch*]

Edgar   This is the foul fiend Flibbertigibbet: he begins at
curfew, and walks till the first cock; he gives the web and
the pin, squinies the eye, and makes the harelip; mildews
the white wheat, and hurts the poor creature of earth.

> Swithold footed thrice the old;
> He met the night-mare, and her nine-fold;
> > Bid her alight,
> > And her troth plight,
> > And aroint thee, witch, aroint thee!

Kent   How fares your Grace?

Lear   What's he?

Kent   Who's there? What is't you seek?

Gloucester   What are you there? Your names?

Edgar   Poor Tom; that eats the swimming frog, the toad, the
tadpole, the wall-newt, and the water; that in the fury of his
heart, when the foul fiend rages, eats cow-dung for sallets;
swallows the old rat and the ditch-dog; drinks the green
mantle of the standing pool; who is whipped from tithing to
tithing, and stock-punished, and imprisoned; who hath had
three suits to his back, six shirts to his body, horse to ride,
and weapon to wear,

> But mice and rats and such small deer,
> Have been Tom's food for seven long year.

Beware my follower. Peace, Smulkin! Peace, thou fiend!

Gloucester   What, hath your Grace no better company?

Edgar   The Prince of Darkness is a gentleman; Modo he's
called, and Mahu.

Gloucester   Our flesh and blood, my lord, is grown so vile,
That it doth hate what gets it.

Edgar   This is the foul fiend Flibbertigibbet; he begins at curfew-time, and walks about till midnight. He gives cataracts, squints eyes, and makes harelips. He mildews the ripening wheat, and hurts the poor creatures of the earth.

> Saint Withold three times walked his land;
> He met a demon and her ninefold band;
>   Her progress he stayed,
>   Her power he allayed,
> And ''Be off with you, witch! Be off!''

Kent   How is your Grace?

Lear   [*peering in the dark*] Who's he?

Kent   [*to* **Gloucester**] Who's there? What are you looking for?

Gloucester   Who are you, there? Your names?

Edmund   Poor Tom, who eats the swimming frog, the toad, the tadpole, the wall-newt and the water-newt. When the foul fiend rages, he eats cowdung instead of salads; swallows dead rats and dead dogs; drinks the scum from standing ponds; is whipped from settlement to settlement, put in the stocks, imprisoned. He once had three suits and six shirts, a horse to ride and weapons to wear,

> But mice and rats and such small game
> Have been Tom's food for seven long year.

Beware of my devil. [*He talks to an invisible companion*] Be quiet, Smulkin! Be quiet, you fiend!

Gloucester   What, has your Grace no better company?

Edgar   The King of the Devils is a gentleman. He's called ''Modo'', and ''Mahu''.

Gloucester   Humanity is so degraded, my lord, it hates its parents.

163

Edgar   Poor Tom's a-cold.

Gloucester   Go in with me. My duty cannot suffer
   T'obey in all your daughters' hard commands;
   Though their injunction be to bar my doors,
   And let this tyrannous night take hold upon you,
   Yet I have ventured to come and seek you out
   And bring you where both fire and food is ready.

Lear   First let me talk with this philosopher.
   What is the cause of thunder?

Kent   Good my lord, take his offer; go into the house.

Lear   I'll talk a word with this same learned Theban.
   What is your study?

Edgar   How to prevent the fiend, and to kill vermin.

Lear   Let me ask you one word in private.

Kent   Importune him once more to go, my lord;
   His wits begin t'unsettle.

Gloucester   Canst thou blame him?
   His daughters seek his death. Ah, that good Kent;
   He said it would be thus, poor banished man!
   Thou say'st the King grows mad; I'll tell thee, friend,
   I am almost mad myself. I had a son,
   Now outlawed from my blood; he sought my life,
   But lately, very late; I loved him, friend,
   No father his son dearer; truth to tell thee,
   The grief hath crazed my wits. What a night's this!
   I do beseech your Grace –

Lear   Oh, cry you mercy, sir:
   Noble philosopher, your company.

Edgar   Tom's a-cold.

Edgar   Poor Tom is cold.

Gloucester   [*to* **Lear**] Come in with me. My sense of duty does not stretch so far as to obey all your daughters' harsh commands. Though their orders are to bar my doors and let this pitiless night have its way with you, I've nevertheless ventured to find you and bring you where warmth and food are ready.

Lear   First let me talk with this philosopher. [*To* **Edgar**] What is the cause of thunder?

Kent   Good my lord, take his offer. Go into the house.

Lear   I'll have a word with this learned professor. What is your subject?

Edgar   How to avoid the fiend, and to kill vermin.

Lear   Let me ask you one word in private.

Kent   Plead with him once more to go in, my lord. His mind is failing.

Gloucester   Can you blame him? [*Claps of thunder are heard overhead*] His daughters want him dead. Ah, that good *Kent*: he said it would be like this, the poor, banished man! You say the King is going insane. I'll tell you this, my friend: I'm almost mad myself. I had a son, now disowned. He sought my life, only recently, recently. I loved him, friend. No father loved his son more. To tell you the truth, the grief has touched my mind. What a night this is! [*To* **Lear**] I beg your Grace –

Lear   Oh, I beg your pardon, sir. [*To* **Edgar**] Noble philosopher, do join us.

Edgar   Tom's cold.

Gloucester   In, fellow, there, into the hovel: keep thee warm.

Lear   Come, let's in all.

Kent   This way, my lord.

Lear   With him;
   I will keep still with my philosopher.

Kent   Good my lord, soothe him; let him take the fellow.

Gloucester   Take him you on.

Kent   Sirrah, come on; go along with us.

Lear   Come, good Athenian.

Gloucester   No words, no words: hush.

Edgar   Child Rowland to the dark tower came,
              His word was still: 'Fie, foh, and fum,
                I smell the blood of a British man.'

                                              [*Exeunt*]

Scene 5

Gloucester's castle. Enter **Cornwall** *and* **Edmund.**

Cornwall   I will have my revenge ere I depart his house.

Edmund   How, my lord, I may be censured, that nature thus
   gives way to loyalty, something fears me to think of.

Gloucester   In, fellow, there − into the shed. Keep yourself warm.

Lear   Come, let's all go in.

Kent   This way, my lord.

Lear   [*his arm around* **Edgar**] With him: I want to be with my philosopher.

Kent   [*to* **Gloucester**] Good my lord, humor him. Let him take the fellow with him.

Gloucester   You take charge of him.

Kent   [*to* **Edgar**] Come on, go with us.

Lear   Come, good Athenian.

Gloucester   [*to* **Edgar**] Don't say anything; don't say anything. Sh!

Edgar   Squire Roland to the dark tower came,
His motto was: Fie, foh, and fum:
I smell the blood of an Englishman.

[*They enter the shed*]

Scene 5

A room in Gloucester's castle. **Cornwall** *and* **Edmund** *enter.*
Cornwall *is waving a letter.*

Cornwall   I'll have my revenge before I leave this house.

Edmund   What people will say about me, in putting loyalty before my feelings as a son, I fear to think.

167

Cornwall   I now perceive it was not altogether your brother's evil disposition made him seek his death; but a provoking merit, set a-work by a reprovable badness in himself.

Edmund   How malicious is my fortune, that I must repent to be just! This is the letter he spoke of, which approves him an intelligent party to the advantages of France. O heavens, that this treason were not, or not I the detector!

Cornwall   Go with me to the Duchess.

Edmund   If the matter of this paper be certain, you have mighty business in hand.

Cornwall   True or false, it hath made thee Earl of Gloucester. Seek out where thy father is, that he may be ready for our apprehension.

Edmund   [*aside*] If I find him comforting the King, it will stuff his suspicion more fully. [*Aloud*] I will persever in my course of loyalty, though the conflict be sore between that and my blood.

Cornwall   I will lay trust upon thee; and thou shalt find a dearer father in my love.

[*Exeunt*]

Scene 6

A chamber in a farmhouse adjoining the castle. Enter **Gloucester** *and* **Kent.**

Gloucester   Here is better than the open air; take it thankfully. I will piece out the comfort with what addition I can: I will not be long from you.

Cornwall   I see now that it wasn't just your brother's evil disposition that made him seek his father's death. He was provoked into it, helped by his wicked nature.

Edmund   How wickedly unfortunate that loyalty to my country should give me a feeling of guilt! This is the letter my father spoke of, which proves he is a spy acting on behalf of France. Oh, heavens! Would that this treason had never happened, and that I wasn't the one to discover it!

Cornwall   Come with me to the Duchess.

Edmund   If the contents of this letter are true, you have important work to do.

Cornwall   True or false, it has made you the Earl of Gloucester. Find your father, so we can arrest him.

Edmund   [aside] If I find him giving aid and comfort to the King, it will make the Duke even more suspicious. [Aloud] I shall continue in my loyal course, in spite of the painful conflict between duty and my feelings as a son.

Cornwall   I have every confidence in you; and you'll find I'll make you a more loving father.

[They go]

Scene 6

A room in a farmhouse near the castle. **Gloucester** *and* **Kent** *enter.*

Gloucester   This is better than the open air. Be thankful for it. I'll try to make it more comfortable with what extras I can find. I won't be away long.

Kent   All the power of his wits have given way to his
impatience. The gods reward your kindness!

[*Exit* **Gloucester**]

[*Enter* **Lear, Edgar,** *and* **Fool**]

Edgar   Frateretto calls me, and tells me Nero is an angler in
the lake of darkness. Pray, innocent, and beware the foul
fiend.

Fool   Prithee, nuncle, tell me whether a madman be a
gentleman or a yeoman?

Lear   A king, a king!

Fool   No; he's a yeoman that has a gentleman to his son; for
he's a mad yeoman that sees his son a gentleman before
him.

Lear   To have a thousand with red burning spits
Come hissing in upon 'em –

Edgar   The foul fiend bites my back.

Fool   He's mad that trusts in the tameness of a wolf, a
horse's health, a boy's love, or a whore's oath.

Lear   It shall be done; I will arraign them straight.
[*To* **Edgar**] Come, sit thou here, most learned justicer;
[*To the* **Fool**] Thou, sapient sir, sit here. Now, you she
foxes!

Edgar   Look where he stands and glares! Want'st thou eyes
at trial, madam?

Kent   His mind has completely gone under the stress. The gods reward your kindness!

[**Gloucester** *goes*]

[**Lear** *enters, with* **Edgar** *and the* **Fool**]

Edgar   Frateretto calls me, and tells me that Nero fishes in the lake of hell. [*To the* **Fool**] Pray, innocent one, and beware of the foul fiend!

Fool   Now, uncle, can you tell me whether a madman is a gentleman, or just someone who is rich?

Lear   A king, a king!

Fool   No. The rich man's son *becomes* a gentleman. Only a madman would have his son a gentleman before he's one himself!

Lear   [*brooding to himself about his ungrateful daughters*] To have a thousand devils armed with red-hot pokers come chasing after them . . .

Edgar   [*jerking about*] The foul fiend is biting my back!

Fool   Anyone's mad who trusts in the tameness of a wolf, or the health of a horse that's for sale, or a boy's love, or a whore's promise.

Lear   [*still in a world of his own*] It shall be done. I'll prosecute them immediately. [*To* **Edgar**] Come, sit you here, most learned judge. [*To the* **Fool**] You, wise sir, sit here. [*Rubbing his hands*] Now, you she foxes!

Edgar   [*pointing to* **Lear**] Look how he stands and glares! [*To the imaginary plaintiff*] Are you showing off in the witness-box, madam?   [*He breaks out into a romantic love-song*]

Come over the stream, Bessy, to me –

171

[Singing] Come o'er the bourn, Bessy, to me –

Fool   *Her boat hath a leak,*
    And she must not speak
    Why she dares not come over to thee!

Edgar   The foul fiend haunts poor Tom in the voice of a
nightingale. Hoppedance cries in Tom's belly for two white
herring. Croak not, black angel; I have no food for thee.

Kent   How do you, sir? Stand you not so amazed:
Will you lie down and rest upon the cushions?

Lear   I'll see their trial first. Bring in their evidence.
[*To* **Edgar**] Thou robed man of justice, take thy place;
[*To the* **Fool**] And thou, his yoke-fellow of equity,
Bench by his side. [*To* **Kent**] You are o' th' commission,
Sit you too.

Edgar   Let us deal justly.

[*Singing*]

    Sleepest or wakest thou, jolly shepherd?
      Thy sheep be in the corn;
    And for one blast of thy minikin mouth,
      Thy sheep shall take no harm.

Purr the cat is grey.

Lear   Arraign her first; 'tis Goneril. I here take my oath
before this honourable assembly, she kicked the poor King
her father.

Fool   Come hither, mistress. Is your name Goneril?

Lear   She cannot deny it.

Fool   Cry you mercy, I took you for a joint-stool.

Lear   And here's another, whose warped looks proclaim
What store her heart is made on. Stop her there!

Fool   [*joining in, picking up his words*]

> Her boat's got a leak,
>   And she must not speak
> Why she dares not come over to you!

Edgar   [*commenting on the quality of the* **Fool's** *singing voice*]
The foul fiend haunts Poor Tom, disguised as a nightingale.
[*He rubs his stomach*] Hoppedance is crying out in Tom's
belly for two pickled herrings. Stop your rumbling, black
angel: I've no food for you.

Kent   [*to* **Lear**] How are you, sir? Don't be dismayed. Will you
lie down and rest on these cushions?

Lear   I'll see their trial first. Bring in the witnesses. [*To* **Edgar,**
who is scantily attired] Take your place, you man of justice,
in your robes. [*To the* **Fool**] And you, his learned colleague,
take your seat on the bench, at his side. [*To* **Kent**] You are
one of the magistrates. You must sit too.

Edgar   Let us handle the case justly. [*He sings*]

> Are you sleeping or awake, jolly shepherd?
>   Your sheep are in the corn.
> If you'd only give one little blast on your whistle,
>   Your sheep would come to no harm.

[*He makes a noise with his mouth*] Purr! [*Explaining*] The cat
is gray.

Lear   [*pointing to an unoccupied seat*] Prosecute her first: it's
Goneril. I here take my oath before this honorable
assembly, that she kicked the poor King, her father.

Fool   Come here, mistress. Is your name Goneril?

Lear   She can't deny it.

Fool   I beg your pardon. I mistook you for a stool!

Lear   And here's another one whose ugly looks reveal what
her heart is made of. [*He jumps up excitedly*] Stop her there!

Arms, arms, sword, fire! Corruption in the place!
False justicer, why hast thou let her 'scape?

Edgar   Bless thy five wits!

Kent   O pity! Sir, where is the patience now
That you so oft have boasted to retain?

Edgar   [*aside*] My tears begin to take his part so much,
They mar my counterfeiting.

Lear   The little dogs and all,
Tray, Blanch, and Sweetheart, see, they bark at me.

Edgar   Tom will throw his head at them. Avaunt, you curs!

Be thy mouth or black or white,
Tooth that poisons if it bite;
Mastiff, greyhound, mongrel grim,
Hound or spaniel, brach or him,
Or bobtail tike or trundle-tail;
Tom will make him weep and wail:
For, with throwing thus my head,
Dogs leap the hatch, and all are fled.

Do de, de, de. Sessa! Come, march to wakes and fairs and
market-towns. Poor Tom, thy horn is dry.

Lear   Then let them anatomize Regan; see what breeds about
her heart. Is there any cause in nature that makes these
hard hearts? [*To* **Edgar**] You, sir, I entertain for one of my
hundred; only I do not like the fashion of your garments:
you will say they are Persian; but let them be changed.

Kent   Now, good my lord, lie here and rest awhile.

Lear   Make no noise, make no noise; draw the curtains: so, so.
We'll go to supper i' th' morning.

Fool   And I'll go to bed at noon.

Arms, arms, sword, fire! There's corruption here! [*To* **Edgar**] False judge – why have you let her escape?

Edgar   Bless your five wits!

Kent   Oh, for pity! Sir, where now is the self-control you have so often boasted of?

Edgar   [*aside, as himself*] My tears of sympathy for him are beginning to ruin my disguise.

Lear   Even the little dogs – Tray, Blanch and Sweetheart – see, they are barking at me!

Edgar   Tom will throw his head at them. Get away, you curs!

Whether your mouth is black or white,
With teeth that poison if they bite,
Mastiff, greyhound, mongrel grim,
Hound or spaniel, her or him,
Or bobtail tike, or droopy-tail –
Tom will make him weep and wail:
'Cos, with throwing thus my head,
Dogs hurry out, and all are fled.

Do de, de, de. Be quiet! Come, let's march to wakes and fairs and market towns! Poor Tom, you need a drink.

Lear   Let them dissect Regan, to see what's festering around her heart. Is there any natural cause for these hard hearts? [*To* **Edgar**] You, sir, I'll engage you as one of my hundred knights, though I don't like the cut of your clothes. You'll say they are Persian-style, but change them.

Kent   Now, good my lord, lie here and rest for a while.

Lear   [*as if at home in bed*] Make no noise, make no noise. Draw the curtains. So, so. We'll have our supper in the morning.

Fool   And I'll go to bed at noon.

[*Re-enter* **Gloucester**]

Gloucester   Come hither, friend: where is the King my
   master?

Kent   Here, sir; but trouble him not: his wits are gone.

Gloucester   Good friend, I prithee, take him in thy arms;
   I have o'erheard a plot of death upon him.
   There is a litter ready; lay him in't,
   And drive toward Dover, friend, where thou shalt meet
   Both welcome and protection. Take up thy master:
   If thou should'st dally half an hour, his life,
   With thine, and all that offer to defend him,
   Stand in assured loss. Take up, take up;
   And follow me, that will to some provision
   Give thee quick conduct.

Kent   Oppressed nature sleeps.
   This rest might yet have blamed thy broken sinews
   Which, if convenience will not allow,
   Stand in hard cure. [*To the* **Fool**] Come, help to bear thy
      master;
   Thou must not stay behind.

Gloucester   Come, come, away.

[*Exeunt* **Kent, Gloucester,** *and the* **Fool,** *bearing off the* **King**]

Edgar   When we our betters see bearing our woes,
   We scarcely think our miseries our foes.
   Who alone suffers, suffers most i' th' mind,
   Leaving free things and happy shows behind;
   But then the mind much sufferance doth o'erskip,
   When grief hath mates, and bearing fellowship.
   How light and portable my pain seems now,
   When that which makes me bend makes the King bow;

[**Gloucester** *returns*]

Gloucester   [*to* **Kent**] Come here, friend. Where is my master the King?

Kent   Here, sir. But don't bother him. His mind has gone.

Gloucester   Good friend, I beg of you: take him in your arms. I've overheard a plot to kill him. There's a stretcher ready: lay him on it, and drive toward Dover, friend, where you'll meet both welcome and protection. Lift your master up. If you dally half an hour, his life, and yours, and all who support him, are certain to be lost. Take him up, take him up, and follow me. I'll give you guidance and provisions.

Kent   Distress has induced sleep. This rest might have soothed your tortured nerves. If circumstances won't allow that, a cure will not be easy. [*To the* **Fool**] Come, help to carry your master. You must not stay behind.

Gloucester   Come: come away.

[**Kent, Gloucester** *and the* **Fool** *leave, carrying* **Lear**]

Edgar   When we see our betters suffering from wretchedness, our own miseries seem more bearable. Lonely suffering is mostly in the mind, which it ceases to be carefree and happy. However, the mind is relieved of much suffering when grief and adversity are shared. How tolerable my pain seems now, when I see the King break beneath a burden

He childed as I fathered! Tom, away!
Mark the high noises, and thyself bewray
When false opinion, whose wrong thoughts defile thee,
In thy just proof repeals and reconciles thee.
What will hap more to-night, safe 'scape the King!
Lurk, lurk.

[*Exit*]

Scene 7

Gloucester's castle. Enter **Cornwall, Regan, Goneril, Edmund,** *and Servants.*

Cornwall   [*to* **Goneril**] Post speedily to my lord your
husband; show him this letter: the army of France is landed.
Seek out the traitor Gloucester.

[*Exeunt some of the Servants*]

Regan   Hang him instantly.

Goneril   Pluck out his eyes.

Cornwall   Leave him to my displeasure. Edmund, keep you
our sister company: the revenges we are bound to take upon
your traitorous father are not fit for your beholding. Advise
the Duke, where you are going, to a most festinate
preparation: we are bound to the like. Our post shall be
swift and intelligent betwixt us. Farewell, dear sister;
farewell, my Lord of Gloucester.

that only puts a strain on me. He suffers from his children, as I do from my father! Tom, away! Note the rumors of great events. Throw off your disguise when you are cleared of the false charges that shame you, and you are reconciled to your father. Whatever else happens tonight, may the King make a safe escape! Meanwhile, stay in hiding!

Scene 7

A room in Gloucester's castle. **Cornwall, Regan, Goneril, Edmund** *and Servants enter.*

Cornwall   [*to* **Goneril**] Send a messenger quickly to my lord, your husband. Show him this letter. [*It is the one* **Gloucester** *mentioned in Act 3 Scene 3*] The French army has landed. Go and find the traitor Gloucester!

[*Several Servants leave*]

Regan   Hang him instantly!

Goneril   Blind him!

Cornwall   Leave him to my displeasure. Edmund, stay with our sister Goneril. The revenge we are proposing to take on your traitorous father is not fit for you to see. Tell the Duke, when you see him, to prepare for war. We'll do the same. Our messengers will keep us fully and swiftly informed. [*To* **Goneril**] Farewell, dear sister. [*To* **Edmund**] Farewell, my Lord of Gloucester.

[*Enter* **Oswald**]

How now! Where's the King?

Oswald   My Lord of Gloucester hath conveyed him hence:
Some five or six and thirty of his knights,
Hot questrists after him, met him at gate;
Who, with some other of the Lord's dependants,
Are gone with him toward Dover, where they boast
To have well-armed friends.

Cornwall   Get horses for your mistress.

Goneril   Farewell, sweet lord, and sister.

Cornwall   Edmund, farewell.

                  [*Exeunt* **Goneril, Edmund,** *and* **Oswald**]

                          Go seek the traitor Gloucester,
Pinion him like a thief, bring him before us.

                          [*Exeunt other Servants*]

Though well we may not pass upon his life
Without the form of justice, yet our power
Shall do a courtesy to our wrath, which men
May blame but not control. Who's there? The traitor?

[*Re-enter Servants, with* **Gloucester** *prisoner*]

Regan   Ingrateful fox, 'tis he.

Cornwall   Bind fast his corky arms.

Gloucester   What means your Graces? Good my friends,
    consider
You are my guests: do me no foul play, friends.

[**Oswald** *enters*]

Well, where's the King?

Oswald   My Lord of Gloucester has taken him away. Some
three dozen or so of his knights, eagerly searching for him,
met him at the castle gate. With some more of Lord
Gloucester's men, they have gone toward Dover, where
they claim they have well-armed friends.

Cornwall   Get horses for your mistress.

Goneril   Farewell, sweet lord, and sister.

Cornwall   Edmund, farewell.

[**Goneril, Edmund** *and* **Oswald** *leave*]

Go and find the traitor Gloucester! Tie him up like a thief,
and bring him to us.

[*Several Servants respond*]

Though we can't condemn him to death without a trial, we
can indulge our anger. Men may deplore it, but not stop it.
Who's there? The traitor?

[*Servants enter with* **Gloucester** *their prisoner*]

Regan   The ungrateful fox! It's him!

Cornwall   Tie his withered arms tight!

Gloucester   What do your Graces mean? My dear friends,
remember you are my guests. Do me no injury, friends.

Cornwall   Bind him, I say.   [*Servants bind him*]

Regan   Hard, hard. O filthy traitor!

Gloucester   Unmerciful lady as you are, I'm none.

Cornwall   To this chair bind him. Villain, thou shalt find –

[**Regan** *plucks his beard*]

Gloucester   By the kind gods, 'tis most ignobly done
To pluck me by the beard.

Regan   So white, and such a traitor!

Gloucester   Naughty lady,
These hairs, which thou dost ravish from my chin,
Will quicken, and accuse thee: I am your host:
With robbers' hands my hospitable favours
You should not ruffle thus. What will you do?

Cornwall   Come, sir, what letters had you late from France?

Regan   Be simple-answered, for we know the truth.

Cornwall   And what confederacy have you with the traitors
Late footed in the kingdom?

Regan   To whose hands have you
sent the lunatic King? Speak.

Gloucester   I have a letter guessingly set down,
Which came from one that's of a neutral heart,
And not from one opposed.

Cornwall   Cunning.

Regan   And false.

Cornwall   Where hast thou sent the King?

Gloucester   To Dover.

Cornwall   Tie him, I say!

[*The Servants tie him up*]

Regan   Tight! Tight! Oh, you filthy traitor!

Gloucester   Merciless lady that you are, I'm not!

Cornwall   Bind him to this chair. Villain, you'll find –

[**Regan** *pulls* **Gloucester's** *beard*]

Gloucester   By the kind gods, it's extremely rude to pull me by the beard!

Regan   [*holding up some hair*] So white, and such a traitor!

Gloucester   Wicked lady, those hairs you've snatched from my chin will come to life and accuse you. I am your host, and as such you shouldn't abuse my hospitality like robbers. What are you going to do?

Cornwall   Come, sir. What letters have you had recently from France?

Regan   A straight answer: we know the truth.

Cornwall   How have you conspired with the traitors who've landed recently in the kingdom?

Regan   To whom have you sent the lunatic King? Speak!

Gloucester   I've had a vague sort of letter from a neutral source, not from an enemy.

Cornwall   Cunning!

Regan   And untrue!

Cornwall   Where have you sent the King?

Gloucester   To Dover.

Regan Wherefore to Dover? Wast thou not charged at peril –

Cornwall Wherefore to Dover? Let him answer that.

Gloucester I am tied to the stake, and I must stand the
course.

Regan Wherefore to Dover?

Gloucester Because I would not see thy
cruel nails
Pluck out his poor old eyes; nor thy fierce sister
In his anointed flesh stick boarish fangs.
The sea, with such a storm as his bare head
In hell-black night endured, would have buoyed up,
And quenched the stelled fires;
Yet, poor old heart, he holp the heavens to rage.
If wolves had at thy gate howled that stern time,
Thou should'st have said, 'Good porter, turn the key.'
All cruels else subscribed: but I shall see
The winged vengeance overtake such children.

Cornwall See't shalt thou never. Fellows, hold the chair.
Upon these eyes of thine I'll set my foot.

Gloucester He that will think to live till he be old,
Give me some help! O cruel! O you gods!

Regan One side will mock another; the other too.

Cornwall If you see vengeance –

1st Servant Hold your hand, my lord.
I have served you ever since I was a child,
But better service have I never done you
Than now to bid you hold.

Regan How now, you dog!

1st Servant If you did wear a beard upon your chin
I'd shake it on this quarrel.

184

Regan   Why to Dover? Weren't you told under threat of
death –

Cornwall   Why to Dover? Let him answer that.

Gloucester   I'm tied to a stake like a bear. I must stand being
baited.

Regan   Why to Dover?

Gloucester   Because I couldn't see your cruel nails pluck out
his poor old eyes, nor your fierce sister's boarish fangs slash
his anointed flesh. Faced with a storm like the one his bare
head endured, during a night as black as hell, the sea itself
would have risen up and quenched the stars. Yet, poor
old heart, he helped the heavens to rage. If wolves had
howled at your gate at that ghastly time, you would have
said, ''Good porter, let them in.'' All other cruel creatures
yield to compassion. I'll see that divine vengeance overtakes
such children as you!

Cornwall   Soo it you never shall. [*To the Servants*] You
fellows, hold the chair. I'll stamp my foot upon those eyes of
yours!

Gloucester   [*struggling*] Anyone who hopes to reach old age:
help me! [**Cornwall** *blinds* **Gloucester** *in one eye with his
boot*] Oh, cruel! Oh, gods!

Regan   One side will mock the other. The other, too!

Cornwall   [*raising his foot*] If you see vengeance –

1st Servant   Hold it, my lord. I've served you ever since I was
a child; but I've never served you better than I do now in
telling you to stop!

Regan   What, you dog!

1st Servant   If you were a man, I'd fight you over this!

Regan   What do you mean?

Cornwall   My villain!   [*They draw and fight*]

1st Servant   Nay then, come on, and take the chance of anger.

Regan   Give me thy sword. A peasant stand up thus!

[*Takes a sword and runs at him behind*]

1st Servant   O, I am slain. My lord, you have one eye left
To see some mischief on him. O!   [*Dies*]

Cornwall   Lest it see more, prevent it. Out, vile jelly!
Where is thy lustre now?

Gloucester   All dark and comfortless. Where's my son
Edmund?
Edmund, enkindle all the sparks of nature
To quit this horrid act.

Regan   Out, treacherous villain!
Thou call'st on him that hates thee; it was he
That made the overture of thy treasons to us,
Who is too good to pity thee.

Gloucester   O my follies! Then Edgar was abused.
Kind gods, forgive me that, and prosper him!

Regan   Go thrust him out at gates, and let him smell
His way to Dover.   [*Exit one with* **Gloucester**]
                              How is't, my lord. How look you?

Cornwall   I have received a hurt. Follow me, lady.
Turn out that eyeless villain; throw this slave
Upon the dunghill. Regan, I bleed apace:
Untimely comes this hurt. Give me your arm.

Regan   What do you mean?

Cornwall   Villain! [*They fight*]

1st Servant   Right, then: come on. Take your chance against an angry man! [*Cornwall is wounded*]

Regan   [*to another Servant*] Give me your sword. A peasant to presume like this? [*She runs him through from behind*]

1st Servant   Oh, you've killed me! My lord, you've one eye left to see him come to a bad end. Oh! [*He dies*]

Cornwall   In case it should see more, we'll prevent it. [*He gouges out* **Gloucester's** remaining eye] Out, you vile piece of jelly! Where's your twinkle now?

Gloucester   [*groaning*] All's dark and comfortless. Where is my son, Edmund? Edmund, summon all the energy of nature to revenge this horrid act!

Regan   Pah! You treacherous villain! You are appealing to someone who hates you. It was Edmund who disclosed your treasons to us. He's too good to pity you.

Gloucester   Oh, my follies! Then Edgar was wronged. Kind gods, forgive me and make him prosper!

Regan   [*to a Servant*] Go and throw him out. Let him smell his way to Dover.

[**Gloucester** *is pushed out*]

How are you, my lord? Are you all right?

Cornwall   I've been hurt. Follow me, lady. Turn that eyeless villain out. Throw this wretch [*the dead servant*] on the dunghill. Regan, I'm bleeding badly. This wound has come at the wrong time. Give me your arm.

[*Exit* **Cornwall,** *led by* **Regan**]

2nd Servant   I'll never care what wickedness I do
If this man come to good.

3rd Servant   If she live long,
And in the end meet the old course of death,
Women will all turn monsters.

2nd Servant   Let's follow the old Earl, and get the Bedlam
To lead him where he would: his roguish madness
Allows itself to any thing.

3rd Servant   Go thou; I'll fetch some flax and whites of eggs
To apply to his bleeding face. Now, heaven help him!

[*Exeunt severally*]

[**Cornwall** *leaves, supported by* **Regan**]

2nd Servant   I don't care what wickedness I do, if this man prospers!

3rd Servant   If she has a long life, and dies a natural death, all women will turn into monsters!

2nd Servant   Let's follow the old Earl, and get the madman to guide him wherever he wants to go. Nobody will criticize what a madman does.

3rd Servant   You go. I'll fetch some flax and whites of eggs to make a plaster for his bleeding face. Now, heaven help him!

[*They go separately*]

Act four

Scene 1

The heath. Enter **Edgar.**

Edgar   Yet better thus, and known to be contemned,
Than, still contemned and flattered, to be worst.
The lowest and most dejected thing of fortune
Stands still in esperance, lives not in fear:
The lamentable change is from the best;
The worst returns to laughter. Welcome, then,
Thou unsubstantial air that I embrace:
The wretch that thou hast blown unto the worst
Owes nothing to thy blasts. But who comes here?

[*Enter* **Gloucester,** *led by an* **Old Man**]

My father, poorly led? World, world, o, world!
But that thy strange mutations make us hate thee,
Life would not yield to age.

Old Man   O my good lord!
I have been your tenant, and your father's tenant,
These fourscore years.

Gloucester   Away, get thee away; good friend, be gone:
Thy comforts can do me no good at all;
Thee they may hurt.

Old Man   You cannot see your way.

Gloucester   I have no way, and therefore want no eyes;
I stumbled when I saw. Full oft 'tis seen,
Our means secure us, and our mere defects
Prove our commodities. Ah, dear son Edgar,

Act four

Scene 1

The heath. **Edgar** *enters.*

Edgar It's better to be like this – openly despised – than what is worse: scorned but deceived by flattery. The most wretched and dejected victim of ill fortune always has some hope, and is proof against fear. What's more distressing is to cease to enjoy life at its best; when things are at their worst, they can only improve. Welcome, then, to the natural elements that surround me. This man you've made so wretched with your fierce winds owes you no thanks. But who comes here?

[**Gloucester** *enters, led by an* **Old Man**]

My father, guided by a commoner? World, world, oh, world! It's hatred of your ups and downs that makes us reconciled to death.

Old Man [*to* **Gloucester**] Oh, my good lord! I've been your tenant, and your father's tenant, these eighty years.

Gloucester Away, go away. Good friend, be gone. Your help can do me no good at all. It may do you some harm.

Old Man You can't see your way.

Gloucester I have no way, and therefore need no eyes. I stumbled when I could see. Very often prosperity makes us complacent, and adversity proves to be an asset. Oh, dear

191

The food of thy abused father's wrath;
Might I but live to see thee in my touch,
I'd say I had eyes again.

Old Man   How now! Who's there?

Edgar [*aside*] O gods! Who is't can say 'I am at the worst'?
I am worse than e'er I was.

Old Man   'Tis poor mad Tom.

Edgar [*aside*] And worse I may be yet; the worst is not
So long as we can say 'This is the worst'.

Old Man Fellow, where goest?

Gloucester   Is it a beggar man?

Old Man Madman and beggar too.

Gloucester He has some reason, else he could not beg.
I' th' last night's storm I such a fellow saw,
Which made me think a man a worm. My son
Came then into my mind; and yet my mind
Was then scarce friends with him. I have heard more since:
As flies to wanton boys, are we to the gods;
They kill us for their sport.

Edgar [*aside*]   How should this be?
Bad is the trade that must play fool to sorrow,
Ang'ring itself and others. [*Aloud*] Bless thee, master!

Gloucester Is that the naked fellow?

Old Man   Ay, my lord.

Gloucester Then, prithee, get thee away. If, for my sake,
Thou wilt o'ertake us, hence a mile or twain,
I' th' way toward Dover, do it for ancient love;
And bring some covering for this naked soul,
Which I'll entreat to lead me.

son Edgar, the object of your deluded father's anger, if I could only live to see you by touching you, I'd say I had my eyes again.

Old Man   [*noticing* **Edgar**] Hello, who's there?

Edgar   [*aside*] Oh, gods! Who can ever say, ''I've hit the bottom?'' I'm worse than I was before.

Old Man   [*to* **Gloucester**] It's poor mad Tom.

Edgar   [*aside*] And worse may still be to come. The worst has not happened as long as we can say, ''This *is* the worst.''

Old Man   Fellow, where are you going?

Gloucester   Is it a beggar man?

Old Man   Lunatic and beggar, too.

Gloucester   He must have some intelligence, or he couldn't beg. In last night's storm I saw such a fellow, which made me think mankind's no better than a worm. My son then came into my mind, though I was angry with him in my thoughts. The gods treat us like naughty boys treat flies; they kill us for the fun of it.

Edgar   [*aside, commenting on his father's blindness*] What has happened? It's a bad business having to joke with a man in distress. Both parties resent it. [*Aloud*] Bless you, master.

Gloucester   Is that the naked fellow?

Old Man   Yes, my lord.

Gloucester   Then, please: go now. If, for my sake, you will catch up with us a mile or two away from here – on the way to Dover – do it for old time's sake. And bring some clothes for this naked soul, whom I shall ask to escort me

Old Man   Alack, sir, he is mad.

Gloucester   'Tis the times' plague, when madmen lead the
   blind.
   Do as I bid thee, or rather do thy pleasure;
   Above the rest, be gone.

Old Man   I'll bring him the best 'parel that I have,
   Come on't what will.

                                            [*Exit*]

Gloucester   Sirrah, naked fellow –

Edgar   Poor Tom's a-cold. [*Aside*] I cannot daub it further.

Gloucester   Come hither, fellow.

Edgar   [*aside*] And yet I must. Bless thy sweet eyes, they
   bleed.

Gloucester   Know'st thou the way to Dover?

Edgar   Both stile and gate, horse-way and foot-path. Poor
   Tom hath been scared out of his good wits: bless thee, good
   man's son, from the foul fiend! Five fiends have been in poor
   Tom at once: as Obidicut, of lust; Hoberdidance, prince of
   dumbness; Mahu, of stealing; Modo, of murder;
   Flibbertigibbet, of mopping and mowing; who since possesses
   chambermaids and waiting-women. So, bless thee, master!

Gloucester   Here, take this purse, thou whom the heavens'
   plagues
   Have humbled to all strokes: that I am wretched
   Makes thee the happier: heavens, deal so still!
   Let the superfluous and lust-dieted man,
   That slaves your ordinance, that will not see
   Because he does not feel, feel your power quickly;
   So distribution should undo excess,
   And each man have enough. Dost thou know Dover?

Old Man   Alas, sir, he is mad.

Gloucester   It's a sign of the sick times, when the mad lead the blind. Do as I say, or rather as you feel inclined. Above all, go!

Old Man   I'll bring him the best clothes I've got, and take the consequences.

[*He goes*]

Gloucester   You there: the naked fellow!

Edgar   Poor Tom is cold. [*Aside*] I can't keep this up –

Gloucester   Come here, fellow.

Edgar   – but I must. [*Resuming his disguise*] Bless your sweet eyes. They are bleeding.

Gloucester   Do you know the way to Dover?

Edgar   Cross-country, bridle-path and footpath. Poor Tom has been scared out of his good wits. Bless you, laddie, from the foul fiend! Five devils have been in Poor Tom together: Bidicut, the lusty one; Hoberdidance, the prince of dumbness; Mahu, of stealing; Modo, of murder; Flibbertigibbet, of making strange faces. They've since possessed chambermaids and serving-women. So, bless you, master!

Gloucester   Here, take this purse, you who've become reconciled to fortune's worst afflictions. My wretchedness makes you the better off. Heavens, stick to your policy! May the man who's well-heeled and overindulgent – who abuses your kind favors – who refuses to see things because he does not feel them personally – quickly experience your power! Spreading the wealth out would remedy excess. Every man would have enough. Do you know Dover?

Edgar   Ay, master.

Gloucester   There is a cliff, whose high and bending head
Looks fearfully in the confined deep;
Bring me but to the very brim of it,
And I'll repair the misery thou dost bear
With something rich about me; from that place
I shall no leading need.

Edgar   Give me thy arm:
Poor Tom shall lead thee.

[*Exeunt*]

Scene 2

Before the Duke of Albany's palace. Enter **Goneril** *and*
Edmund.

Goneril   Welcome, my lord; I marvel our mild husband
Not met us on the way.

[*Enter* **Oswald**]

                    Now, where's your master?

Oswald   Madam, within; but never man so changed.
I told him of the army that was landed;
He smiled at it: I told him you were coming;
His answer was 'The worse': of Gloucester's treachery,
And of the loyal service of his son,
When I informed him, then he called me sot,
And told me I had turned the wrong side out:
What most he should dislike seems pleasant to him;
What like, offensive.

Edgar   Yes, master.

Gloucester   There is a cliff whose great and brooding height peers fearfully into the pounding sea below. Just take me to the very edge of it, and I'll help to remedy your misery with something valuable I'm carrying. From there I'll need no guide.

Edgar   Give me your arm. Poor Tom will lead you.

[*They go*]

Scene 2

Near the Duke of Albany's palace. Enter **Goneril** *and* **Edmund**, *who have traveled from Gloucester's castle together.*

Goneril   Welcome, my lord. I'm amazed that my meek and mild husband didn't meet us on the way.

[**Oswald** *enters*]

Where's your master?

Oswald   Madam, he's indoors. But never was a man so changed. I told him about the army that has landed; he smiled at it. I told him you were coming; his answer was, "So much the worse." When I informed him of Gloucester's treachery, and of the loyal services of his son, he called me an idiot and told me I'd got it wrong way round. What he ought to dislike seems pleasant to him; what he should like, offensive.

Goneril   [*to* **Edmund**]   Then shall you go no further.
  It is the cowish terror of his spirit
  That dares not undertake; he'll not feel wrongs
  Which tie him to an answer. Our wishes on the way
  May prove effects. Back, Edmund, to my brother;
  Hasten his musters and conduct his powers:
  I must change arms at home, and give the distaff
  Into my husband's hands. This trusty servant
  Shall pass between us; ere long you are like to hear,
  If you dare venture on your own behalf,
  A mistress's command. Wear this; spare speech;
  Decline your head: this kiss, if it durst speak,
  Would stretch thy spirits up into the air.
  Conceive, and fare thee well.

Edmund   Yours in the ranks of death.

Goneril   My most dear Gloucester!

                                 [*Exit* **Edmund**]

  O, the difference of man and man!
  To thee a woman's services are due:
  A fool usurps my bed.

Oswald   Madam, here comes my lord.

                                       [*Exit*]

[*Enter* **Albany**]

Goneril   I have been worth the whistle.

Albany   O Goneril!
  You are not worth the dust which the rude wind
  Blows in your face. I fear your disposition:
  That nature, which contemns its origin,
  Cannot be bordered certain in itself;

Goneril   [*to* **Edmund**] Then you must go no further. He's too cowardly to take any action; he'll avoid provocation. The hopes we expressed on the way here may be fulfilled. Go back, Edmund, to my brother-in-law. Speed up recruitment and lead his army. I must change roles at home, and give my husband the embroidery to do. [*Pointing to* **Oswald**] This trusty servant will be our go-between. Soon you may well hear – if you're not afraid to do yourself some good – a certain command from your mistress . . . [**Edmund's** *hand goes to his dagger; he realizes* **Goneril** *is hinting at the murder of* **Albany**] Wear this; there's no need to say anything. [*She puts a chain around his neck*] Lower your head. [*She kisses him*] This kiss, if it dared to speak, would rouse you . . . Keep me in your thoughts, and goodbye.

Edmund   Yours ever, until death!

Goneril   My dearest Gloucester!

[**Edmund** *leaves*]

Oh, the difference between one man and another! You deserve what a woman has to give. I have a fool for my bedfellow.

Oswald   Madam, here comes my lord.

[*He goes*]

[**Albany** *enters*]

Goneril   You would once have thought I was worth the trouble of coming to meet me.

Albany   Oh, Goneril! You are not worth the dust that the harsh wind blows in your face! I distrust your character. A nature that can deny a parent cannot hold itself in check. As one

She that herself will sliver and disbranch
From her material sap, perforce must wither
And come to deadly use.

Goneril   No more; the text is foolish.

Albany   Wisdom and goodness to the vile seem vile;
Filths savour but themselves. What have you done?
Tigers, not daughters, what have you performed?
A father, and a gracious aged man,
Whose reverence even the head-lugged bear would lick,
Most barbarous, most degenerate, have you madded.
Could my good brother suffer you to do it?
A man, a prince, by him so benefited!
If that the heavens do not their visible spirits
Send quickly down to tame these vile offences,
It will come,
Humanity must perforce prey on itself,
Like monsters of the deep.

Goneril   Milk-livered man!
That bear'st a cheek for blows, a head for wrongs;
Who hast not in thy brows an eye discerning
Thine honour from thy suffering; that not know'st
Fools do those villains pity who are punished
Ere they have done their mischief. Where's thy drum?
France spreads his banners in our noiseless land,
With plumed helm thy state begins to threat,
Whilst thou, a moral fool, sits still, and cries
'Alack! why does he so?'

Albany   See thyself, devil!
Proper deformity shows not in the fiend
So horrid as in woman.

Goneril   O vain fool!

Albany   Thou changed and self-covered thing, for shame,

who has cut herself off from the main branch, you must of necessity wither and die.

Goneril   Say no more. Your sermon is a silly one.

Albany   Wisdom and goodness always seem vile to the vile. To the filthy everything seems filthy. What have you done? Tigers rather than daughters, what have you been up to? A father, and a gracious elderly man – that even a captive bear would lick with reverence – you have barbarously and degenerately made insane. How could my brother-in-law allow you to do it? A man – a prince – who owed so much to him! If the gods don't quickly intervene by sending down their agents to punish these vile offenses, then surely men will start eating each other, like the monsters of the sea!

Goneril   You coward, you'll let anyone push you around! You can't distinguish between the tolerable and the insufferable. You don't realize that only fools pity villains who are punished before they do their mischief. Where's your call to arms? The King of France raises his flags in our docile land; the threat of war hangs over your country while you, a moralizing fool, sit there and cry, ''Alas, why is he doing this?''

Albany   See yourself for what you are, devil! Depravity, bad enough when seen in the fiend, is even more horrid in a woman!

Goneril   You worthless idiot!

Albany   You transformed and self-deceiving thing, for shame!

Be-monster not thy feature. Were't my fitness
To let these hands obey my blood,
They are apt enough to dislocate and tear
Thy flesh and bones; howe'er thou art a fiend,
A woman's shape doth shield thee.

Goneril   Marry, your manhood mew –

[*Enter a* **Messenger**]

Albany   What news?

Messenger   O my good lord, the Duke of Cornwall's dead;
Slain by his servant, going to put out
The other eye of Gloucester.

Albany   Gloucester's eyes!

Messenger   A servant that he bred, thrilled with remorse,
Opposed against the act, bending his sword
To his great master: who, thereat enraged,
Flew on him, and amongst them felled him dead;
But not without that harmful stroke, which since
Hath plucked him after.

Albany   This shows you are above,
You justicers, that these our nether crimes
So speedily can venge! But, O poor Gloucester!
Lost he his other eye?

Messenger   Both, both, my lord.
This letter, madam, craves a speedy answer;
'Tis from your sister.

Goneril   [*aside*]   One way I like this well;
But being widow, and my Gloucester with her,
May all the building in my fancy pluck
Upon my hateful life: another way,

Stop acting like a monster! If I were inclined to let my
emotions govern my behavior, these hands would tear your
flesh and bones apart! Fiend though you are, your female
form protects you.

Goneril   [*contemptuously*] You and your manhood! Pah!

[*A* **Messenger** *enters*]

Albany   What's your news?

Messenger   Oh, my good lord, the Duke of Cornwall is dead:
killed by his servant as he was putting out Gloucester's
other eye.

Albany   Gloucester's eyes!

Messenger   One of his servants, moved by compassion, made
objection, raising his sword against his great master.
Furious at this, he [*the Duke*] attacked him, and the man
was struck dead; but not before the Duke sustained a mortal
wound that later took his life.

Albany   [*addressing the heavens*] This proves you are there
above, you judges, in that our worldly crimes are so
speedily revenged! But oh, poor Gloucester! Did he lose
his other eye?

Messenger   Both, my lord, both. [*To* **Goneril**] This letter,
madam, requires a speedy answer. It's from your sister.

Goneril   [*aside*] In one sense, I like this. However, she being a
widow and my Gloucester with her, all my dreams for the
future could collapse in ruins. Looking at it another way, the

The news is not so tart. [*Aloud*] I'll read, and answer.

[*Exit*]

Albany   Where was his son when they did take his eyes?

Messenger   Come with my lady hither.

Albany   He is not here.

Messenger   No, my good lord; I met him back again.

Albany   Knows he the wickedness?

Messenger   Ay, my good lord; 'twas he informed against him,
And quit the house on purpose that their punishment
Might have the freer course.

Albany   Gloucester, I live
To thank thee for the love thou show'dst the King,
And to revenge thine eyes. Come hither, friend:
Tell me what more thou know'st.

[*Exeunt*]

Scene 3

The French camp near Dover. Enter **Kent** *and a* **Gentleman.**

Kent   Why the King of France is so suddenly gone back know
you the reason?

Gentleman   Something he left imperfect in the state, which
since his coming forth is thought of; which imports to the

news is not so grievous. [*Aloud*] I'll read it and answer it.

[*She goes*]

Albany   Where was his son when they blinded him?

Messenger   On his way here with my lady.

Albany   He isn't here.

Messenger   No, my good lord. I met him on his way back.

Albany   Does he know about the wickedness?

Messenger   Yes, my good lord. It was he who informed against him [*his father*]. He left the house on purpose so that they would have a free hand with their punishment.

Albany   Gloucester, I live to thank you for the love that you have shown the King, and to revenge your eyes! [*To the Messenger*] Come here, friend. Tell me what more you know.

[*They go*]

Scene 3

The French camp near Dover. Enter **Kent** *and a* **Gentleman**.

Kent   Have you no idea why the King of France has returned so suddenly?

Gentleman   He remembered something he'd forgotten to do in his own kingdom which had such risky complications that kingdom so much fear and danger that his personal return was most required and necessary.

Kent   Who hath he left behind him general?

Gentleman   The Marshal of France, Monsieur La Far.

Kent   Did your letters pierce the Queen to any demonstration of grief?

Gentleman   Ay, sir; she took them, read them in my presence;
And now and then an ample tear trilled down
Her delicate cheek; it seemed she was a queen
Over her passion; who, most rebel-like,
Sought to be king o'er her.

Kent   O, then, it moved her.

Gentleman   Not to a rage; patience and sorrow strove
Who should express her goodliest. You have seen
Sunshine and rain at once; her smiles and tears
Were like, a better way; those happy smilets
That played on her ripe lip seemed not to know
What guests were in her eyes; which parted thence,
As pearls from diamonds dropped. In brief,
Sorrow would be a rarity most beloved,
If all could so become it.

Kent   Made she no verbal question?

Gentleman   Faith, once or twice she heaved the name of
'father'
Pantingly forth, as if it pressed her heart;
Cried 'Sisters! sisters! Shame of ladies! sisters!
Kent! father! sisters! What, i' th' storm! i' th' night?
Let pity not believe it!' There she shook
The holy water from her heavenly eyes,
And clamour moistened, then away she started
To deal with grief alone.

his return was vital and necessary.

Kent   Which general has he left in charge?

Gentleman   The Marshal of France, Monsieur La Far.

Kent   Did your letters move Cordelia to any show of grief?

Gentleman   Yes, sir. She took them, and read them in my presence. Every now and then a large tear trickled down her soft cheek. She governed her emotions like a queen; they, like rebels, tried to play the superior role of king.

Kent   Oh, then she was moved by it?

Gentleman   Not to distraction. Self-control vied with sorrow as to which should show more attractively in her face. You have seen sunshine and rain happen together. Her smiles and tears were similar, but more attractive. The happy little smiles that played on her ruby lips seemed unaware of the tears that lodged in her eyes. They fell like pearls dropping from diamonds. In short, sorrow would be a precious rarity if it were always as becoming as it was in her case.

Kent   Did she ask no questions?

Gentleman   Indeed, once or twice she gasped the name ''Father'' as if it pressed upon her heart. She cried, ''Sisters! Sisters! Disgrace to womanhood! Sisters! Kent! Father! Sisters! What – in the storm? At night? For pity's sake, it's unbelievable!'' At that point she let her holy tears fall from her heavenly eyes. Then away she went, calmed by her outburst, to cope with her grief in private.

Kent   It is the stars,
   The stars above us, govern our conditions;
   Else one self mate and make could not beget
   Such different issues. You spoke not with her since?

Gentleman   No.

Kent   Was this before the King returned?

Gentleman   No, since.

Kent   Well, sir, the poor distressed Lear's i' th' town;
   Who sometime, in his better tune, remembers
   What we are come about, and by no means
   Will yield to see his daughter.

Gentleman   Why, good sir?

Kent   A sovereign shame so elbows him: his own unkindness,
   That stripped her from his benediction, turned her
   To foreign casualties, gave her dear rights
   To his dog-hearted daughters: these things sting
   His mind so venomously that burning shame
   Detains him from Cordelia.

Gentleman   Alack, poor gentleman!

Kent   Of Albany's and Cornwall's powers you heard not?

Gentleman   'Tis so, they are afoot.

Kent   Well, sir, I'll bring you to our master Lear,
   And leave you to attend him. Some dear cause
   Will in concealment wrap me up awhile;
   When I am known aright, you shall not grieve
   Lending me this acquaintance. I pray you, go
   Along with me.

                                             [*Exeunt*]

Kent   It's the stars, the stars above us, who decide our characters! Otherwise parents couldn't beget such different children. You've not spoken to her since?

Gentleman   No.

Kent   Was this before the King returned to France?

Gentleman   No, after.

Kent   Well, sir, the poor distressed Lear has reached Dover. Sometimes in his more lucid moments he remembers why we are here, and won't in any circumstances consent to see his daughter.

Gentleman   Why, sir?

Kent   An overpowering shame pushes him away. His own unkindness – which lost her his blessing, turned her out to live abroad as best she could, and gave her dowry to his pitiless daughters – these things sting his mind so poisonously that he's held back from Cordelia by a burning sense of shame.

Gentleman   Alas, poor gentleman!

Kent   You haven't heard anything of the armies of Albany and Cornwall?

Gentleman   Yes. They are on the march.

Kent   Well, sir, I'll bring you to our master, Lear, and leave you to look after him. Important business will keep me privately occupied for some time. When I resume my real name, you won't be sorry you associated with me like this. Please, come with me.

[They go]

Scene 4

The same. Enter, with drum and colours, **Cordelia, Doctor,** *and Soldiers.*

Cordelia   Alack, 'tis he: why, he was met even now
As mad as the vexed sea; singing aloud;
Crowned with rank fumiter and furrow-weeds,
With hardocks, hemlock, nettles, cuckoo-flowers,
Darnel, and all the idle weeds that grow
In our sustaining corn. A century send forth;
Search every acre in the high-grown field,
And bring him to our eye.   [*Exit an Officer*]
                                    What can man's wisdom
In the restoring his bereaved sense?
He that helps him take all my outward worth.

Doctor   There is means, madam;
Our foster-nurse of nature is repose,
The which he lacks; that to provoke in him,
Are many simples operative, whose power
Will close the eye of anguish.

Cordelia   All blest secrets,
All you unpublished virtues of the earth,
Spring with my tears! be aidant and remediate
In the good man's distress! Seek, seek for him,
Lest this ungoverned rage dissolve the life
That wants the means to lead it.

[*Enter a* **Messenger**]

Messenger   News, madam;
The British powers are marching hitherward.

Cordelia   'Tis known before; our preparation stands
In expectation of them. O dear father!

Scene 4

The French camp near Dover. **Cordelia** *enters with a* **Doctor** *and Soldiers.*

Cordelia   Alas, it's he. He was found just now, as mad as the raging sea, singing aloud, with a crown of luxuriant fumitory [*an herb*] and common weeds – burdocks, hemlock, nettles, cuckoo-flowers, coarse grasses, and all the worthless weeds that grow among our health-giving corn. Send out a troop of soldiers; search every acre in the fields of crops, and bring him to our sight.

[An Officer leaves]

What can man's learning do to restore his lost reason? I'd give all I possess to the man who can cure him.

Doctor   There is a way, madam. Sleep is nature's nourishment, which he lacks. To induce it, there are many effective medicinal herbs, with the power to put pain to sleep.

Cordelia   May all the blessed secrets and little-known remedies of the earth germinate with my tears! Be helpful and curative in the good man's distress! Look, look for him, in case in his frenzy he ends a life that lacks the means to survive.

[**Messenger** *enters*]

Messenger   News, madam. The British army is marching toward you.

Cordelia   We know that. We are ready for them. Oh, dear

It is thy business that I go about;
Therefore great France
My mourning and importuned tears hath pitied.
No blown ambition doth our arms incite,
But love, dear love, and our aged father's right.
Soon may I hear and see him!

[*Exeunt*]

Scene 5

Gloucester's castle. Enter **Regan** *and* **Oswald.**

Regan   But are my brother's powers set forth?

Oswald   Ay, madam.

Regan   Himself in person there?

Oswald   Madam, with much ado:
    Your sister is the better soldier.

Regan   Lord Edmund spake not with your lord at home?

Oswald   No, madam.

Regan   What might import my sister's letter to him?

Oswald   I know not, lady.

Regan   Faith, he is posted hence on serious matter.
    It was great ignorance, Gloucester's eyes being out,
    To let him live; where he arrives he moves
    All hearts against us. Edmund, I think, is gone,
    In pity of his misery, to dispatch

father! It is *your* interests I'm pursuing. That's why my royal
husband has pitied my sorrowful and pleading tears. We
aren't roused to war by puffed-up ambition, but by love,
dear love, and our old father's rights. May I soon hear and
see him!

[*They go*]

Scene 5

A room in Gloucester's castle. **Regan** *enters, followed by*
Oswald, *who is carrying a letter.*

Regan   Have my brother-in-law's troops set out?

Oswald   Yes, madam.

Regan   Himself there in person?

Oswald   Madam, after a lot of fuss. Your sister is the better
soldier.

Regan   Lord Edmund didn't speak to your lord at his home?

Oswald   No, madam.

Regan   What was behind my sister's letter to him?

Oswald   I don't know, lady.

Regan   Indeed, he has gone off on important business. It was
stupid to let Gloucester live after he was blinded. Wherever
he goes he turns all hearts against us. Edmund, I think, has
gone to end his father's darkened life out of pity for his

His nighted life; moreover, to descry
The strength o'th'enemy.

Oswald   I needs must after him, madam, with my letter.

Regan   Our troops set forth to-morrow; stay with us,
The ways are dangerous.

Oswald   I may not, madam;
My lady charged my duty in this business.

Regan   Why should she write to Edmund? Might not you
Transport her purposes by word? Belike,
Something – I know not what: I'll love thee much,
Let me unseal the letter.

Oswald   Madam, I had rather –

Regan   I know your lady does not love her husband;
I am sure of that; and at her late being here
She gave strange eliads and most speaking looks
To noble Edmund. I know you are of her bosom.

Oswald   I, madam!

Regan   I speak in understanding: y'are, I know't:
Therefore I do advise you, take this note:
My lord is dead; Edmund and I have talked;
And more convenient is he for my hand
Than for your lady's. You may gather more.
If you do find him, pray you give him this,
And when your mistress hears thus much from you,
I pray desire her call her wisdom to her:
So, fare you well.
If you do chance to hear of that blind traitor,
Preferment falls on him that cuts him off.

Oswald   Would I could meet him, madam: I should show
What party I do follow.

misery, as well as to determine the strength of the enemy.

Oswald   I must go after him, madam, with my letter.

Regan   Our troops set out tomorrow. Stay with us. It's dangerous outside.

Oswald   I must not, madam. My lady put me on special trust with this business.

Regan   Why should she write to Edmund? Couldn't you convey her message by word of mouth? Probably some things – [*she breaks off, not wishing to express her suspicion that* **Goneril** *and* **Edmund** *are lovers*] I don't know what . . . I'd very much appreciate it . . . Let me open the letter.

Oswald   Madam, I'd rather –

Regan   I know your lady doesn't love her husband. I'm sure of that. When she was here recently, she gave knowing glances and meaningful looks to noble Edmund. I know you have her confidence.

Oswald   I, madam?

Regan   I know what I'm talking about. You have, I know it. Therefore I advise you: take note of this. My lord is dead. Edmund and I have come to an understanding, and he's more available to me than he is to your lady. You know what I'm getting at. If you find him, give him this. [*She hands* **Oswald** *a ring*] And when your mistress hears what I've told you, I suggest you advise her to act sensibly. So, goodbye. If you happen to hear of that blind traitor, there's promotion for the one who ends his life.

Oswald   If only I could meet him, madam. I'd show where my loyalty lies.

Regan   Fare thee well.

                                        [*Exeunt*]

Scene 6

The country near Dover. Enter **Gloucester,** *and* **Edgar** *dressed like a peasant.*

Gloucester   When shall I come to the top of that same hill?

Edgar   You do climb up it now; look how we labour.

Gloucester   Methinks the ground is even.

Edgar   Horrible steep.
   Hark! Do you hear the sea?

Gloucester   No, truly.

Edgar   Why, then your other senses grow imperfect
   By your eyes' anguish.

Gloucester   So may it be, indeed.
   Methinks thy voice is altered, and thou speak'st
   In better phrase and matter than thou didst.

Edgar   You're much deceived; in nothing am I changed
   But in my garments.

Gloucester   Methinks you're better spoken.

Edgar   Come on, sir; here's the place: stand still. How fearful
   And dizzy 'tis to cast one's eyes so low!
   The crows and choughs that wing the midway air
   Show scarce so gross as beetles; half way down

Regan   Fare you well.

[*They go*]

Scene 6

The countryside near Dover. **Gloucester** *enters, led by* **Edgar**, *who is now dressed like a peasant.*

Gloucester   When shall I reach the top of the hill?

Edgar   You're climbing up it now. Notice how hard it's getting.

Gloucester   I think the ground is level.

Edgar   It's horribly steep. Listen! Do you hear the sea?

Gloucester   Frankly, no.

Edgar   Well then, your other senses are growing imperfect through the pain in your eyes.

Gloucester   It may be so, indeed. I think your voice is altered, and that you speak more coherently than you used to.

Edgar   You've got it wrong. I'm the same as before except for my clothing.

Gloucester   I think you are better spoken.

Edgar   Come on, sir. Here's the place. Stand still. [*He has stopped in the middle of a field, though he pretends he is at the edge of a cliff*] How frightening and dizzy-making it is to look so far down! The crows and jackdaws that fly a middling height look hardly as big as beetles. Halfway down

Hangs one that gathers samphire, dreadful trade!
Methinks he seems no bigger than his head.
The fishermen that walk upon the beach
Appear like mice, and yond tall anchoring bark
Diminished to her cock; her cock a buoy
Almost too small for sight. The murmuring surge,
That on the unnumbered idle pebbles chafes,
Cannot be heard so high. I'll look no more,
Lest my brain turn, and the deficient sight
Topple down headlong.

Gloucester   Set me where you stand.

Edgar   Give me your hand; you are now within a foot
Of the extreme verge: for all beneath the moon
Would I not leap upright.

Gloucester   Let go my hand.
Here, friend, 's another purse; in it a jewel
Well worth a poor man's taking: fairies and gods
Prosper it with thee! Go thou further off;
Bid me farewell, and let me hear thee going.

Edgar   Now fare ye well, good sir.

Gloucester   With all my heart.

Edgar   [*aside*] Why I do trifle thus with his despair
Is done to cure it.

Gloucester   [*kneeling*] O you mighty gods!
This world I do renounce, and in your sights
Shake patiently my great affliction off;
If I could bear it longer, and not fall
To quarrel with your great opposeless wills,
My snuff and loathed part of nature should
Burn itself out. If Edgar live, O bless him!
Now, fellow, fare thee well.

there's a man gathering samphire [*a European plant*]. What
a dreadful job! He looks to me no bigger than his head. The
fishermen walking on the beach look like mice, and that tall
ship at anchor over there is reduced to the size of her tender,
and her tender a buoy almost too small to be seen. The
murmuring waves that agitate the countless, useless
pebbles cannot be heard from this height. I'll look no more,
in case it turns my head, and blurred sight makes me topple
headlong down.

Gloucester   Put me where you are.

Edgar   Give me your hand. You are now within a foot of the
extreme edge. For all the world, I wouldn't jump up and
down.

Gloucester   Let go my hand. Here, friend, is another purse. In
it there's a jewel worth a lot to a poor man. May good
fortune see you enjoy it! Go further away. Say goodbye, and
let me hear you go.

Edgar   [*pretending to go*] Goodbye, good sir.

Gloucester   With all my heart.

Edgar   [*aside*] The reason I'm trifling with his misery like this is
to cure it.

Gloucester   [*kneeling*] Oh, you mighty gods! I renounce the
world, and in your sight uncomplainingly rid myself of my
great suffering. Even if I could bear it longer, and not fall
into quarreling with your great and absolute decrees, the
smoldering wick and hatred end of my life would fizzle out.
If Edgar is alive, oh, bless him! [*To* **Edgar**] Now, fellow:
fare you well.

[He falls forward]

Edgar   Gone, sir: farewell.
And yet I know how conceit may rob
The treasury of life when life itself
Yields to the theft; had he been where he thought
By this had thought been past. Alive or dead?
Ho, you sir! Friend! Hear you, sir! Speak!
Thus might he pass indeed; yet he revives.
What are you, sir?

Gloucester   Away, and let me die.

Edgar Hadst thou been aught but gossamer, feathers, air,
So many fathom down precipitating,
Thou˙dst shivered like an egg; but thou dost breathe,
Hast heavy substance, bleed'st not, speak'st, art sound.
Ten masts at each make not the altitude
Which thou hast perpendicularly fell:
Thy life's a miracle. Speak yet again.

Gloucester But have I fallen or no?

Edgar From the dread summit of this chalky bourn.
Look up a-height: the shrill-gorged lark so far
Cannot be seen or heard: do but look up.

Gloucester Alack! I have no eyes.
Is wretchedness deprived that benefit
To end itself by death? 'Twas yet some comfort,
When misery could beguile the tyrant's rage,
And frustrate his proud will.

Edgar   Give me your arm:
Up: so; how is't? Feel you your legs? You stand.

Gloucester Too well, too well.

[*He throws himself forward, as if over a cliff*]

Edgar   [*pretending to be at a distance*] Gone, sir. Farewell!

[*To himself*] Possibly one can be deluded into death when there's no will to live. If he had been where he thought he was, thought would by now be a thing of the past. Is he alive, or dead? [*To* **Gloucester**] Hello, sir! Friend! Do you hear me, sir? Speak! [*To himself*] He might indeed have died. [**Gloucester** *stirs*] But he's recovering! [*Now pretending he is a fisherman at the foot of the cliff*] Who are you, sir?

Gloucester   Go away, and leave me to die.

Edgar   If you'd been anything other than gossamer, feathers, or air, you'd be shattered like an egg after falling from such a height! But you are breathing; you are solid; you aren't bleeding; you can speak; you are in one piece. You have fallen more than the height of ten ships' masts. It's a miracle you are alive. Say something more

Gloucester   Have I fallen, or not?

Edgar   From the very top of this chalky cliff. Look right up there: you can't see or hear the shrill-voiced lark at that distance. Just look up!

Gloucester   Alas, I have no eyes. Is wretchedness deprived of the benefit of ending itself by death? It was some small comfort when misery could thwart the anger of a tyrant, and frustrate his lofty plans.

Edgar   Give me your arm. [*He helps* **Gloucester** *to stand*] Up, so; how goes it? Can you feel your legs? You are standing up!

Gloucester   Only too well, too well.

Edgar   This is above all strangeness.
Upon the crown o' th' cliff what thing was that
Which parted from you?

Gloucester   A poor unfortunate beggar.

Edgar   As I stood here below, methought his eyes
Were two full moons; he had a thousand noses,
Horns whelked and waved like the enridged sea:
It was some fiend; therefore, thou happy father,
Think that the clearest gods, who make them honours
Of men's impossibilities, have preserved thee.

Gloucester   I do remember now; henceforth I'll bear
Affliction till it do cry out itself
'Enough, enough,' and die. That thing you speak of
I took it for a man; often 'twould say
'The fiend, the fiend': he led me to that place.

Edgar   Bear free and patient thoughts. But who comes here?

[*Enter* **Lear,** *fantastically dressed with wild flowers*]

The safer sense will ne'er accommodate
His master thus.

Lear   No, they cannot touch me for coining; I am the King
himself.

Edgar   O, thou side-piercing sight!

Lear   Nature's above art in that respect. There's your press-
money. That fellow handles his bow like a crow-keeper: draw
me a clothier's yard. Look, look! a mouse. Peace, peace! This
piece of toasted cheese will do't. There's my gauntlet; I'll
prove it on a giant. Bring up the brown bills. Oh, well flown

Edgar   This is quite remarkable. On the edge of the cliff, what was that object who left you?

Gloucester   A poor unfortunate beggar.

Edgar   As I stood here below, I thought his eyes were two full moons. He had a thousand noses. He had horns that were bent and twisted like the wavy sea. It was some devil. Therefore, you lucky old man, assume that the righteous gods, who are revered for doing the impossible, have preserved you.

Gloucester   I remember now. In future, I'll bear suffering till it decides I've endured enough, and lets me die. That thing you spoke of I thought was a man. It often said, ''The fiend, the fiend.'' He led me to that place.

Edgar   Put your mind at rest. But who comes here?

[**Lear** *enters, ornately dressed with wild flowers. He has lost his reason*]

No man in his right mind would ever get himself up like this.

Lear   No, they can't accuse me of counterfeiting. I am the King himself!

Edgar   What a heartbreaking sight!

Lear   In matters of that sort, art takes second place to the real thing! [*As if to a recruit*] There's your King's shilling! [*Jumping from one delusion to another*] That man there handles his bow like a scarecrow. Draw that bowstring out a full arm's length! [*He spots something at his feet*] Look, look, a mouse! Sh! Sh! This piece of toasted cheese will catch it. [*He tears off an imaginary chunk, then suddenly throws it to the ground*] There's my gauntlet; I'd challenge a giant even. [*He's a general now*] Bring up the pikemen! [*He follows an imaginary arrow in its flight*] Oh, well-flown, bird!

bird; i' th' clout, i' th' clout: hewgh! Give the word.

Edgar   Sweet marjoram.

Lear   Pass.

Gloucester   I know that voice.

Lear   Ha! Goneril, with a white beard! They flattered me
like a dog, and told me I had the white hairs in my beard ere
the black ones were there. To say 'ay' and 'no' to every thing
that I said! 'Ay' and 'no' too was no good divinity. When the
rain came to wet me once and the wind to make me chatter,
when the thunder would not peace at my bidding, there I
found 'em, there I smelt 'em out. Go to, they are not men
o' their words: they told me I was every thing; 'tis a lie, I am
not ague-proof.

Gloucester   The trick of that voice I do well remember:
Is't not the King?

Lear   Ay, every inch a king:
When I do stare, see how the subject quakes.
I pardon that man's life. What was thy cause?
Adultery?
Thou shalt not die; die for adultery! No:
The wren goes to't, and the small gilded fly
Does lecher in my sight.
Let copulation thrive; for Gloucester's bastard son
Was kinder to his father than my daughters
Got 'tween the lawful sheets.
To't, luxury, pell-mell! For I lack soldiers.
Behold yond simp'ring dame,
Whose face between her forks presages snow;
That minces virtue, and does shake the head
To hear of pleasure's name;
The fitchew nor the soiled horse goes to't
With a more riotous appetite.
Down from the waist they are Centaurs,

A bull's eye, a bull's eye! Swish! [*Noticing* **Edgar**] Give the password.

Edgar   Sweet marjoram.

Lear   Pass.

Gloucester   I know that voice.

Lear   [*peering at him*] Aha, Goneril with a white beard! They flattered me like fawning dogs, and told me I was a shrewd one even before I grew my first beard. To think they said "Yes" and "No" to everything I said! "Yes" and "No" isn't sound theology. When the rain came to drench me once, and the wind made me shiver, when the thunder wouldn't stop when I told it to, then I rumbled them; that's when I smelt them out! Pah, they're not men of their words. They told me I was all powerful. It was a lie. I'm not immune from sickness.

Gloucester   The tone of that voice I well remember. Are you not the King?

Lear   Yes, every inch a king! When I look hard at a man, see how he trembles! I pardon that man's life. What was your crime? Adultery? You shall not die. Die for adultery? No, even the wren goes to it, and the little gold-colored fly does it in front of my eyes. Let copulation prosper; Gloucester's bastard son was kinder to his father than my legitimate daughters. Get at it, lust, flat out. I need soldiers! Look at that innocent-looking female, whose face suggests she's frigid, who looks so goody-goody, who deplores all sexy talk; polecats and stallions aren't so hungry for it! From the waist down they're animals, albeit they're women higher up.

Though women all above:
But to the girdle do the gods inherit,
Beneath is all the fiends': there's hell, there's darkness,
There is the sulphurous pit, burning, scalding,
Stench, consumption; fie, fie, fie! pah, pah!
Give me an ounce of civet, good apothecary,
To sweeten my imagination.
There's money for thee.

Gloucester   O, let me kiss that hand.

Lear   Let me wipe it first; it smells of mortality.

Gloucester   O ruined piece of nature! This great world
Shall so wear out to nought. Dost thou know me?

Lear   I remember thine eyes well enough. Dost thou squiny
    at me?
No, do thy worst, blind Cupid; I'll not love.
Read thou this challenge; mark but the penning of it.

Gloucester   Were all thy letters suns, I could not see.

Edgar   [*aside*] I would not take this from report; it is,
And my heart breaks at it.

Lear   Read.

Gloucester   What, with the case of eyes?

Lear   O, ho! are you there with me? No eyes in your head,
    nor no money in your purse? Your eyes are in a heavy case,
    your purse in a light: yet you see how this world goes.

Gloucester   I see it feelingly.

Lear   What, art mad? A man may see how this world goes
    with no eyes. Look with thine ears: see how yond justice rails
    upon simple thief. Hark, in thine ear: change places,
    and, handy-dandy, which is the justice, which is the thief?
    Thou hast seen a farmer's dog bark at a beggar?

The gods hold sway down to the belt; below is all the devil's. *There* is hell; *there* is darkness; *there* is the sulphurous pit – burning, scalding; stench, corruption! [*His mind is tormented with horror and repugnance*] Ugh, ugh, ugh! Pah! Pah! [*To* **Gloucester**] Give me an ounce of perfume, dear chemist, to sweeten my imagination! There's some money for you.

Gloucester   Oh, let me kiss your hand.

Lear   Let me wipe it first. It smells of death.

Gloucester   Oh, what a ruin of a man! So too will the universe come to its end. Do you know me?

Lear   I remember your eyes well enough. Are you squinting at me? No, do your worst, blind sinfulness; I won't indulge. [*Obsessed with* **Gloucester's** *affliction*] Read this challenge. Note how it's written.

Gloucester   If all the letters were suns, I could not see them.

Edgar   [*aside*] I wouldn't believe this if I heard about it. But it's a fact, and my heart breaks at it.

Lear   Read.

Gloucester   What, with holes for eyes?

Lear   Oh, ho! Is that your game? No eyes in your head, and no money in your purse? Sad for your eyes; bad for your purse. But that's the way of the world, you see.

Gloucester   I see by the feel of things.

Lear   What, are you mad? A man doesn't need eyes to see how this world goes. Look with your ears. See how that magistrate rebukes that humble thief. A word in your ear: Switch places, and – take your choice – which is the magistrate, which the thief? You've seen a farmer's dog bark at a beggar?

Gloucester   Ay, sir.

Lear   And the creature run from the cur? There thou
    might'st behold
    The great image of Authority:
    A dog's obeyed in office.
    Thou rascal beadle, hold thy bloody hand!
    Why dost thou lash that whore? Strip thine own back;
    Thou hotly lusts to use her in that kind
    For which thou whip'st her. The usurer hangs the
        cozener.
    Through tattered clothes small vices do appear;
    Robes and furred gowns hide all. Plate sin with gold,
    And the strong lance of justice hurtless breaks:
    Arm it in rags, a pigmy's straw does pierce it.
    None does offend, none, I say, none; I'll able 'em:
    Take that of me, my friend, who have the power
    To seal the accuser's lips. Get thee glass eyes;
    And, like a scurvy politician, seem
    To see the things thou dost not. Now, now, now, now;
    Pull off my boots; harder, harder; so.

Edgar   [*aside*] O, matter and impertinency mixed;
    Reason in madness.

Lear   If thou wilt weep my fortunes, take my eyes;
    I know thee well enough; thy name is Gloucester;
    Thou must be patient; we came crying hither:
    Thou know'st the first time that we smell the air
    We wawl and cry. I will preach to thee: mark.

Gloucester   Alack, alack the day!

Lear   When we are born, we cry that we are come
    To this great stage of fools. This's a good block!
    It were a delicate stratagem to shoe
    A troop of horse with felt; I'll put't in proof,

Gloucester   Yes, sir.

Lear   And the man run away from the cur? That symbolizes Authority: a dog is obeyed when it's got an official position. [*Addressing an imaginary officer of the law*] You rascally constable, stay your blood-stained hand! Why are you lashing that whore? Strip the skin off your own back; you're lusting for the very thing you're whipping her for. The big crook hangs the petty one. The petty crimes of the poor are always obvious; robes and fur-lined gowns hide everything. Cover sin with gold armor, and the strong lance of justice shatters on contact. Cover it with rags, and the puny weapon of a pigmy will pierce through it. Nobody sins: nobody, I say, nobody; I'll vouch for them. Take my word for it, my friend: I who have the power to silence all prosecutors. Get youself glass eyes. Like a vile opportunist, pretend to see what you actually cannot. [*As if talking to his valet*] Now, now, now, now – pull off my boots! Harder, harder; that's right.

Edgar   [*aside*] Sense and nonsense combined. Sanity in madness!

Lear   If you want to weep for my misfortunes, have my eyes. I know you well enough. Your name is Gloucester. You must be patient. We came crying into this world; you know, the first time that we smell the air we wail and cry. I'll preach to you – listen.

Gloucester   Alas, alas the day!

Lear   When we are born, we cry because we've come to this great stage of fools. [*He stands on a tree stump to continue his "sermon"*] This is a good mounting-block! It would be an ingenious idea to shoe a troop of horses with felt. I must

And when I have stolen upon these sons-in-law,
Then, kill, kill, kill, kill, kill, kill!

[*Enter a* **Gentleman**, *with Attendants*]

Gentleman   O, here he is; lay hand upon him. Sir,
Your most dear daughter –

Lear   No rescue? What! a prisoner! I am even
The natural fool of fortune. Use me well;
You shall have ransom. Let me have surgeons;
I am cut to the brains.

Gentleman   You shall have any thing.

Lear   No seconds? All myself?
Why this would make a man a man of salt,
To use his eyes for garden water-pots,
Ay, and laying autumn's dust. I will die bravely,
Like a smug bridegroom. What! I will be jovial:
Come, come; I am a king, masters, know you that?

Gentleman   You are a royal one, and we obey you.

Lear   Then there's life in't. Nay, an you get it, you shall get
it by running. Sa, sa, sa, sa.

[*Exit running. Attendants follow*]

Gentleman   A sight most pitiful in the meanest wretch,
Past speaking of in a king! Thou hast one daughter,
Who redeems nature from the general curse
Which twain have brought her to.

Edgar   Hail, gentle sir!

Gentleman   Sir, speed you: what's your will?

Edgar   Do you hear aught, sir, of a battle toward?

give it a try. And when I've crept up behind these
sons-in-law, then [*he jumps down, shouting*] kill, kill, kill,
kill, kill, kill!

[*A* **Gentleman** *enters, with Attendants*]

Gentleman   Oh, here he is. Take hold of him. Sir, your most
dear daughter –

Lear   [*thinking he has been captured in war*] No rescue? What,
a prisoner? I was born unlucky. Treat me well. You shall
have ransom. Get me doctors. My head's split.

Gentleman   You shall have whatever you want.

Lear   No supporters? Just me alone? Why, this would make a
man cry salt tears, to have his eyes used for garden
watering-cans, yes, and to lay the dust of autumn. I shall die
splendidly, like a bridegroom all dressed up. What, I'll be
jovial! Come, come, I am a king, gentlemen. Do you realize
that?

Gentleman   You are a royal person, and we obey you.

Lear   Then there's still hope. Come, if you want it, you'll have
to run for it! [*He runs off, making noises like a hunter*] Sa,
sa, sa, sa! [*The Attendants pursue him*]

Gentleman   A most pitiful sight even if it featured the lowliest
of wretches: it's beyond words when it involves a king! You
have one daughter who redeems nature from the universal
curse her two sisters have brought upon it.

Edgar   Greetings, sir!

Gentleman   Sir, my compliments: what can I do for you?

Edgar   Have you heard anything, sir, of an impending battle?

231

Gentleman   Most sure and vulgar; every one hears that,
Which can distinguish sound.

Edgar   But, by your favour,
How near's the other army?

Gentleman   Near, and on speedy foot; the main descry
Stands on the hourly thought.

Edgar   I thank you, sir: that's all.

Gentleman   Though that the Queen on special cause is here,
Her army is moved on.

Edgar   I thank you, sir.

[*Exit* **Gentleman**]

Gloucester   You ever-gentle gods, take my breath from me:
Let not my worser spirit tempt me again
To die before you please!

Edgar   Well pray you, father.

Gloucester   Now, good sir, what are you?

Edgar   A most poor man, made tame to fortune's blows;
Who, by the art of known and feeling sorrows,
Am pregnant to good pity. Give me your hand,
I'll lead you to some biding.

Gloucester   Hearty thanks:
The bounty and the benison of heaven
To boot, and boot!

[*Enter* **Oswald**]

Oswald   A proclaimed prize! Most happy!
That eyeless head of thine was first framed flesh
To raise my fortunes. Thou old unhappy traitor,

Gentleman   Certainly; it's common knowledge. Everyone's heard about it who isn't deaf.

Edgar   But, if I may ask: how near is the other army?

Gentleman   Very near, and advancing swiftly. We expect to see the main body any hour now.

Edgar   Thank you, sir: that's all.

Gentleman   Though the Queen is here for special reasons, her army has moved on.

Edgar   I thank you, sir.

[*The* **Gentleman** *leaves*]

Gloucester   You ever-merciful gods, take my life. Don't let my evil side tempt me again to die before it's your will!

Edgar   Well prayed, father.

Gloucester   Now, good sir, who are you?

Edgar   A very poor man, broken by misfortune. Experience of sorrow has predisposed me toward pity. Give me your hand. I'll lead you to some shelter.

Gloucester   Hearty thanks. May the bounty and blessing of heaven reward you, in addition to my gratitude.

[**Oswald** *enters*]

Oswald   A man with a price on his head! Most fortunate! That eyeless head of yours was preordained to make my fortune! You miserable old traitor, think of your sins. [*He draws his*

Briefly thyself remember: the sword is out
That must destroy thee.

Gloucester   Now let thy friendly hand
Put strength enough to't.   [**Edgar** *interposes*]

Oswald   Wherefore, bold peasant,
Dar'st thou support a published traitor? Hence;
Lest that the infection of his fortune take
Like hold on thee. Let go his arm.

Edgar   Chill not let go, zir, without vurther 'casion.

Oswald   Let go, slave, or thou diest.

Edgar   Good gentleman, go your gait, and let poor volk pass.
An chud ha' bin zwaggered out of my life, 'twould not ha'
been zo long as 'tis by a vortnight. Nay, come not near th'old
man: keep out, che vor' ye, or 'se try whither your costard or
my ballow be the harder. Chill be plain with you.

Oswald   Out, dunghill!

Edgar   Chill pick your teeth, zir. Come; no matter vor your
foins.

[*They fight, and* **Edgar** *knocks him down*]

Oswald   Slave, thou hast slain me. Villain, take my purse.
If ever thou wilt thrive, bury my body;
And give the letters which thou find'st about me
To Edmund Earl of Gloucester; seek him out
Upon the British party. O untimely death.
Death!   [*Dies*]

Edgar   I know thee well: a serviceable villain;
As duteous to the vices of thy mistress
As badness would desire.

Gloucester   What, is he dead?

sword from its scabbard] The sword is out that must
destroy you.

Gloucester   [*ready to die*] Thrust hard with your friendly hand.

[**Edgar** *steps forward in his father's defense*]

Oswald   You impertinent peasant, how dare you defend an
outlawed traitor? Go, before you suffer the same fate as
him. Let go his arm.

Edgar   [*assuming a regional accent*] I'll not let go, sir, without
a better reason.

Oswald   Let go, wretch, or you'll die.

Edgar   Good gentleman, be on your way, and let us poor folk
move on. If I could have been cheated out of my life, I'd
have lost it weeks ago. No, don't come near the old man.
Keep off, I tell you, or I'll test which is harder – your head or
my stick. That's the truth.

Oswald   Get away, you slob!

Edgar   I'll pick your teeth for you, sir. Come on, I'm not scared
of your sword-thrusts. [*They fight;* **Edgar** *knocks* **Oswald**
down]

Oswald   Wretch, you've killed me. Peasant, take my purse. If
you ever hope to prosper, bury my body. Give the letters
you'll find on me to Edmund, Earl of Gloucester. Find him on
the English side. Oh, such untimely death! Death . . . [*He
dies*]

Edgar   I know you well. An unscrupulous villain, as dutiful in
serving the vices of your mistress as wickedness could
desire.

Gloucester   What, is he dead?

Edgar   Sit you down, father; rest you.
Let's see these pockets: the letters that he speaks of
May be my friends. He's dead; I am only sorry
He had no other deathsman. Let us see:
Leave, gentle wax; and, manners, blame us not:
To know our enemies' minds, we rip their hearts;
Their papers is more lawful.   [*Reads*]

> *Let our reciprocal vows be remembered. You have many*
> *opportunities to cut him off; if your will want not, time*
> *and place will be fruitfully offered. There is nothing done*
> *if he return the conqueror; then am I the prisoner, and his*
> *bed my gaol; from the loathed warmth whereof deliver*
> *me, and supply the place for your labour.*
> > *Your wife, so I would say –*
> > *Affectionate servant,*
> > > Goneril.

O undistinguished space of woman's will!
A plot upon her virtuous husband's life,
And the exchange my brother! Here, in the sands,
Thee I'll rake up, the post unsanctified
Of murderous lechers; and in the mature time
With this ungracious paper strike the sight
Of the death-practised Duke: for him 'tis well
That of thy death and business I can tell.

Gloucester   The King is mad: how stiff is my vile sense
That I stand up, and have ingenious feeling
Of my huge sorrows! Better I were distract:
So should my thoughts be severed from my griefs,
And woes by wrong imaginations lose
The knowledge of themselves.

[*Drum afar off*]

236

Edgar   Sit down, father, and rest. Let's see what's in these pockets; the letters he referred to might do me some good. [*As he searches, he answers* **Gloucester's** *question*] He's dead. I am only sorry he didn't have some other executioner. [*He finds the letter*] Let's see. [*He breaks the seal*] If I may, dear wax! Don't say this is bad manners; to know what's in our enemies' minds, we rip their hearts. Ripping open their letters is more lawful. [*He reads the contents aloud*]

> *Remember our mutual vows. You'll have many chances to do away with him. If you've got the determination, there'll be ample time and opportunity. If he comes back the victor, we shall have achieved nothing. Then I would be his prisoner, and our marital bed would be my jail. Save me from the intimate horror of that, and assure yourself of physical contentment.*
>> *Your wife, as I would wish, and*
>>> *Devoted lover,*
>>>> *Goneril.*

Oh, how infinite is woman's lust! A plot to kill her virtuous husband, and my brother to replace him! [*Addressing* **Oswald**] Here, in these sands, the unholy burial-place of murderous lechers, I'll cover your body up. When the time is ripe, I'll show this wicked letter to the Duke, whose life is threatened. It's fortunate for him that I can report both your death and the business you were about.

Gloucester   The King is mad. How obstinate my mind is, that I should stay sane, and be conscious of my great distress! It would be better if I were mad; then my thoughts and my griefs would be separated, and in my fantasies woes would cease to have any meaning.

[*The sound of drums is heard*]

Edgar   Give me your hand:
Far off, methinks, I hear the beaten drum.
Come, father, I'll bestow you with a friend.

[*Exeunt*]

Scene 7

A tent in the French camp. Enter **Cordelia, Kent, Doctor,** *and* **Gentleman.**

Cordelia   O thou good Kent! How shall I live and work
To match thy goodness? My life will be too short,
And every measure fail me.

Kent   To be acknowledged, madam, is o'er-paid.
All my reports go with the modest truth,
No more nor clipped, but so.

Cordelia   Be better suited:
These weeds are memories of those worser hours:
I prithee, put them off.

Kent   Pardon, dear madam;
Yet to be known shortens my made intent:
My boon I make it that you know me not
Till time and I think meet.

Cordelia   Then be't so, my good lord. [*To the Doctor*]
How does the King?

Doctor   Madam, sleeps still.

Cordelia   O you kind gods,
Cure this great breach in his abused nature!

Edgar   Give me your hand. I think I can hear drum-beats in the distance. Come, father: I'll leave you with a friend.

[*They go*]

Scene 7

A tent in the French camp. **Cordelia, Kent, Doctor** *and a* **Gentleman** *enter.*

Cordelia   Oh good Kent! How shall I live and work to equal your goodness? My life will be too short, and I'll fail by every standard.

Kent   To be appreciated, madam, is to be overpaid. All I've described is the honest truth, no more, no less, just as it is.

Cordelia   Change your clothes. These garments are reminders of those bad times. Please, take them off.

Kent   With respect, madam, to be recognized now runs counter to my plans. I'd ask the favor of your not knowing me till I think the time is right.

Cordelia   So be it, my good lord. [*To the* **Doctor**] How is the King?

Doctor   Madam, he's still sleeping.

Cordelia   Oh, you kind gods, cure this great fracture in his

Th'untuned and jarring senses, O, wind up
Of this child-changed father!

Doctor   So please your Majesty
That we may wake the King? He hath slept long.

Cordelia   Be governed by your knowledge, and proceed
I' th' sway of your own will. Is he arrayed?

[*Enter* **Lear** *in a chair carried by Servants*]

Gentleman   Ay, madam, in the heaviness of sleep
We put fresh garments on him.

Doctor   Be by, good madam, when we do awake him;
I doubt not of his temperance.

Cordelia   Very well.

Doctor   Please you draw near. Louder the music there!

Cordelia   O my dear father! Restoration hang
Thy medicine on my lips, and let this kiss
Repair those violent harms that my two sisters
Have in thy reverence made!

Kent   Kind and dear Princess!

Cordelia   Had you not been their father, these white flakes
Did challenge pity of them. Was this a face
To be opposed against the warring winds?
To stand against the deep dread-bolted thunder?
In the most terrible and nimble stroke
Of quick, cross lightning? To watch – poor perdu! –
With this thin helm? Mine enemy's dog,
Though he had bit me, should have stood that night
Against my fire. And wast thou fain, poor father,
To hovel thee with swine and rogues forlorn,

tormented mind! Tune the discordant senses of this childlike father!

Doctor   Would your Majesty allow us to wake the King? He has slept long.

Cordelia   Act according to your knowledge of these things. Do as you think best. Is he dressed?

[**Lear** *enters in a chair carried by Servants*]

Gentleman   Yes, madam. While he was fast asleep we put clean clothes on him.

Doctor   Be at his side, good madam, when we waken him. I do not doubt that he'll be normal.

Cordelia   Very well.

[*Soft music is played*]

Doctor   [*to the Servants*] Come nearer. Play louder there!

Cordelia   Oh, my dear father! May my lips convey healing, and let this kiss cure the damage that my two sisters have done to you. [*She kisses him on the forehead*]

Kent   Kind and dear Princess!

Cordelia   [*stroking his hair*] Even if they were not of your own begetting, these snowy locks would merit pity. Was this a face to battle with antagonistic winds? To withstand the thunderbolts of deep-throated thunder? To be in the midst of flashes of terrifying lightning? To be up at night – poor hopeless one! – with this thin head-covering? My enemy's dog, even if it had bitten me, would have had a place in front of my fire that night. Were you obliged, poor father, to slum it with swine and homeless vagabonds, in scanty and

In short and musty straw? Alack, alack!
'Tis wonder that thy life and wits at once
Had not concluded all. He wakes; speak to him.

Doctor   Madam, do you; 'tis fittest.

Cordelia   How does my royal lord? How fares your Majesty?

Lear   You do me wrong to take me out o' th' grave;
Thou art a soul in bliss; but I am bound
Upon a wheel of fire, that mine own tears
Do scald like molten lead.

Cordelia   Sir, do you know me?

Lear   You are a spirit, I know; where did you die?

Cordelia   Still, still, far wide.

Doctor   He's scarce awake; let him alone awhile.

Lear   Where have I been? Where am I? Fair daylight?
I am mightily abused. I should e'en die with pity
To see another thus. I know not what to say.
I will not swear these are my hands: let's see;
I feel this pin prick. Would I were assured
Of my condition!

Cordelia   O, look upon me, sir,
And hold your hand in benediction o'er me.
No, sir, you must not kneel.

Lear   Pray, do not mock me:
I am a very foolish fond old man,
Fourscore and upward, not an hour more or less;
And, to deal plainly,
I fear I am not in my perfect mind.
Methinks I should know you and know this man;
Yet I am doubtful: for I am mainly ignorant
What place this is, and all the skill I have
Remembers not these garments; nor I know not

musty-smelling straw? Alas, alas! It's amazing that your life and your sanity didn't succumb together. He is waking. Speak to him.

Doctor   Madam, do you. It's best.

Cordelia   How is my royal lord? How fares your Majesty?

Lear   It's wrong of you to take me out of the grave. You are a soul in a state of bliss; but I am in hell, tied to a wheel of fire. My own tears scald like molten lead.

Cordelia   Sir, do you know me?

Lear   You are a spirit, I know. Where did you die?

Cordelia   [*to the* **Doctor**] He is still confused.

Doctor   He's hardly awake. Leave him alone a moment.

Lear   Where have I been? Where am I? Is this real daylight? I was mightily deluded. I'd die with pity to see someone else like this. I don't know what to say. I'm not sure these are my hands – let's see. [*He winces as he tests with the point of a brooch*] I feel this pin-prick. I wish I could sort things out.

Cordelia   Oh, look at me, sir, and hold your hand in blessing over me!

[**Lear** *looks at her, then falls at her feet*]

No, sir: you must not kneel!

Lear   Please, do not mock me. I am a very foolish old man, in his dotage; over 80 years old, not an hour more or less. To tell you frankly, I'm afraid I'm not in my right mind. I think I should know you and this man, but I am uncertain. I'm entirely ignorant about what this place is, and even if I try very hard I can't remember these clothes; nor do I know

243

Where I did lodge last night. Do not laugh at me;
For, as I am man, I think this lady
To be my child Cordelia.

Cordelia   And so I am, I am.

Lear   Be your tears wet? Yes, faith. I pray, weep not:
If you have poison for me, I will drink it.
I know you do not love me; for your sisters
Have, as I do remember, done me wrong:
You have some cause, they have not.

Cordelia   No cause, no cause.

Lear   Am I in France?

Kent   In your own kingdom, sir.

Lear   Do not abuse me.

Doctor   Be comforted, good madam; the great rage,
You see, is killed in him: and yet it is danger
To make him even o'er the time he has lost.
Desire him to go in; trouble him no more
Till further settling.

Cordelia   Will't please your Highness walk?

Lear   You must bear with me.
Pray you now, forget and forgive: I am old and foolish.

[*Exeunt* **Lear, Cordelia, Doctor,** *and Attendants*]

Gentleman   Holds it true, sir, that the Duke of Cornwall was
so slain?

Kent   Most certain, sir.

Gentleman   Who is conductor of his people?

Kent   As 'tis said, the bastard son of Gloucester.

where I stayed last night. Do not laugh at me; as I'm a man,
I think this lady is my child Cordelia.

Cordelia   And so I am, I am!

Lear   Are your tears wet? [*He tries them*] Yes, indeed. Please
don't weep. If you have poison for me, I will drink it. I know
you do not love me. Your sisters have, now I remember,
done me wrong. You have some cause. They have not.

Cordelia   [*shaking her head, weeping*] No cause, no cause.

Lear   [*to* **Kent**] Am I in France?

Kent   In your own kingdom, sir.

Lear   Do not mock me.

Doctor   Take comfort, madam. The delirium, you see, has
subsided in him. It's dangerous to fill in the gaps in his
memory. Request him to go in. Don't trouble him any more
till he's calmer.

Cordelia   Would your Highness like to walk? [*She offers her
arm*]

Lear   You must be patient with me. Please now: forget and
forgive. I am old and foolish.

[**Lear, Cordelia, Doctor** *and Attendants leave*]

Gentleman   Is it a fact that the Duke of Cornwall was killed
like that?

Kent   Absolutely, sir.

Gentleman   Who has taken command of his people?

Kent   The bastard son of Gloucester, so it's said,

Gentleman   They say Edgar, his banished son, is with the
   Earl of Kent in Germany.

Kent   Report is changeable. 'Tis time to look about; the
   powers of the kingdom approach apace.

Gentleman   The arbitrement is like to be bloody. Fare you
   well, sir.

[*Exit*]

Kent   My point and period will be throughly wrought,
   Or well or ill, as this day's battle's fought.

[*Exit*]

Gentleman   They say Edgar, his banished son, is with the Earl of Kent in Germany.

Kent   Rumors come and go. We must prepare. The armies of the kingdom will soon be here.

Gentleman   The battle is likely to be a bloody one. Farewell, sir.

[*He goes*]

Kent   The full stop at the end of my life will be placed for good or ill according to the outcome of today's battle.

[*He goes*]

Act five

Scene 1

The British camp near Dover. Enter, with drum and colours,
Edmund, Regan, *Officers, Soldiers, and Others.*

Edmund   Know of the Duke if his last purpose hold,
Or whether since he is advised by aught
To change the course; he's full of alteration
And self-reproving; bring his constant pleasure.

[To an Officer, who goes out]

Regan   Our sister's man is certainly miscarried.

Edmund   'Tis to be doubted, madam.

Regan   Now, sweet lord,
You know the goodness I intend upon you:
Tell me, but truly, but then speak the truth,
Do you not love my sister?

Edmund   In honoured love.

Regan   But have you never found my brother's way
To the forfended place?

Edmund   That thought abuses you.

Regan   I am doubtful that you have been conjunct
And bosomed with her, as far as we call hers.

Edmund   No, by mine honour, madam.

Regan   I never shall endure her: dear my lord,
Be not familiar with her.

Act five

Scene 1

The British camp at Dover. Enter **Edmund**, **Regan**, *Officers, Soldiers and others.*

Edmund   [*to an Officer*] Find out from the Duke if he's sticking to his last plan, or whether he's had any reason to alter course. He changes his mind all the time and is full of insecurity. Bring his final decision.

[*The Officer salutes and goes*]

Regan   Our sister's steward has come to some harm.

Edmund   I'm afraid so, madam.

Regan   Now, sweet lord, you know that I intend to do you some good. Tell me, honestly, even if it's unpalatable: don't you love my sister?

Edmund   In an honorable way.

Regan   [*trying to be delicate about personal matters*] But have you never trespassed on my brother-in-law's territory?

Edmund   That thought is worrying you.

Regan   I suspect you may have got very close to her . . . gone all the way . . .

Edmund   No, on my honor, madam!

Regan   I couldn't tolerate her. Dear my lord, don't be intimate with her.

Edmund   Fear me not.
  She and the Duke her husband!

[*Enter, with drum and colours,* **Albany, Goneril,** *and Soldiers*]

Goneril   [*aside*] I had rather lose the battle than that sister
  Should loosen him and me.

Albany   Our very loving sister, well be-met.
  Sir, this I hear; the King is come to his daughter,
  With others whom the rigour of our state
  Forced to cry out. Where I could not be honest,
  I never yet was valiant: for this business,
  It touches us, as France invades our land,
  Not bolds the King, with others, whom, I fear,
  Most just and heavy causes make oppose.

Edmund   Sir, you speak nobly.

Regan   Why is this reasoned?

Goneril   Combine together 'gainst the enemy;
  For these domestic and particular broils
  Are not the question here.

Albany   Let's then determine
  With the ancient of war on our proceeding.

Edmund   I shall attend you presently at your tent.

Regan   Sister, you'll go with us?

Goneril   No.

Regan   'Tis most convenient; pray go with us.

Goneril   [*aside*] O, ho! I know the riddle. I will go.

  [*As they are going out, enter* **Edgar,** *disguised*]

Edmund   Don't worry about me. [*A drum sounds*] Here she is, with the Duke her husband!

[**Albany** *and* **Goneril** *enter, followed by Soldiers*]

Goneril   [*aside*] I'd rather lose the battle than have my sister come between him and me.

Albany   [*bowing politely to* **Regan**] Our very loving sister: greetings. [*To* **Edmund**] Sir, I hear this: the King has gone to his daughter, along with others forced to defect as a result of our harsh rule. I've never had any stomach for shady matters. As for this business, it concerns us only because France invades our land: not that we wish to confront the King and those others whose genuine grievances, I fear, make them opposed to us.

Edmund   Sir, you speak nobly.

Regan   Why bother to say all this?

Goneril   Unite against the enemy; these family and private quarrels are irrelevant.

Albany   Then let's consult the experts on our tactics.

Edmund   I'll join you at your tent immediately. [*He makes to leave*]

Regan   Sister, you'll go with us?

Goneril   No.

Regan   It's only right that you should. Go with us.

Goneril   [*aside*] Oh, yes. I know your game . . . [*She suspects her sister does not trust her alone with* **Edmund**] I'll go.

[*Before anyone can leave,* **Edgar** *enters, disguised*]

Edgar   If e'er your Grace had speech with man so poor,
Hear me one word.

Albany   I'll overtake you.

[Exeunt all but **Albany** *and* **Edgar***]*

                              Speak.

Edgar   Before you fight the battle, ope this letter.
If you have victory, let the trumpet sound
For him that brought it: wretched though I seem,
I can produce a champion that will prove
What is avouched there. If you miscarry,
Your business of the world hath so an end,
And machination ceases. Fortune love you!

Albany   Stay till I have read the letter.

Edgar   I was forbid it.
When time shall serve, let but the herald cry,
And I'll appear again.

Albany   Why, fare thee well;
I will o'erlook thy paper.

[Exit **Edgar***]*

[Re-enter **Edmund***]*

Edmund   The enemy's in view; draw up your powers.
Here is the guess for their true strength and forces
By diligent discovery; but your haste
Is now urged on you.

Albany   We will greet the time.

[Exit]

Edgar   [*to* **Albany**] If your Grace would deign to speak to so poor a man, may I have a word with you?

Albany   [*indicating to the others to carry on*] I'll catch up with you.

[**Edmund, Regan, Goneril,** *Officers, Soldiers and Attendants leave*]

Edgar   [*to* **Albany**] Before you fight the battle, open this letter. If you win, sound the trumpet to summon me. Humble though I seem, I can produce a champion who will prove what is said here. If you lose, you won't be concerned about worldly things, and there all matters will end. Good luck!

Albany   Stay till I've read the letter.

Edgar   I was forbidden to. At the appropriate time, just let the herald's trumpet sound, and I'll appear again.

Albany   Well, fare you well. I'll read your letter.

[**Edgar** *goes*]

[**Edmund** *returns*]

Edmund   The enemy is in sight. Bring up your troops. [*Handing* **Albany** *a note*] Here's the estimate of their equipment and numbers, determined by our scouts. You must be quick now.

Albany   We'll rise to the challenge.

[*He goes*]

Edmund   To both these sisters have I sworn my love;
    Each jealous of the other, as the stung
    Are of the adder. Which of them shall I take?
    Both? one? or neither? Neither can be enjoyed
    If both remain alive: to take the widow
    Exasperates, make mad her sister Goneril;
    And hardly shall I carry out my side,
    Her husband being alive. Now then, we'll use
    His countenance for the battle; which being done,
    Let her who would be rid of him devise
    His speedy taking off. As for the mercy
    Which he intends to Lear and to Cordelia,
    The battle done, and they within our power,
    Shall never see his pardon; for my state
    Stands on me to defend, not to debate.

[*Exit*]

Scene 2

*A field between the two camps. Alarum within. Enter, with drum
and colours,* **Lear, Cordelia,** *and their forces; and exeunt.*

[*Enter* **Edgar** *and* **Gloucester**]

Edgar   Here, father, take the shadow of this tree
    For your good host; pray that the right may thrive.
    If ever I return to you again,
    I'll bring you comfort.

Gloucester   Grace go with you, sir!

[*Exit Edgar*]

Edmund   I have sworn my love to both these sisters. Each is
suspicious of the other, as those who are stung are wary
of the snake. Which of them shall I have? Both? One? Or
neither? Neither can be enjoyed if both remain alive. To take
the widow would exasperate, infuriate, her sister Goneril.
But with *her* husband still alive, I wouldn't find it easy to
play a winning game. So for now we'll use him as a front
man in the battle. When that's over, it's up to her who
wants to be rid of him to work out how to see him off. As
for the mercy he intends to show Lear and Cordelia, once
the battle's over and they are at our mercy, they'll never see
his pardon. My interests are best served by action rather
than thought.

[*He goes*]

Scene 2

A field between the two camps. Noises of war. **Lear** *and*
Cordelia *cross the stage with some of their army, and leave.*
Edgar *enters with* **Gloucester**.

Edgar   Here, father, shelter in the shade of this hospitable
tree. Pray that right triumphs. If ever I return to you again,
I'll bring you comforting news.

Gloucester   Grace go with you, sir!

[*Edgar leaves*]

[*Alarum; afterwards a retreat. Re-enter* **Edgar**]

Edgar   Away, old man! Give me thy hand: away!
King Lear hath lost, he and his daughter ta'en.
Give me thy hand; come on.

Gloucester   No further, sir; a man may rot even here.

Edgar   What, in ill thoughts again? Men must endure
Their going hence, even as their coming hither;
Ripeness is all. Come on.

Gloucester   And that's true too.

                                                    [*Exeunt*]

Scene 3

*The British camp near Dover. Enter, in conquest, with drum and
colours,* **Edmund; Lear** *and* **Cordelia** *as prisoners; Officers,
Soldiers, etc.*

Edmund   Some officers take them away: good guard,
Until their greater pleasures first be known
That are to censure them.

Cordelia   We are not the first
Who, with best meaning, have incurred the worst.
For thee, oppressed King, I am cast down;
Myself could else out-frown false fortune's frown.
Shall we not see these daughters and these sisters?

[*The sounds of war grow louder. A retreat is sounded.*
Edgar *returns, dismayed*]

Edgar   We must go, old man! Give me your hand. [*He tries to
pull* **Gloucester** *to his feet*] Let's go! King Lear has lost. He
and his daughter have been captured. Give me your hand.
Come on!

Gloucester   [*resisting*] No further, sir. A man can die well
enough here.

Edgar   What, depressed again? Men must endure dying just as
they do being born. Being prepared for it is what matters.
Come on.

Gloucester   That's true, too.

[*He rises to his feet and they leave*]

Scene 3

*The British camp near Dover. Drums and flags herald the
entrance of* **Edmund** *in victory, and* **Lear** *and* **Cordelia** *in defeat,
as prisoners. Soldiers guard them.*

Edmund   Some officers take them away. Guard them well, till
the wishes of our leaders, who will decide their fate, are
known.

Cordelia   We are not the first to suffer the worst from the best
of intentions. For you – a suffering King – I am defeated: for
myself I could have faced ill fortune and won. Shall we see
these ''daughters,'' these ''sisters''?

Lear   No, no, no, no! Come, let's away to prison;
    We two alone will sing like birds i' th' cage:
    When thou dost ask me blessing, I'll kneel down,
    And ask of thee forgiveness: so we'll live,
    And pray, and sing, and tell old tales, and laugh
    At gilded butterflies, and hear poor rogues
    Talk of court news; and we'll talk with them too,
    Who loses and who wins; who's in, who's out;
    And take upon's the mystery of things,
    As if we were God's spies: and we'll wear out,
    In a walled prison, packs and sects of great ones
    That ebb and flow by th'moon.

Edmund   Take them away.

Lear   Upon such sacrifices, my Cordelia,
    The gods themselves throw incense. Have I caught thee?
    He that parts us shall bring a brand from heaven,
    And fire us hence like foxes. Wipe thine eyes:
    The good years shall devour them, flesh and fell,
    Ere they shall make us weep: we'll see 'em starve first.
    Come.

                    [*Exeunt* **Lear** *and* **Cordelia,** *guarded*]

Edmund   Come hither, captain; hark.
    Take thou this note   [*giving a paper*];
                    Go follow them to prison.
    One step I have advanced thee; if thou dost
    As this instructs thee, thou dost make thy way
    To noble fortunes; know thou this, that men
    Are as the time is; to be tender-minded
    Does not become a sword; thy great employment
    Will not bear question; either say thou'lt do't,
    Or thrive by other means.

Lear   No, no, no, no! Come, let's be off to prison. We two, alone, will sing like birds in a cage. When you ask a blessing of me, I'll kneel down and ask your forgiveness. That way we'll live, and pray, and sing; and tell each other tales of days gone by; and laugh at courtiers in their fancy clothes; and hear poor wretches discusss the news from court. And we'll talk with them, too: who has failed, and who succeeded; who's in favor, and who's out; and – as if we were God's spies – solve the mysteries of the universe. In the confines of our prison, we'll outlast many a gang of high and mighty ones, who come and go by the month.

Edmund   [*to the Officers*] Take them away.

Lear   The gods themselves endorse such sacrifices as yours, Cordelia. [*She starts to weep*] Have I made you cry? [*He puts his arm around her*] To separate us, a man would need a burning torch from heaven – to drive us apart with fire, like a fox smoked from its lair. Wipe your eyes. They'll rot before they'll make us weep! We'll see them starved first! Come!

[**Lear** *and* **Cordelia** *leave under guard*]

Edmund   [*to an* **Officer**] Come here, Captain. Listen. [*Giving him a paper*] Take this note. Follow them to prison. I've promoted you once already. If you follow these instructions, you'll do well for yourself. Know this: men must take advantage of their opportunities. To be tender-hearted is not becoming in a soldier. This great assignment brooks no argument: either say you'll do it, or prosper by some other means.

Officer   I'll do't, my lord.

Edmund   About it; and write happy when thou hast done.
Mark, I say, instantly, and carry it so
As I have set it down.

Officer   I cannot draw a cart nor eat dried oats;
If it be man's work I'll do't.

[*Exit*]

[*Flourish. Enter* **Albany, Goneril, Regan,** *Officers, and
Soldiers*]

Albany   Sir, you have showed to-day your valiant strain,
And fortune led you well; you have the captives
Who were the opposites of this day's strife;
I do require them of you, so to use them
As we shall find their merits and our safety
May equally determine.

Edmund   Sir, I thought it fit
To send the old and miserable King
To some retention and appointed guard;
Whose age had charms in it, whose title more,
To pluck the common bosom on his side,
And turn our impressed lances in our eyes
Which do command them. With him I sent the Queen:
My reason all the same; and they are ready
To-morrow, or at further space, t'appear
Where you shall hold your session. At this time
We sweat and bleed; the friend hath lost his friend,
And the best quarrels, in the heat, are cursed
By those that feel their sharpness;
The question of Cordelia and her father
Requires a fitter place.

Officer   I'll do it, my lord.

Edmund   Get on with it then. Consider yourself lucky when
you've done it. Note – I say *immediately*. Carry it out
according to my instructions.

Officer   I can't pull a cart, or live on dried oats like a horse:
so if it's man's work, I'll do it.

[*He goes*]

[*Trumpets sound. Enter* **Albany, Goneril, Regan,** *Officers
and Soldiers*]

Albany   [*to* **Edmund**] Sir, you've shown your valiant side
today, and fortune has taken care of you. You have the
captives who were our enemies in today's battle: I require
them from you, to do with them what their deserts, and our
safety, shall equally determine.

Edmund   Sir, I thought it appropriate to send the old and
miserable King to some confinement, under guard. The
emotional appeal of his age, and even more so his title,
could win the hearts of the common people, and turn
against us the lances of the conscripted soldiers under our
command. With him I sent the Queen, for the same reason.
They are ready tomorrow, or later, to appear wherever you
intend to hold your trial. Right now, we sweat and bleed.
Friend has lost friend. Even the best of causes can be
misjudged by injured parties acting in the heat of passion.
The issue of Cordelia and her father requires a more suitable
place.

Albany   Sir, by your patience,
I hold you but a subject of this war,
Not as a brother.

Regan   That's as we list to grace him;
Methinks our pleasure might have been demanded,
Ere you had spoke so far. He led our powers,
Bore the commission of my place and person;
The which immediately may well stand up,
And call itself your brother.

Goneril   Not so hot;
In his own grace he doth exalt himself
More than in your addition.

Regan   In my rights,
By me invested, he compeers the best.

Albany   That were the most, if he should husband you.

Regan   Jesters do oft prove prophets.

Goneril   Holla, holla!
That eye that told you so looked but a-squint.

Regan   Lady, I am not well; else I should answer
From a full-flowing stomach. General,
Take thou my soldiers, prisoners, patrimony;
Dispose of them, of me; the walls are thine;
Witness the world, that I create thee here
My lord and master.

Goneril   Mean you to enjoy him?

Albany   The let-alone lies not in your good will.

Edmund   Nor in thine, lord.

Albany   Half-blooded fellow, yes.

Regan   [*to* **Edmund**] Let the drum strike, and prove my title
thine.

Albany   Sir, just a moment. I regard you as a subject in this war – not as an equal.

Regan   It's up to us to decide how to rank him. I think our wishes might have been consulted before you had said so much. He led our armies, and acted with the authority of my rank and person. Such representation might well stand up and call itself your equal.

Goneril   Not so fast. He ranks higher in his own right than because of any titles *you* have given him!

Regan   In exercising my rights, with my approval, he equates with the best.

Albany   That would only be so if he married you.

Regan   Many a true word is spoken in jest!

Goneril   [*sarcastically*] Well, well, well . . . That's seeing things straight!

Regan   Madam, I am not well: otherwise I'd give you a piece of my mind. [*To* **Edmund**] General, take my soldiers, my prisoners, my inheritance. Do as you wish with them, and me. I surrender myself: may the world be witness that I hereby create you my lord and master.

Goneril   Do you intend to marry him?

Albany   [*rebuking his wife sharply*] It's not for you to say yes or no!

Edmund   Or you, lord –

Albany   Bastard, it is!

Regan   [to **Edmund**] Let the drum sound and proclaim that what is mine, is yours.

Albany   Stay yet; hear reason. Edmund, I arrest thee
On capital treason; and, in thy attaint,
This gilded serpent   [*pointing to* **Goneril**].
                              For your claim, fair sister,
I bar it in the interest of my wife;
'Tis she is sub-contracted to this lord,
And I, her husband, contradict your banns.
If you will marry, make your loves to me;
My lady is bespoke.

Goneril   An interlude!

Albany   Thou art armed, Gloucester; let the trumpet sound:
If none appear to prove upon thy person
Thy heinous, manifest, and many treasons,
There is my pledge   [*throws down a glove*]:
                              I'll make it on thy heart,
Ere I taste bread, thou art in nothing less
Than I have here proclaimed thee.

Regan   Sick! O, sick!

Goneril   [*aside*] If not, I'll ne'er trust poison.

Edmund   There's my exchange   [*throws down a glove*].
                              What in the world he is
That names me traitor, villain-like he lies.
Call by the trumpet: he that dares approach,
On him, on you – who not? – I will maintain
My truth and honour firmly.

Albany   A herald, ho!

Edmund   A herald, ho, a herald!

Albany   Trust to thy single virtue; for thy soldiers,
All levied in my name, have in my name
Took their discharge.

Regan   My sickness grows upon me.

Albany   Hold it: listen to reason! Edmund, I arrest you for
capital treason; and as your accessory [*he points to*
Goneril], this deceptively beautiful serpent. [*To* **Regan**] As
for your claim, fair sister, I rule it out of order in the interests
of my wife. She's the one who is under contract to this lord,
and I – her husband – contradict your banns. If you want to
marry, address your proposals to me. My lady is already
spoken for.

Goneril   Such drama!

Albany   You are armed, Gloucester. Let the trumpet sound. If
no one appears to prove in combat with you your vile,
undeniable and many treasons, there is my challenge! [*He
throws down a gauntlet*] I'll prove it on peril of your life,
before ever I break bread again, that you are in every way
what I have here described you.

Regan   [*holding her forehead*] Sick, oh, I'm sick!

Goneril   [*aside*] If not, I'll never trust poison.

Edmund   There's my response. [*He throws down his own
gauntlet in exchange*] No matter who he is that calls me
traitor, he lies like a villain! Let the trumpet sound a call.
Whoever dares to come forward, I will defend my truth and
honor against him, against you, and against anybody.

Albany   [*calling*] A herald, there!

Edmund   A herald there, a herald!

Albany   Trust to your personal valor, because your soldiers –
all levied in my name – have accepted their discharge
from me.

Regan   [*about to fall*] I'm feeling worse.

Albany   She is not well; convey her to my tent.

[*Exit* **Regan,** *led*]

[*Enter a* **Herald**]

Come hither, herald. Let the trumpet sound,
And read out this.

Officer   Sound, trumpet!   [*A trumpet sounds*]

Herald   [*reads*] *If any man of quality or degree within the lists
of the army will maintain upon Edmund, supposed Earl of
Gloucester, that he is a manifold traitor, let him appear by the
third sound of the trumpet. He is bold in his defence.*

Sound!   [*First trumpet*]
Again!   [*Second trumpet*]
Again!   [*Third trumpet*]
                [*Trumpet answers within*]

[*Enter* **Edgar,** *armed, with a trumpet before him*]

Albany   Ask him his purposes, why he appears
Upon this call o' th' trumpet.

Herald   What are you?
Your name, your quality, and why you answer
This present summons?

Edgar   Know, my name is lost;
By treason's tooth bare-gnawn, and canker-bit:
Yet am I noble as the adversary
I come to cope.

Albany   Which is that adversary?

Edgar   What's he that speaks for Edmund, Earl of
Gloucester?

Albany   She isn't well. Convey her to my tent. [*Officers support her and lead her out*]

[*A* **Herald** *enters*]

Come here, herald. Let the trumpet sound, and read this out. [*He hands over* **Edgar's** *challenge*]

Officer   Sound, trumpet! [*A trumpet sounds*]

Herald   [*reading*] *If any man of rank or distinction, presently enlisted in the army, will maintain that Edmund, supposed Earl of Gloucester, is an all-around traitor, let him appear by the third sound of the trumpet. He will defend himself boldly.*

Sound!

[*The trumpet sounds for the first time*]

Again!

[*The second trumpet sounds*]

Again!

[*The third trumpet sounds. There is a pause, and then an answering trumpet is heard from nearby.* **Edgar** *enters, armed, preceded by a trumpeter*]

Albany   [*to the* **Herald**] Ask him what is his purpose in appearing upon the trumpet call.

Herald   Who are you? Your name? Your rank? Why do you respond to this summons?

Edgar   Know that my name is not on record. Treason has destroyed it. Yet I am as noble as the adversary I come to fight.

Albany   Who is that adversary?

Edgar   Who represents Edmund, Earl of Gloucester?

Edmund   Himself: what say'st thou to him?

Edgar   Draw thy sword,
That, if my speech offend a noble heart,
Thy arm may do thee justice; here is mine:
Behold, it is the privilege of mine honours,
My oath, and my profession: I protest,
Maugre thy strength, place, youth, and eminence,
Despite thy victor sword and fire-new fortune,
Thy valour and thy heart, thou art a traitor,
False to thy gods, thy brother, and thy father,
Conspirant 'gainst this high illustrious prince,
And, from the extremest upward of thy head
To the descent and dust below thy foot,
A most toad-spotted traitor. Say thou 'No,'
This sword, this arm, and my best spirits are bent
To prove upon thy heart, whereto I speak,
Thou liest.

Edmund   In wisdom I should ask thy name;
But since thy outside looks so fair and war-like,
Ad that thy tongue some say of breeding breathes,
What safe and nicely I might well delay
By rule of knighthood, I disdain and spurn;
Back do I toss these treasons to thy head,
With the hell-hated lie o'erwhelm thy heart,
Which, for they yet glance by and scarcely bruise,
This sword of mine shall give them instant way,
Where they shall rest for ever. Trumpets, speak!

[*Alarums. They fight.* **Edmund** *falls*]

Albany   Save him! Save him!

Goneril   This is practice, Gloucester:
By the law of war thou wast not bound to answer

Edmund [*stepping forward*] He himself. What have you to say to him?

Edgar Draw your sword, so that, if what I have to say offends a noble heart, your valor may bring you justice. Here is mine. [*He draws his sword from its scabbard*] Behold! To draw it is the privilege of my rank, my vows, and my knighthood. I declare – notwithstanding your strength, position, youth, and eminence, despite your victorious sword, your brand-new good fortune, your valor and your courage – that you are a traitor! You have betrayed your gods, your brother and your father. You have conspired against this illustrious high-born prince, and from the top of your head to the dust below your feet, you are a most infamous traitor! Deny it, and this sword, this arm, and my best endeavors are determined to prove to that heart of yours, to which I speak, that you lie!

Edmund Common sense tells me I should ask your name. But as your exterior looks so good and valiant, and because your speech has a touch of good breeding about it, though I could with all propriety postpone this combat – according to the rules of knighthood – this I disdainfully refuse to do. I throw these accusations of treason back at you, together with the hateful-as-hell charge of lying. Though right now they pass you by unscathed, my sword will thrust them home where they belong, and put them to rest forever. Trumpets, speak!

[**Edmund** *and* **Edgar** *fight.* **Edmund** *falls, wounded*]

Albany Save him! Save him!

Goneril This is trickery, Gloucester. By the code of arms, you were not obliged to fight with an unknown enemy. You are

An unknown opposite; thou art not vanquished,
But cozened and beguiled.

Albany   Shut your mouth, dame,
Or with this paper shall I stop it. Hold, sir;
Thou worse than any name, read thine own evil:
No tearing, lady; I perceive you know it.

Goneril   Say, if I do, the laws are mine, not thine:
Who can arraign me for't?

Albany   Most monstrous! O!
Know'st thou this paper?

Goneril   Ask me not what I know.

[*Exit*]

Albany   Go after her: she's desperate; govern her.

[*Exit an Officer*]

Edmund   What you have charged me with, that have I done,
And more, much more; the time will bring it out:
'Tis past, and so am I. But what art thou
That hast this fortune on me? If thou'rt noble,
I do forgive thee.

Edgar   Let's exchange charity.
I am no less in blood than thou art, Edmund;
If more, the more thou hast wronged me.
My name is Edgar, and thy father's son.
The gods are just, and of our pleasant vices
Make instruments to plague us;
The dark and vicious place where thee he got
Cost him his eyes.

not defeated, but cheated and deceived!

Albany   Shut your mouth, woman, or I'll stop it with this letter. [*It is* **Goneril's** *to* **Edmund**, *the one which* **Edgar** *found on* **Oswald** *in Act 4 Scene 6. To* **Edgar**] Hold your sword, sir. [*To* **Goneril**] Wicked beyond all words: read your own evil! [**Goneril** *tries to grab the paper*] No snatching, lady! I suspect you know what it is.

Goneril   What if I do? The law belongs to me, not you. Who could prosecute me for it?

Albany   How utterly monstrous! Oh! *Do* you know this letter?

Goneril   [*hysterical now*] Don't ask me what I know!

[*She leaves, distraught*]

Albany   Follow her. She's desperate. Take charge of her.

[*An Officer leaves*]

Edmund   [*to* **Albany**] What you have charged me with, I have done: and more, much more. Time will reveal all. It's over now, and so am I. [*To* **Edgar**] But who are you, who has the advantage over me? If you are noble, I forgive you.

Edgar   Let's exchange courtesies. I am no less noble than you are, Edmund. If I'm more, you have wronged me all the more. My name is Edgar, and I'm your father's son. The gods are just. They use the vices we take pleasure in as the means to punish us; conceiving you cost him his eyes.

Edmund   Thou hast spoken right, 'tis true.
    The wheel is come full circle; I am here.

Albany   Methought thy very gait did prophesy
    A royal nobleness: I must embrace thee:
    Let sorrow split my heart, if ever I
    Did hate thee or thy father.

Edgar   Worthy prince, I know't.

Albany   Where have you hid yourself?
    How have you known the miseries of your father?

Edgar   By nursing them, my lord. List a brief tale;
    And when 'tis told, O that my heart would burst!
    The bloody proclamation to escape
    That followed me so near – O, our lives' sweetness,
    That we the pain of death would hourly die
    Rather than die at once! – taught me to shift
    Into a madman's rags, assume a semblance
    That very dogs disdained: and in this habit
    Met I my father with his bleeding rings,
    Their precious stones new lost; became his guide,
    Led him, begged for him, saved him from despair;
    Never – O fault! – revealed myself unto him,
    Until some half-hour past, when I was armed;
    Not sure, though hoping, of this good success,
    I asked his blessing, and from first to last
    Told him my pilgrimage: but his flawed heart,
    Alack, too weak the conflict to support,
    'Twixt two extremes of passion, joy and grief,
    Burst smilingly.

Edmund   This speech of yours hath moved me,
    And shall perchance do good; but speak you on;
    You look as you had something more to say.

Edmund   You've said right. It's true. The wheel of fortune has turned a full circle. I am back at the bottom.

Albany   [*to* **Edgar**] I thought your very walk suggested a royal nobleness. My welcome to you. [*They embrace in soldierly fashion*] May sorrow be my lot if ever I hated you or your father.

Edgar   Wise prince, I know that.

Albany   Where did you hide yourself? How did you know about your father's sufferings?

Edgar   By nursing them, my lord. Listen to a brief story, and when I've told it, would that my heart would burst! To escape the threat of death that was so close upon me – oh, how sweet life is, in that we suffer the pain of death by the hour rather than die suddenly! – I learned to dress in the rags of a madman, and to assume a character that even dogs despised. And in this clothing I met my father with his bleeding sockets, his eyes newly blinded. I became his guide, led him, begged for him, and saved him from despair. I never, foolishly, revealed myself to him till some half hour ago, when I was in armor. Not certain of this fortunate outcome, though hoping for it, I asked his blessing, and told him of my journeying from first to last. But his injured heart, alas, too weak to carry the strain, torn between the two extremes of passion – joy and grief – burst with happiness.

Edmund   This speech of yours has touched me, and it could perhaps do some good. Proceed. You look as though you have more to say.

Albany   If there be more, more woeful, hold it in;
For I am almost ready to dissolve,
Hearing of this.

Edgar   This would have seemed a period
To such as love not sorrow; but another,
To amplify too much, would make much more,
And top extremity.
Whilst I was big in clamour, came there in a man,
Who, having seen me in my worst estate,
Shunned my abhorred society; but then, finding
Who 'twas that so endured, with his strong arms
He fastened on my neck, and bellowed out
As he'ld burst heaven; threw him on my father;
Told the most piteous tale of Lear and him
That ever ear received; which in recounting
His grief grew puissant, and the strings of life
Began to crack: twice then the trumpets sounded,
And there I left him tranced.

Albany   But who was this?

Edgar   Kent, sir, the banished Kent; who in disguise
Followed his enemy king, and did him service
Improper for a slave.

[*Enter a* **Gentleman,** *with a bloody knife*]

Gentleman   Help, help! O, help!

Edgar   What kind of help?

Albany   Speak, man.

Edgar   What means this bloody knife?

Gentleman   'Tis hot, it smokes;
It came even from the heart of – O, she's dead!

Albany   [*to* Edgar] If there's more to report that's more
harrowing, keep it to yourself. I'm almost at the point of
tears, hearing of this.

Edgar   Those who cannot cope with sorrow would think of
this as a breaking-point. To add more woe by giving details
would generate further suffering, and go beyond all bearing.
While I was bawling out my grief, a man arrived who, having
seen me in my wretchedness, would have avoided my
loathsome company. But seeing who it was that suffered
so, he wrapped his strong arms around my neck, and
bellowed out as if he'd burst the heavens. He embraced my
father, and told the most pitiful tale about Lear and himself
that ever anyone heard. In the telling of it, his grief
overwhelmed him, and his hold on life began to slip. Then
the trumpet sounded twice; and there I left him,
unconscious.

Albany   But who was this?

Edgar   Kent, sir, the banished Kent, who in disguise followed
the King from whom he was alienated, serving him beyond
the duties even of a slave.

[*A* **Gentleman** *enters, carrying a bloodstained knife*]

Gentleman   Help, help, oh, help!

Edgar   What kind of help?

[*The* **Gentleman** *is too choked to answer*]

Albany   Speak up, man!

Edgar   Why this bloodstained knife?

Gentleman   It's warm . . . it's steaming . . . it came from the
heart of . . . [*He cannot find the words*] Oh, she's dead!

275

Albany   Who dead? Speak, man.

Gentleman   Your lady, sir, your lady: and her sister
By her is poisoned; she confesses it.

Edmund   I was contracted to them both: all three
Now marry in an instant.

Edgar   Here comes Kent.

[*Enter* **Kent**]

Albany   Produce the bodies, be they alive or dead;

[*Exit* **Gentleman**]

This judgment of the heavens, that makes us tremble,
Touches us not with pity. [*To* **Kent**] O, is this he?
The time will not allow the compliment
Which very manners urges.

Kent   I am come
To bid my King and master aye good night;
Is he not here?

Albany   Great thing of us forgot!
Speak, Edmund, where's the King? And where's Cordelia?

[*The bodies of* **Goneril** *and* **Regan** *are brought in*]

Seest thou this object, Kent?

Kent   Alack, why thus?

Edmund   Yet Edmund was beloved;
The one the other poisoned for my sake,
And after slew herself.

Albany   Even so. Cover their faces.

Edmund   I pant for life; some good I mean to do
Despite of mine own nature. Quickly send,
276

Albany   Who is dead? Speak, man!

Gentleman   Your wife, sir, your wife. And she has poisoned your sister-in-law. She confessed it.

Edmund   I was engaged to them both. All three of us will now be married at the same time.

Edgar   Here comes Kent.

[**Kent** *enters*]

Albany   Bring in the bodies, alive or dead.

[*A* **Gentleman** *leaves*]

This judgment of heaven, tearful though it is, does not arouse our pity. [*To* **Kent**] Oh, is this the man? This is not the right time for the normal courtesies.

Kent   I have come to bid my King and master an everlasting good night. Is he not here?

Albany   A serious oversight! Speak, Edmund! Where is the King? And where is Cordelia? [*The bodies of* **Goneril** *and* **Regan** *are brought in*] Do you see this, Kent?

Kent   Alas: what's caused this?

Edmund   So Edmund was indeed loved! One poisoned the other for my sake, and afterwards killed herself.

Albany   Indeed so. Cover their faces.

Edmund   I pant for life. I mean to do some good, in spite of my nature. Send quickly – hurry now! – to the castle. I've given

    Be brief in it, to th' castle; for my writ
    Is on the life of Lear and on Cordelia.
    Nay, send in time.

Albany   Run, run! O, run!

Edgar   To who, my lord? Who has the office? Send
    Thy token of reprieve.

Edmund   Well thought on: take my sword,
    Give it the captain.

Edgar   Haste thee, for thy life.

                                        [*Exit Officer*]

Edmund   He hath commission from thy wife and me
    To hang Cordelia in the prison, and
    To lay the blame upon her own despair,
    That she fordid herself.

Albany   The gods defend her!
    Bear him hence awhile.

                                    [*Edmund is borne off*]

[*Enter* **Lear,** *with* **Cordelia** *dead in his arms*]

Lear   Howl, howl, howl! O, you are men of stones!
    Had I your tongues and eyes, I'd use them so
    That heaven's vault should crack. She's gone for ever.
    I know when one is dead, and when one lives;
    She's dead as earth. Lend me a looking-glass;
    If that her breath will mist or stain the stone,
    Why, then she lives.

Kent   Is this the promised end?

Edgar   Or image of that horror?

278

orders for the deaths of Lear and Cordelia. Get there in time.

Albany   Run – run! Oh, run!

Edgar   To whom, my lord? Who is in charge? Send your token, indicating a reprieve.

Edmund   A good idea: take my sword. Give it to the captain.

Edgar   [*passing the sword to an Officer*] Hurry, on your life! [*The Officer runs off*]

Edmund   [*to* **Albany**] He has orders from your wife and me to hang Cordelia in the prison, and to say her despair led to her suicide.

Albany   The gods protect her! [*To Servants*] Take him away for the moment. [**Edmund** *is carried off*]

[**Lear** *enters, with* **Cordelia** *dead in his arms*]

Lear   Howl, howl, howl! Oh, you are men of stone! If I had your tongues and eyes, I'd use them so the roof of heaven would crack! She's gone forever. I know when one is dead, and when one lives. She's as dead as earth. Lend me a mirror. If her breath will mist or stain the glass, why, then she lives!

Kent   Is this the end of the world?

Edgar   Or a copy of that horror?

Albany   Fall and cease.

Lear   This feather stirs; she lives! If it be so,
It is a chance which does redeem all sorrows
That ever I have felt.

Kent   [*kneeling*]   O my good master!

Lear   Prithee, away.

Edgar   'Tis noble Kent, your friend.

Lear   A plague upon you, murderers, traitors all!
I might have saved her; now she's gone for ever!
Cordelia, Cordelia! stay a little. Ha!
What is't thou say'st? Her voice was ever soft,
Gentle and low, an excellent thing in woman.
I killed the slave that was a-hanging thee.

Officer   'Tis true, my lords, he did.

Lear   Did I not, fellow?
I have seen the day, with my good biting falchion
I would have made them skip: I am old now,
And these same crosses spoil me. Who are you?
Mine eyes are not o' th' best: I'll tell you straight.

Kent   If Fortune brag of two she loved and hated,
One of them we behold.

Lear   This is a dull sight. Are you not Kent?

Kent   The same:
Your servant Kent. Where is your servant Caius?

Lear   He's a good fellow, I can tell you that;
He'll strike, and quickly too. He's dead and rotten.

Kent   No, my good lord; I am the very man –

Lear   I'll see that straight.

Albany May the heavens fall, and all things cease!

Lear [*testing to see whether* **Cordelia** *is breathing*] This feather moves! She's alive! If so, it is a piece of luck that cancels out all the sorrows that I have ever felt.

Kent [*kneeling*] Oh, my good master!

Lear [*pushing him aside anxiously*] Go away!

Edgar [*explaining*] It's the noble Kent, your friend.

Lear Damn you! Murderers, traitors, all of you! I might have saved her. Now she's gone forever. Cordelia, Cordelia, stay a while! [*He puts his ear to her lips*] What's that you say? Her voice was always soft, gentle and low: an excellent thing in a woman. [*Proudly*] I killed the wretch who was hanging you!

Officer It's true, my lords: he did.

Lear Didn't I, man? I've seen the day when, with my good sharp sword I would have made them jump! I am old now, and these ailments of mine got in the way. [*He peers at* **Kent**] Who are you? My eyes are not as good as they might be; I'll tell you straight –

Kent If Fortune should boast of two men she both loved and hated, we are looking at one of them now.

Lear – my sight is poor. [*After a pause*] Aren't you Kent?

Kent I am. Your servant, Kent. Where is your servant called Caius?

Lear [*recognizing the name* **Kent** *used when disguised*] He's a good fellow, I can tell you that! He'll fight, and quickly, too! [*Sadly*] He's dead and decayed.

Kent No, my good lord. I am the man –

Lear [*not able to grasp what* **Kent** *says*] I'll see to that in a moment.

281

Kent   That from your first of difference and decay
Have followed your sad steps –

Lear   You are welcome hither.

Kent   Nor no man else. All's cheerless, dark, and deadly:
Your eldest daughters have fordone themselves,
And desperately are dead.

Lear   Ay, so I think.

Albany   He knows not what he says, and vain is it
That we present us to him.

Edgar   Very bootless.

[*Enter an* **Officer**]

Officer   Edmund is dead, my lord.

Albany   That's but a trifle here.
You lords and noble friends, know our intent;
What comfort to this great decay may come
Shall be applied: for us, we will resign,
During the life of this old majesty,
To him our absolute power: [*To* **Edgar** *and* **Kent**]
                              You, to your rights,
With boot and such addition as your honours
Have more than merited. All friends shall taste
The wages of their virtue, and all foes
The cup of their deservings. O, see, see!

Lear   And my poor fool is hanged! No, no, no life!
Why should a dog, a horse, a rat, have life,
And thou no breath at all? Thou'lt come no more,
Never, never, never, never, never!
Pray you, undo this button: thank you, sir.
Do you see this? Look on her, look, her lips,
Look there, look there!   [*Dies*]

Kent   – who has followed in your sad steps from the very beginning of your declining fortunes.

Lear   You are welcome here.

Kent   The very man. All is dreary, dark, and funereal. Your eldest daughters have put an end to themselves, and in hopeless desperation are dead.

Lear   [*uncomprehending*] Yes, so I believe.

Albany   He doesn't know what he is saying. It's no use our talking to him.

Edgar   None whatever.

[*An* **Officer** *enters*]

Officer   Edmund is dead, my lord.

Albany   That's of small importance here. Lords and noble friends, know our intentions. We shall provide what comfort we can for this noble ruin of mankind. As for us, we shall abdicate our absolute power to this old majesty during the remainder of his life. [*To* **Edgar** *and* **Kent**] As for you: resume your rightful places, with such additional titles as your noble deeds have more than earned. All friends shall be rewarded for their loyalty, and all foes punished as they deserve to be. Oh, look, look!

Lear   And my poor child is hanged! No, no, no life! Why should a dog, or a horse, or a rat have life, and you no breath at all? You'll come no more: never, never, never, never, never! [*He struggles with his collar*] Please, undo this button. [**Albany** *helps him*] Thank you, sir. [*He imagines* **Cordelia** *is showing signs of life*] Do you see this? Look at her – look – her lips! Look there, look there! [*The excitement overwhelms him, and he dies*]

Edgar   He faints! My lord, my lord!

Kent   Break, heart; I prithee, break!
Edgar   Look up, my lord.

Kent   Vex not his ghost: O, let him pass; he hates him
That would upon the rack of this tough world
Stretch him out longer.

Edgar   He is gone, indeed.

Kent   The wonder is he hath endured so long;
He but usurped his life.

Albany   Bear them from hence. Our present business
Is general woe. [*To* **Kent** *and* **Edgar**] Friends of my soul,
   you twain
Rule in this realm, and the gored state sustain.

Kent   I have a journey, sir, shortly to go;
My master calls me, I must not say no.

Edgar   The weight of this sad time we must obey;
Speak what we feel, not what we ought to say.
The oldest hath borne most: we that are young
Shall never see so much, nor live so long.

                    [*Exeunt, with a dead march*]

Edgar   He's fainted! [*Shaking* **Lear**] My lord, my lord!

Kent   May he suffer no more!

Edgar   Come on, my lord!

Kent   [*drawing him away*] Don't trouble his parting soul. Let him go. Only an enemy would prolong the torture.

Edgar   He's really gone.

Kent   The surprising thing is that he endured his suffering so long. He lived on borrowed time.

Albany   Bear them away. General mourning is now our immediate concern. [*To* **Kent** *and* **Edgar**] Kindred souls: you two shall rule in this kingdom, to shoulder the burden of our ruined state.

Kent   [*hinting at his death*] I have a journey to make, sir, soon. My master calls me. I must not deny him.

Edgar   We must respond to the burdens of these sad times, and speak frankly, not expediently. The oldest have suffered most. We who are young will never see as much as they have seen, or live so long.

[*The bodies are all taken up, and everyone leaves at a dead march*]

Activities

Characters

Search the text (either the original or the modern version) to find answers to the following questions. They will help you to form personal opinions about the major characters in the play. *Record any relevant quotations in Shakespeare's own words.*

King Lear

1   At the beginning of the play Lear (aged "fourscore and upward, not an hour more or less") is "every inch a King." In his opening speech in *Act I Scene 1*

    a How does he display the "authority" which Kent (in *Act I Scene 4*) recognizes as one of Lear's major characteristics?

    b At what point does "majesty fall to folly"?

2   Kent accuses Lear of "hideous rashness." Why was it unwise to

    a subdivide the kingdom?

    b subdivide it unequally?

    c subdivide it according to "how nature doth with merit challenge"?

3   **a** At the end of *Act I Scene 1*, what do we learn from Goneril and Regan of Lear's

       i   temper,

      ii   judgment,

     iii   parental partiality,

    in former days?

    b Give specific examples of Lear's "imperfections of long-engraffed condition" as demonstrated in this scene.

c Show from two of Gloucester's comments in *Act I Scene 2* that Kent was not alone in thinking Lear acted rashly.

4 "By day and night he wrongs me," says Goneril in *Act I Scene 3*. List the "gross crimes" of which Lear is accused in this scene and decide whether Goneril is

a speaking the truth;

b justified in her actions.

5 a At the beginning of *Act I Scene 4*, Lear is seen enjoying retirement.

    i In what ways is he still acting like a king?

    ii What evidence is there that his happiness is clouded?

    iii Why does the dialogue with the Fool create conflict in his mind?

b By the end of the scene, Lear is emotionally distraught. Find examples of his use of

(i) sarcasm (ii) anger (iii) threats (iv) curses (v) tears (vi) self-reproach (vii) self pity

In responding to Goneril's provocations.

6 a Lear's progress towards madness is accelerated in *Act II Scene 4*. Show how stress is evident in

(i) his expressions of incredulity (ii) his physical discomfort (iii) his sense of impotence (iv) his attempts at self-control.

b By the end of the scene, Lear's "let me not be mad" of *Act I Scene 5* has changed to "O Fool, I shall go mad." Find evidence of mental torment in his reactions to

i) the stocking of Kent ii) Regan and Cornwall's delayed appearance iii) Regan's defense of Goneril iv) Goneril and Regan's progressive reduction of Lear's hundred knights.

Activities

7 In *Act III Scene 2* Lear's rage and sorrow is directed at the storm.

   a Show how he is obsessed with

      i the theme of ingratitude. What does he call upon nature to do?

      ii his weakness and old age. What is his plea before the justice of the gods?

   b Of what is his resolution to "say nothing" an ironic echo?

   c i Why might his speech denouncing hypocrites and sinners be said to mark the beginning of his redemption?

      ii How does his treatment of the Fool confirm that Lear is beginning to look upon his fellow men in a new way?

8 **a** At the beginning of *Act III Scene 3*, in the midst of the storm and suffering from "this tempest in my mind," Lear's understanding increases. How is this shown by

      i the order in which Lear invites his companions to enter the hovel?

      ii his thoughts on "poor unaccommodated man"?

      iii his actions?

   b Identify the points at which

      i Lear's "wits begin t'unsettle" in *Act III Scene 3*;

      ii revenge is replaced by justice as a means of dealing with the "she foxes," in *Act III Scene 6*.

   c What do the three "justices" have in common who "try" Goneril and Regan?

9 Lear's next appearance is in *Act IV Scene 6*. He is mad. As a result of his experiences and losing his mind, what has he learned about

   a flattery?

b the limitations of power?

c tolerance?

d the nature of authority?

e the nature of vice?

f the nature of justice?

g hypocrisy?

h patience?

10 In *Act IV Scene 7* Lear recovers from his madness in the company of Cordelia.

    a What, according to Kent in *Act IV Scene 3*, has kept Lear from Cordelia until now?

    b At their reunion, the Doctor observes: "the great rage, you see, is killed in him." Illustrate the truth of this, from Lear's awakening to his exit on Cordelia's arm.

11 The battle over and lost, Lear is a prisoner in *Act V Scene 3*. Which of his lines show that he

      i has learned humility?

      ii has rejected the false values of court life?

      iii has regained his dignity?

12 At the end of the play, Lear enters carrying the dead body of Cordelia.

    a There is evidence that he has once again retreated from reality as a result of suffering. Give examples.

    b What has he done which is reminiscent of Lear in his prime?

    c Why is the moment of his death an apt one?

Goneril and Regan

1 Their public speeches near the beginning of *Act I Scene 1* contrast sharply with their private ones at the end.

Activities

a Goneril appears to take flattery as far as it will go in expressing her love for her father.

    i How does Regan succeed in topping her?

    ii At this point, is there any recognizable difference in the characters of the two sisters?

b What evidence is there

    i that they have been keeping a critical eye on their father?

    ii that they do not respect him?

    iii that they do not appreciate what he has given them?

c From the evidence in this dialogue, and especially the last two lines of the scene, decide which sister is the dominant one.

2 It is to his eldest daughter Goneril that Lear first goes after resigning the throne.

  a Read *Act I Scene 3*, and list

    i Lear's alleged offenses;

    ii Goneril's plans for dealing with him.

  b What do you deduce about her character?

3 **a** Goneril challenges Lear in *Act I Scene 4*.

    i Compare her accusations with those in *Act I Scene 3*. Have they changed?

    ii What is consistent about her manner toward her father?

  b She also stands up to her husband, Albany. How is it made clear that she is the dominant partner?

4 In *Act IV Scene 1* Regan and her husband visit Gloucester.

  a How does Regan's relationship with Cornwall differ from her sister's with Albany?

  b How can we tell that Regan has a prejudiced and distorted attitude toward her father and his knights?

  c At this point in the play, how would you describe Regan's attitude toward Gloucester?

5 **a** Find evidence in *Act II Scene 2* and *Act II Scene 4* to confirm Regan's assertion in *Act I Scene 1*: "I am made of that self metal as my sister."

b i How do the two sisters act in concert in *Act II Scene 4*?

ii Which sister seems, on balance, to be the more obsessed with the danger of Lear's followers?

6 **a** Both sisters take a life during the course of the play.

i Compare the circumstances and contrast the methods employed by each.

ii Is Goneril's suicide consistent with her character?

b Both sisters fall in love with Edmund.

i Deduce from this the qualities they both admire in a man.

ii Examine Goneril's attitude to her husband in *Act I Scene 4*, *Act IV Scene 1*, and *Act V Scene 3*. What qualities in a man does she despise?

c The two sisters are "jealous of the other, as the stung are of the adder" (Edmund, *Act V Scene 1*).

i Check the meaning of these words in the modern translation, then trace the course of the "jealousy" in *Act IV Scene 2*, *Act IV Scene 5*, *Act V Scene 1* and *Act V Scene 3*.

ii Both Goneril and Regan are demonstrably bad daughters and bad sisters. One plans to have her husband murdered (check *Act IV Scene 2* and *Act IV Scene 6*); the other has a sadistic trait (check *Act II Scene 2* and *Act III Scene 7*). Is either less pernicious than the other?

Cordelia

1 That Cordelia was Lear's favorite daughter is confirmed three times in *Act I Scene 1*: find the relevant evidence in speeches by

(a) Goneril; (b) the King of France; (c) Lear himself.

2 That Cordelia is Lear's most virtuous and loving daughter is confirmed

    a in *Act IV Scene 3*. How does Cordelia's reported response to the news of Lear's maltreatment show both her feelings, and her natural disinclination to reveal them in public?

    b in *Act IV Scene 4*. How does Cordelia show her love both emotionally and practically?

    c in *Act IV Scene 7*. What examples are there of her (i) goodness (ii) kindness (iii) compassion (iv) tenderness (v) forgiving nature?

3 That Cordelia is loved and respected by others is demonstrated in *Act I Scenes 1* and *4*

    a by Kent. How does he compliment her?

    b by the King of France. What value does he put upon her?

    c by the Fool. What effect does Cordelia's departure have on him?

4 **a** Twice in *Act I Scene 1* Cordelia refers to her natural reticence. Find the lines, and

    b check them against Lear's description of her speaking voice in *Act V Scene 3*. Then

    c comment on the aptness of the King of France's analysis of her character in *Act I Scene 1*.

5 In spite of saying so little, and appearing only four times in the play, Cordelia shows she has several very positive characteristics.

    a She is honest. What is the best example of this?

    b She deplores insincerity. How does she make this plain (i) to the Duke of Burgundy? (ii) to her sisters?

    c She respects integrity. How do we know she recognizes the goodness of Kent?

d She is loyal. Where does Lear say she has good reason not to be?

e She is philosophical. How is this demonstrated by her last speech in the play?

Kent

1 Kent has the first words in the play, and almost the last. In *Act I Scene 1*, he is fearlessly outspoken; from his speeches choose

    a three words or phrases which confirm his loyalty to the King;

    b three words or phrases which show his clear understanding of Lear's wrongheadedness;

    c three words or phrases which indicate his understanding of Goneril and Regan.

2 **a** Outspokenness is also a major characteristic of Kent in disguise. How does this work

        i to his advantage in *Act I Scene 4* and

        ii to his disadvantage in *Act II Scene 2*?

    b In the latter scene, Cornwall speaks of Kent's "saucy roughness." Find examples of this in

        i his argument with Oswald;

        ii his retorts to Cornwall and Regan.

3 Between *Act III Scene 1* and *Act V Scene 3*, Kent's role is one of protector and correspondent, working on behalf of Lear's cause.

    a In the storm scene (*Act III Scene 6*) he stands out as being the only rational man at the trial. His suggested cure for Lear's insanity is the same as the Doctor's in *Act IV Scene 4*: what is it?

    b In *Act III Scene 1* and *Act IV Scene 3*, Kent establishes links with Cordelia and the French invading army at Dover.

What is said at the beginning of *Act IV Scene 3* and the end of *Act IV Scene 4* to clear Kent of the charge of treason?

4 What is the evidence in *Act V Scene 3* that Kent sees his service to the King as extending beyond the grave?

The Fool

1 a The Fool first appears in *Act I Scene 4*.

   i   How many times does Lear have to call for him before he appears?

   ii What is the Knight's explanation for the Fool's absence, and what does it tell us about the latter's feelings?

   b Immediately, the Fool begins to jest about foolishness

   i   to Kent (and again in *Act II Scene 4*). Explain why.

   ii to Lear. What does he say that merits Kent's remark: "This is not altogether fool, my lord"?

   c Collect further examples of the Fool's oft-reiterated theme, in this scene and the others in which he appears.

2 a Another of his targets is Truth (and its counterpart, Falsehood). How many references to it can you find in *Act I Scene 4*?

   b Find examples of Truth conveyed by means of

   i   jokes and conundrums;

   ii songs;

   iii wise sayings.

   c In the circumstances, why does Goneril say he is "more knave than fool"?

3 The Fool's second appearance, in *Act I Scene 5*, follows Lear's humiliation at the hands of Goneril.

   a Why do you think the Fool's first joke is about brains?

b What message is he trying to convey in his jokes about crab-apples, noses, and snails?

c Which of the Fool's remarks is close to the unvarnished truth?

d Mark the text at points where the Fool diverts Lear from brooding about his troubles.

4 a As Lear becomes more isolated and tormented, the Fool works harder to sustain him, maintaining his pointed jokes, puns and witticisms as the King progresses toward madness. In *Act II Scene 4*

    i How many jokes does he make at Lear's expense?

    ii How many at Kent's?

    iii Is there a significance in the switch of emphasis?

b As Lear departs into the storm, the Fool is his only companion. According to the Gentleman in *Act III Scene 1*, what is his function now?

5 The storm scenes (*Act III Scenes 2; 4; 6*) are those in which Lear's "wits begin to turn" and he goes mad.

a The Fool suffers from the same physical discomfort as his master. Which lines in *Act III Scene 2* show that they have come close together through hardship?

b What incident in *Act III Scene 4* is close enough to farce to relieve the dramatic tension?

c Which line spoken by the Fool in Edgar's presence emphasizes the leveling effect of their situation?

d How does the Fool's presence at the mock trial of Goneril and Regan help to bring out the full pathos and tragedy of Lear's condition?

6 The Fool's last words in the play ("And I'll go to bed at noon") can be interpreted many ways. Here are two of them:

a "If you are having your evening meal in the morning, then my bedtime will be noon" (i.e., a straightforward quip).

b "I shall not live much longer" (i.e., using the word "bed" as a euphemism for "grave").

Those who favor (a) point out that the Fool's dramatic usefulness is at an end, so Shakespeare gives him no more lines to say. Those who favor (b) say Lear's "And my poor fool is hanged" (*Act V Scene 3*) proves that he committed suicide, though the word "fool" could mean "child" and therefore refer to Cordelia.

What is your opinion?

Gloucester

1 Gloucester opens the play by making light of a "pleasant vice" which resulted in the birth of the illegitimate Edmund. Look up Edgar's words to the dying Edmund in *Act V Scene 3*: show how they confirm the former's belief that "the gods are just" in dealing with immorality.

2 Edmund describes Gloucester as "a credulous father." Trace the tricks Edmund uses to deceive Gloucester in *Act I Scene 1* and *Act II Scene 2*.

   a Is his success due entirely to his manipulative skills, or have recent events made the old Earl vulnerable?

   b Show that Gloucester's mind is in a state of turmoil after Lear's abdication.

3 Gloucester seems weak, letting others make decisions for him.

   a To Edmund, he says "frame the business after your own wisdom" in *Act I Scene 2*; and he refers to Cornwall as "The noble Duke my master" in *Act II Scene 1*. What is ironic about his dependence on these two men?

   b Consider his protest at the stocking of Kent. Do you think he did all he could in the circumstances?

c Read the dialogue between Lear and Gloucester in *Act II Scene 4* concerning Cornwall's slighting of the King. Does Gloucester's exit line imply that he lacks the courage to take sides?

4 By *Act III Scene 2* Gloucester has had further experience of Goneril and Regan, and time to think.

    a Explain what is praiseworthy about his resolution.

    b Explain what is unfortunate about his choice of confidant.

    c Explain how he puts his decision to aid Lear into practice.

5 In *Act III Scene 7* Gloucester suffers cruelly for his loyalty.

    a Illustrate

       i his dignity while being threatened;

      ii his strong moral values.

    b Later, in *Act IV Scene 1*, he says "I stumbled when I saw." What is the first truth he learns after losing his sight?

6 Blindness brings despair to Gloucester.

    a In *Act IV Scene 1*, which lines sum up his pessimistic philosophy?

    b What is his purpose in seeking to be guided toward Dover?

7 *Act IV Scene 6* sees Gloucester, led by Edgar, "at the top of that same hill" which, he is told, overlooks the sea.

    a Explain why it is necessary for Edgar to mislead his father.

    b Choose two statements by Gloucester, one after Edgar's successful ruse, and one after his meeting with Lear, to show that he has rejected the pessimism of *Act IV Scene 1*.

    c i On what occasion in *Act V Scene 2* does Gloucester relapse into melancholy?

      ii What observation revives him?

8 Gloucester's death is reported by Edgar in *Act V Scene 3*. What was the cause of it?

Edmund

1 We meet Edmund at the very beginning of the play, when Gloucester speaks for him, and we learn of his illegitimacy. Find two reasons why

  a he might be forgiven for having a jaundiced view of society;

  b he might be forgiven for his subsequent lack of filial loyalty.

2 In his soliloquy in *Act I Scene 2, lines 1–22* Edmund speaks for himself.

  a To whose "law" does he say his "services are bound"?

  b List his arguments for appealing to the gods to "stand up for bastards."

3 a Edmund's villainy has a strong element of wit about it. Find examples in *Act I Scene 2*, with reference to

   i his deception of Gloucester and manipulation of Edgar;

   ii his skeptical references to astrology;

   iii his use of irony.

  b Which lines summarize his case for intrigue against "a credulous father and a brother noble"?

  c In *Act II Scene 1*,

   i how many examples of his cunning trickery can you find?

   ii which of Gloucester's lines indicate that Edmund has succeeded?

   iii which lines of Cornwall's advance his prospects even further?

4 In *Act III Scene 5*, Edmund tells Cornwall: "I will perserver in my course of loyalty, though the conflict be sore between that and my blood."

  a Consider

   i what he has previously said in *Act III Scene 3*;

   ii his behavior in *Act III Scene 7*;

      iii   Regan's report of his murderous intentions in *Act IV Scene 5*.

  b Is there any evidence of conflicting loyalty?

5 Both Goneril and Regan fall in love with Edmund.

  a Find the evidence in *Act IV Scene 2*, *Act IV Scene 5*, and *Act V Scene 1*.

  b Decide from Edmund's soliloquy at the end of *Act V Scene 1* how far their love is reciprocated.

6 By the end of the play, Edmund has been both victor and vanquished.

  a In victory, what is his most wicked deed?

  b In defeat, what good does he do "despite of mine own nature"?

  c Do the words he utters in his dying moments – "Yet Edmund was beloved" – provide any clue about either his past behavior or his deathbed reformation?

Edgar

1 Edgar plays a number of roles throughout the play.

  a In *Act I Scene 1* he is simply the Earl of Gloucester's legitimate son. How much older is he than Edmund?

  b In *Act I Scene 2* he is in disgrace. How does Edmund account for the ease with which this was accomplished?

  c By *Act II Scene 3* he is Poor Tom: "Edgar I nothing am."

      i   Describe his appearance.

      ii   Using the information in *Act III Scene 4*, list his sufferings and show why "unaccommodated man is no more but such a poor, bare, forked animal" as he is.

      iii   Explain why Lear finds him a congenial companion, and how Lear's suffering helps Edgar endure his own.

iv Show from Edgar's words in *Act IV Scene 1* that he has the courage and the philosophy to overcome despair.

2   a   Edgar is changed for the better when he appears in *Act IV Scene 6*, although he denies this to his blind father.

      i   From whom did he obtain his superior clothes?

      ii   In what ways is his speech different?

  b   i   What is Edgar's purpose in "trifling thus with his [i.e., Gloucester's] despair"?

      ii   Explain his method of procedure.

  c   Which lines of Gloucester's prove that the ruse has worked?

3   a   In his final role in the play, Edgar is a man of action.

      i   What is his first valorous deed on behalf of his father in *Act IV Scene 6*?

      ii   What is the second, before the battle, in *Act V Scene 1*?

      iii   What is the third, after the battle?

  b   i   Show from the speeches of Edmund and Albany at the end of the play that Edgar has royal dignity.

      ii   In the Quarto edition of the play (1608), the last lines of *King Lear* are given to Albany. Do you agree with the Folio editors that the words are more appropriately given to Edgar?

Structure, themes and imagery

1 The play has both a main plot and a subplot. Identify the main characters in each.

2 Show how in each there is

   a a foolish father
   b loyalty
   c disloyalty
   d rejection of the good
   e trust in the bad
   f banishment
   g greed
   h deceit
   i disguise
   j homelessness

   k madness, real or feigned
   l redemption through suffering
   m experience of abject poverty
   n loving care shown by a rejected child
   o violent death
   p death caused by emotional stress

3 Complete the following:

   a Whereas one father has all daughters, the other has . . .
   b Whereas one suffers madness, the other suffers . . .
   c Whereas there is rivalry between sisters in one, there is rivalry between . . . in the other.
   d Whereas in one a son leaves home, in the other . . .
   e Whereas daughters betray their father in one, a . . . betrays his father in the other.
   f Whereas one family is wiped out, in the other . . . survives.
   g Whereas in one, a Fool helps a King, in the other a madman helps . . .

4 The theme that initiates events in the play is that of the generation gap; the relationship of parent and child, and the duties and obligations that flow from the blood-bond. Find examples of parent/child relationships involving

(a) gratitude/ingratitude (b) kindness/cruelty (c) trust/deceit (d) legitimacy/illegitimacy (e) duties/freedoms (f) respect/contempt (g) hatred/love

5 Self-knowledge, and the pursuit of truth, go hand-in-hand with the development of the plot.

   a Lear goes mad before he comes to his senses. Find examples of his progress from folly to wisdom in the following scenes:

   (i) *Act 1 Scene 1* (ii) *Act 1 Scene 4* (iii) *Act 2 Scene 4* (iv) *Act 3 Scenes 2 and 6* (iv) *Act 4 Scenes 6 and 7*

   b Gloucester loses his sight before he can "see." Trace the stages through which he passes (noting in particular how he learns to accept Edgar's dictum "Ripeness is all") in the following scenes:

   (i) *Act 1 Scenes 1 and 2* (ii) *Act 2 Scene 1* (iii) *Act 3 Scenes 3 and 4* (iv) *Act 3 Scene 7* (v) *Act 4 Scene 1* (vi) *Act 4 Scene 6* (vii) *Act 5 Scene 2*.

6 a The largest theme of all is that of the nature of man, in terms both of the individual and of the way he behaves (often hypocritically) in organized society. The following speeches are central; they are all spoken by Lear:

      i "Reason not the need . . ." (*Act 2 Scene 4*). What *is* "the need"?

      ii "Let the great gods . . . find out their enemies now" (*Act 3 Scene 2*). Who are their enemies?

      iii "Poor naked wretches . . ." (*Act 3 Scene 4*). What is to be learned from them?

      iv "What, art mad? . . . harder, harder; so." (*Act 4*

Scene 6) What has Lear learned about power, corruption, and the dispensation of justice?

b How many relevant pieces of wisdom can you find among the songs and sayings of the Fool?

7 Animal imagery abounds in *King Lear*. To convey the inhumanity of human behavior and its similarity to wild life, over sixty different creatures are mentioned. Trace the following to their sources, and explain their significance in the context of the play:

(**a**) "monster ingratitude" (**b**) "serpent's tooth" (**c**) "wolvish visage" (**d**) "like a vulture" (**e**) "most serpent-like" (**f**) "like rats . . . like dogs" (**g**) "those pelican daughters" (**h**) "rash boarish fangs" (**i**) "Tigers, not daughters" (**j**) "be-monster not thy feature" (**k**) "dog-hearted daughters".

How many more can you find?

8 a Look up Gloucester's speech in *Act 1 Scene 2*: "These late eclipses in the sun and moon. . . ." How many words can you find that imply discord, social breakdown, and fractured relationships?

b "Division" is echoed in figurative expressions throughout the play. Place the following examples in context and explain the force of the imagery:

  i "These hot tears which break from me perforce . . ." (*Act 1*)

  ii "Like rats, oft bite the holy cords a-twain . . ." (*Act 2*)

  iii "Crack Nature's moulds . . ." (*Act 3*)

  iv "She that herself will silver and disbranch from her material sap . . ." (*Act 4*)

  v "The strings of life begin to crack . . ." (*Act 5*)

9 Imagery based on physical suffering is recurrent in *King Lear*. The torment endured by Lear and Gloucester, and the savagery of the play as a whole, are reflected in terms of "a human body in anguished movement: tugged, wrenched, beaten, pierced, stung, scourged, dislocated, flayed, gashed, scalded, tortured and finally broken on the rack" (Caroline Spurgeon: *Shakespeare's Imagery*).

a Trace the following examples to their contexts, and explain their appositeness. They are all from Act One.

  i ... "wrenched my frame of nature from the fixed place"

  ii ... 'Th'untented woundings of a father's curse Pierce every sense about thee!'

  iii ... "with her nails she'll flay thy wolvish visage"

b Find further examples, guided by Miss Spurgeon's list.

10 In his opening address to the court in *Act 1 Scene 1*, Lear says he will "divest" himself of "rule, Interest of territory, cares of state." Imagery based on clothing (or references to it) can be found throughout the play.

a Find examples from speeches by the following:

  i France, in *Act 1 Scene 1*;

  ii Cornwall, in *Act 2 Scene 2*;

  iii Lear, in *Act 3 Scene 4*;

  iv Lear in *Act 3 Scene 6*.

b Explain why clothes have a symbolic significance in relation to the play's major themes.

Textual questions

Read the original Shakespeare and (if necessary) the modern transcription, to gain an understanding of the speeches and extracts below. Then concentrate entirely on the original in answering the questions.

1   *Thou, Nature, art my goddess (Act 1 Scene 2)*

    a   Edmund has said very little up to this point, and what he has said would accord with customs in polite society. What is the element of shock built into these first words of his soliloquy?

    b   A soliloquy can either be regarded as "thinking aloud, alone" or "confiding inner thoughts to a wider audience." If you were playing the part of Edmund, would you treat these lines as private musing, or as an opportunity to address the audience?

    c   Why is custom said to be "a plague"?

    d   Why is "moonshines Lag of a brother" more wittily suggestive than "younger than a brother"?

    e   Edmund repeats "base" five times, "bastard" three times, and "bastardy" and "baseness" once each, all in the space of twenty-two lines. What effect does this have on what in former times would have been a series of words with derogatory connotations?

    f   What effect on the meaning of "legitimate" does Edmund's (i) reference to conception in and out of wedlock and (ii) repetition of the word as adjective and noun five times have on its normally favorable meaning?

    g   Why might an audience at this stage in the play's development side with a character who has announced his villainous intentions?

Activities

2   *These late eclipses in the sun and moon (Act 1 Scene 2)*

   a   Gloucester believes there is an astrological explanation for the troubles of his time. What is Edmund's viewpoint on the subject?

   b   "Nature" is a word frequently used throughout the play; here it means "man's reason." Collect as many references to nature as you can find, and interpret each one according to the context in which it appears.

   c   Several items in Gloucester's catalogue of woe are directly related to the circumstances of the play. Explain each.

   d   Gloucester uses the word "nothing." So do Lear and Cordelia in *Act 1 Scene 1*. (i) How many times can you find the word employed in *King Lear* and (ii) can you explain why it should be so significant a word?

3   *I heard myself proclaimed (Act 2 Scene 3)*

   a   Why "happy" hollow?

   b   Edgar uses mostly words of one or two syllables in this soliloquy. (i) How does this help to emphasize important information and (ii) how does this help to emphasize the words which are exceptions to the rule?

   c   Edgar is planning to be "Poor Tom" here. Compare what is said of him, and by him, in *Act 3 Scene 4*. Does he carry out his plans to the letter?

   d   The play is set in ancient Britain: what evidence is there here that Elizabethan audiences did not object to anachronisms?

   e   Reread *Act 1 Scene 2*: what is ironic about Edgar's choice of name for his new identity?

4   *I prithee, daughter, do not make me mad (Act 2 Scene 4)*

   a   In this speech, Lear says "I can be patient." "Patient" and "patience" are words with many echoes throughout the play. Find as many as you can.

b Here patience is shown in the way Lear's outbursts are followed by checks. Mark the text (i) where you believe Lear raises his voice in anger, and (ii) where he disciplines himself with self-control.

c (i) Some lines are effective here because they are antithetical: that is, one half of the line is balanced against the other. Find examples, and say how they add to the pathos of Lear's words.

(ii) Sometimes Lear's mounting anger results in repetition in sets of three words or phrases. Find two examples.

d How does Lear make his critical points perfectly clear while affecting not to?

5 *O, reason not the need (Act 2 Scene 4)*

a The first lines relate significantly to the process whereby Lear's folly is redeemed. Explain why.

b Lear only once refers to "God" in his speeches. Here, as elsewhere, he addresses "heavens" and "you gods." Sometimes in the play the gods are regarded as malevolent (find Gloucester's anguished cry in *Act 4 Scene 1*) and sometimes benign (note his retraction in *Act 4 Scene 6*). What position does Lear take here?

c How is Lear's pathetic impotence conveyed (i) in disjointed sentences and (ii) by a short line?

d If you were producing the play, would you have Lear leave the stage in tears, or not? Discuss the alternatives and give reasons for your decision.

6 *Blow, winds, and crack your cheeks! (Act 3 Scene 2)*

a The Elizabethan theater had primitive sound effects, and performances took place on fine days in the open air. How does Shakespeare

  i create the illusion of a storm by means of words?

  ii succeed in conveying a sense of Lear's impending mental breakdown?

    b The passionate force of Lear's raging is conveyed by the verbs he uses to command the elements.

      i List them, and

      ii show how water, fire, explosion and destruction are called upon to carry out his orders.

    c In this speech, some lines are composed of multisyllabic and/or hyphenated words; others are mainly monosyllabic.

      i List them, and

      ii show how water, fire, explosion and destruction are called upon to carry out his orders.

7 Examine the following key speeches in similar detail:

    a *Poor naked wretches, whereso'er you are (Act 3 Scene 4)*

    b *Wisdom and goodness to the vile seem vile (Act 4 Scene 2)*

    c *Come on, sir, here's the place: stand still (Act 4 Scene 6)*

    d *Ay, every inch a king (Act 4 Scene 6)*

    e *And the creature run from the cur (Act 4 Scene 6)*

    f *Pray do not mock me (Act 4 Scene 7)*

    g *No, no, no, no! Come, let's away to prison (Act 5 Scene 3)*

    h Lear's last speeches, from *Howl, howl, howl* to *Look there, look there! (Act 5 Scene 3)*

Examination questions

1. *King Lear* is a play based on family relationships. How do the parallel stories of Lear and Gloucester support this viewpoint?

2. "The essence of tragedy is the vindication of human nobility and greatness." How far is this true of *King Lear*?

3. To what extent was Lear "a man more sinned against than sinning"?

4. What resemblances and differences does Shakespeare display in the characters of Lear's three daughters?

5. In what ways do the Fool and Gloucester add to the dramatic effect of *King Lear*?

6. Show by means of precise reference and illustration how the subplot emphasizes the central theme of *King Lear*.

7. Discuss any *two* of the following: (i) the animal imagery in *King Lear* (ii) the importance of the Fool's patter before and during the storm (iii) Edgar's feigned madness (iv) Kent's loyalty.

8. The following remarks are applied to King Lear; say what you think they mean and how far they are true: (i) "He hath ever but slenderly known himself" (ii) "The best and soundest of his time hath been but rash" (iii) "He but usurped his life."

9. How does Shakespeare achieve both intense horror and acute pathos in the storm scenes of *King Lear*?

10. Show how suffering is an integral part of the tragedy of *King Lear*.

11. What part does Nature play in *King Lear*?

12. Consider *two* of the following as examples of different kinds of villainy: (i) Edmund (ii) Goneril (iii) Regan (iv) Cornwall.

13 "This is not altogether fool, my lord." In what ways is the Fool wiser than Lear?

14 "You do me wrong to take me out o' th' grave." In what ways is the reborn Lear a better man than the one who died in the storm?

15 For over 100 years, *King Lear* was performed with a happy ending and the storm scene cut. Assess the importance of what was lost.

One-word-answer quiz

1 Into how many parts did Lear originally divide his kingdom?
2 How many knights did Lear wish to have in his train?
3 How many were denied him in his first fortnight of retirement?
4 How many did Regan offer him at first?
5 What was her final offer?
6 Until what time was Kent to sit in the stocks, according to Cornwall?
7 In the storm scene, who is first to find Edgar in the hovel?
8 What was Edgar wearing when disguised as Poor Tom?
9 Who "oft prove prophets"?
10 To how many of his daughters does Lear kneel?
11 What was the Prince of Darkness called, besides Modo?
12 What did Lear have in his countenance that Kent would fain call master?
13 What is obeyed in office?
14 How many "red burning spits" would Lear have liked to hiss in upon his daughters?
15 What was the surname of the Marshal of France?
16 What did Edmund give to the Captain who went to save the lives of Lear and Cordelia?
17 What did Kent give to the Gentleman who went to see Cordelia at Dover?
18 How many days was Kent allowed to prepare for banishment?
19 For how many days did the Fool pine after Cordelia?

20 For how many years had Poor Tom been mad, according to Edgar?

21 For how many years had Edmund been abroad?

22 What article did Lear ask for in his dying moments?

23 What did the Fool take Goneril for in the trial scene?

24 Who showed his father "a child-like office"?

25 Who said she had been "worth the whistle"?

26 What was Kent's assumed name?

27 How many times did the trumpet sound before Edgar appeared to fight Edmund?

28 Who does Lear call the "hot Duke"?

29 What was Edmund's goddess?

30 How many knights were "not questrists" after Gloucester?

31 Who signed herself "Your wife, so I would say, Affectionate servant"?

32 How old was Kent?

33 What did Lear say can be made out of nothing?

34 Who told Edgar that Nero was an angler in the Lake of Darkness?

35 Who wrote the letter which Kent held when in the stocks?

What's missing?

Complete the following quotations:

1   O! How this mother swells up toward my heart; . . .
2   I have no way, and therefore want no eyes; . . .
3   Come, let's away to prison; We two . . .
4   The gods are just, and of our pleasant vices . . .
5   This shows you are above, You justicers . . .
6   As flies to wanton boys are we to the gods . . .
7   This is the excellent foppery of the world . . .
8   Her voice was ever soft, Gentle and low . . .
9   Let it be so; . . .
10   Nor only, sir, this your all-licensed Fool . . .
11   They durst not do't; They could not, would not do't . . .
12   No, they cannot touch me for coining . . .
13   Cry to it, nuncle, as the cockney did to the eels . . .
14   This is most strange, That she . . .
15   Poor naked wretches, whereso'er you are . . .
16   Pray, do not mock me: I am a very foolish fond old man . . .
17   Howl, howl, howl! O, you are men of stones: . . .
18   Return to her? and fifty men dismissed? No, . . .
19   There thou might'st behold The great image of Authority . . .
20   How, how, Cordelia! Mend your speech a little . . .
21   Men must endure Their going hence, even as . . .
22   I am made of that self metal as my sister . . .
23   Truth's a dog must to kennel; . . .
24   Yet better thus, and known to be contemned, Than . . .
25   Better thou Hadst not been born than . . .

26 Ay, every inch a King: . . .

27 Wisdom and goodness to the vile seem vile; . . .

28 Thy dowerless daughter, King, thrown to my chance . . .

29 Idle old man, that . . .

30 I am a man More . . .

31 It is the stars, The stars above us, govern our conditions . . .

32 Thou, Nature, art my goddess . . .

33 O, reason not the need: . . .

34 When we our betters see bearing our woes . . .

35 Pat he comes, like the catastrophe of the old comedy: . . .

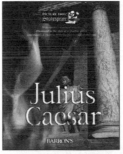